Lecture Notes in Computer Science 7055

Commenced Publication in 1973
Founding and Former Series Editors:
Gerhard Goos, Juris Hartmanis, and Jan van Leeuwen

Ari Juels   Christof Paar (Eds.)

RFID
Security and Privacy

7th International Workshop, RFIDSec 2011
Amherst, MA, USA, June 26-28, 2011
Revised Selected Papers

 Springer

Volume Editors

Ari Juels
RSA Laboratories/EMC
11 Cambridge Center
Cambridge, MA 02142, USA
E-mail: ajuels@rsa.com

Christof Paar
Ruhr University Bochum
Horst Görtz Institute for IT-Security
44780 Bochum, Germany
E-mail: christof.paar@rub.de

ISSN 0302-9743   e-ISSN 1611-3349
ISBN 978-3-642-25285-3   e-ISBN 978-3-642-25286-0
DOI 10.1007/978-3-642-25286-0
Springer Heidelberg Dordrecht London New York

Library of Congress Control Number: 2011944230

CR Subject Classification (1998): C.2, K.6.5, D.4.6, E.3, H.4, J.1

LNCS Sublibrary: SL 2 – Programming and Software Engineering

Typesetting: Camera-ready by author, data conversion by Scientific Publishing Services, Chennai, India

Printed on acid-free paper

Springer is part of Springer Science+Business Media (www.springer.com)

Preface

RFIDSec 2011, the 7th workshop on RFID Security and Privacy, was held in Amherst and Northampton, Massachusetts, USA, during June 26–28, 2011.

The workshop attracted 21 submissions, of which the Program Committee selected 12 for publication in the workshop proceedings. The accepted papers dealt with the topics of on-tag cryptography, attacks, security through physics, and protocol-level security. The Program Committee included 26 subject-matter experts from 14 countries, and represented academia, industry, and government.

An excellent array of invited talks complemented the paper sessions. Adi Shamir of the Weizmann Institute of Science (Israel) gave the RFIDSec 2011 keynote talk, "Minimalism in Cryptography," an overview of his recent results in the theory of cipher design. Srdjan Capkun highlighted the limitations of logical-layer privacy protections in his invited talk, "On Physical-Layer Identification of RFID Tags." At the workshop banquet, Collin Mulliner gave an update on NFC security ("Hacking Your NFC Phone and Service: The Good News and the Bad News"). Offering an industry perspective on the work of RFID (and other) standards bodies, Ravi Pappu informed and regaled workshop attendees with a talk entitled "The Making of Camels."

For the first time, RFIDSec offered tutorials in highly relevant areas. The four tutorials preceding the workshop were: Matt Reynolds and Ravi Pappu taught "The Physics of RFID," David Oswald and Timo Kasper, "Hands-on Side Channel Attacks Against Smart Cards and Other Tokens," Shane Clark, Ben Ransford, Mastooreh Salajegheh, and Hong Zhang, "Hands-on Programming of Batteryless, RFID-Scale Computers with Sensors," and Ari Juels, "Introduction to RFID Security and Privacy."

We wish to thank the generous sponsors of RFIDSec 2011: Microsoft Research, Mocana, Cryptography Research, the National Science Foundation, the Institute for Information Infrastructure Protection (I3P), the *RFID Journal*, DIFRwear, and UMass Amherst. Deep thanks are also due to Kevin Fu for his outstanding organizational efforts as General Chair, and to Wendy Cooper for her tireless support as Conference Coordinator.

August 2011
Ari Juels
Christof Paar

Organization

General Chair

Kevin Fu — UMass Amherst, USA

Program Chairs

Ari Juels — RSA Laboratories, USA
Christof Paar — Ruhr University Bochum, Germany

Program Committee

Gildas Avoine — UCL, Louvain-la-Neuve, Belgium
Lejla Batina — Radboud University Nijmegen, The Netherlands
Wayne Burleson — UMass Amherst, USA
Vanesa Daza — Universitat Pompeu Fabra, Spain
Josep Domingo-Ferrer — Univ.Rovira i Virgili, Spain
Henri Gilbert — France
Jorge Guajardo — Philips Research, The Netherlands
Julio César Hernández Castro — University of Portmouth, UK
Christian Damsgaard Jensen — DTU, Denmark
Süleyman Kardas — Tubitak Uekae, Turkey
Tom Karygiannis — NIST, USA
Farinaz Koushanfar — Rice University, USA
Kerstin Lemke-Rust — Universität Bonn-Rhein-Sieg, Germany
Antoni Martinez-Balleste — Rovira i Virgili University, Spain
Florian Michahelles — ETHZ, Switzerland
David Molnar — Microsoft Research Redmond, USA
Karsten Nohl — Security Research Labs, Germany
Berna Ors — Istanbul Technical University, Turkey
Axel Poschmann — Nanyang Technical University, Singapore
Kazuo Sakiyama — Univ.of Electro Communic., Japan
Nitesh Saxena — NYU-Poly, USA
Joshua Smith — University of Washington, USA
Agusti Solanas — Rovira i Virgili University, Spain
Juan E. Tapiador — University of York, UK
Ingrid Verbauwhede — KU Leuven, Belgium
Avishai Wool — Tel Aviv University, Israel

External Reviewers

T. Akishita	P. Peris-Lopez	M. Valis
M.A. Bingol	B. Martin	M.G. Vasco
X. Carpent	A. Mirhoseini	J. Voris
T. Halevi	J.M. Seguí	A. Vosoughi
Y. Hanatani	J. Takahashi	Y. Oren
C.H. Kim	R. Trujillo-Rasúa	

RFIDSec 2011 Sponsors

Cryptography Research	Mocana
DIFRwear	National Science Foundation
I3P	RFID Journal
Microsoft Research	UMass Amherst

RFIDSec Steering Committee

Manfred Aigner	TU Graz, Austria
Gildas Avoine (Chair)	UCL, Louvain-la-Neuve, Belgium
Kevin Fu	UMass Amherst, USA
Yingjiu Li	Singapore Management University, Singapore
Christof Paar	Ruhr University Bochum, Germany
Bart Preneel	KU Leuven, Belgium
Vincent Rijmen	TU Graz, Austria; KU Leuven, Belgium

Table of Contents

KLEIN: A New Family of Lightweight Block Ciphers

Zheng Gong[1], Svetla Nikova[2,3], and Yee Wei Law[4]

[1] School of Computer Science, South China Normal University, China
cis.gong@gmail.com
[2] Faculty of EWI, University of Twente, The Netherlands
[3] Dept. ESAT/SCD-COSIC, Katholieke Universiteit Leuven, Belgium
s.i.nikova@utwente.nl
[4] Department of EEE, The University of Melbourne, Australia
yee.wei.law@gmail.com

Abstract. Resource-efficient cryptographic primitives are essential for realizing both security and efficiency in embedded systems like RFID tags and sensor nodes. Among those primitives, lightweight block cipher plays a major role as a building block for security protocols. In this paper, we describe a new family of lightweight block ciphers named KLEIN, which is designed for resource-constrained devices such as wireless sensors and RFID tags. Compared to related proposals, KLEIN has advantage in the software performance on legacy sensor platforms, while its hardware implementation can be compact as well.

1 Introduction

With the rapid advances in wireless communication and embedded systems, we are becoming increasingly dependent on the so-called pervasive computing, evidence of which can be found in ubiquitous smart cards, RFID tags, public transport systems, smart meters, etc. Wireless sensor networks (WSNs), due to its potential in pushing the envelope of pervasive computing to areas such as environment monitoring, military surveillance and healthcare, is attracting more and more attention. When choosing security algorithms for resource-limited devices the implementation costs should be taken into account. Symmetric-key algorithms, especially block ciphers, still play an important role in the security of embedded systems. Moreover recent results have shown that lightweight block ciphers can be used not only for encryption, but also for hash [4] and authentication [21] on devices with highly constrained resources. For security and performance concerns, some types of sensors are equipped with a hardware implementation of AES-128 [14], e.g. the Chipcon CC2420 transceiver chip [7]. But for resource-constrained devices, AES could be too expensive, despite the various approaches that have been proposed to reduce the costs of AES hardware and software implementations [20,24,25,31].

In the literature, quite a few lightweight block ciphers with various design strategies have been proposed [3,6,13,18,22,27,33,35,42,52]. Skipjack is a lightweight block cipher designed by the U.S. National Security Agency (NSA) for embedded applications [42]. The algorithm of Skipjack has an 80-bit key with a 64-bit block length based on an unbalanced Feistel network. NOEKEON is a hardware-efficient block cipher, which

A. Juels and C. Paar (Eds.): RFIDSec 2011, LNCS 7055, pp. 1–18, 2012.

was proposed by Daemen *et al.* [13] and submitted to the NESSIE project in 2000. HIGHT was designed by Hong *et al.* [22] as a generalized Feistel-like cipher, which is suitable for low-resource devices. mCrypton [35] is designed by following the overall architecture of Crypton [34] but with redesign and simplifications of each component function to enable much compact implementation in both hardware and software. SEA is a software-oriented block cipher which was proposed by Standaert et al. [52]. At FSE 2007, Leander *et al.* [33] proposed a family of new lightweight variants of DES, which are called DESL and DESXL. The main idea of the new variants of DES is to use just one S-box recursively, instead of eight different S-boxes. Bogdanov *et al.* proposed [3] an ultra-lightweight block cipher which is called PRESENT. The design of PRESENT is extremely hardware efficient, since it uses a fully wired diffusion layer without any algebraic unit. KATAN and KTANTAN are designed as a family of ultra-lightweight block ciphers by De Cannière *et al.* [6]. Both KATAN and KTANTAN use an 80-bit key length with 32, 48, or 64-bit block size, while KTANTAN is more compact in hardware since its key will be unchangeably burnt on devices. In [18], Engels *et al.* proposed a novel ultra-lightweight cryptographic algorithm with 256-bit key length and 16-bit block size, referred to as Hummingbird, for resource-constrained devices.

The security of any block cipher should be extensively analyzed before its wide implementation. Biham *et al.* have discovered an impossible differential attack on 31 of the 32 rounds [1] of Skipjack. A truncated differential attack was also published against 28 rounds of Skipjack by Knudsen *et al.* [29]. Granboulan [23] presented a revised result in the differential analysis of Skipjack. By exploiting its periodic key schedule, a complementation slide attack is mounted on the full 32 rounds of Skipjack [46]. The attack requires only $2^{32.5}$ known texts and 2^{44} encryptions of Skipjack. In a NESSIE report, Knudsen and Raddum [28] showed that "indirect mode" NOEKEON was still vulnerable to certain peculiar kinds of related-key cryptanalysis, and discovered weaknesses in NOEKEON-variant ciphers which cast doubt on the design strategy behind NOEKEON and thus on its security. As a result NOEKEON was not selected by NESSIE. Although PRESENT has a hardware-efficient diffusion layer, different attacks have been applied to the reduced-round variants of PRESENT due to its diffusion property, e.g. the weak key attack [43,44], the linear attack [8] and the saturation attack [9]. Recently, Bogdanov and Rechberger [5] have proposed a meet-in-the-middle attack on KTANTAN. At FSE 2011, Saarinen [50] presented a chosen-IV, chosen-message differential attack which can break full-round Hummingbird in practice.

The performance of a block cipher is also a key factor for resource-constrained devices. Efficiency in hardware is a major design criterion for lightweight block ciphers. The area in *gate equivalents* (GE) is often used as a measure for the compactness of the hardware implementation. Generally speaking, one GE is equal to the area which is required by two-input NAND gate with the lowest driving strength of the appropriate technology [45]. PRESENT, for example, has a compact implementation with 1570 GE in a 64-bit datapath [4], as well as a very lightweight implementation with 1000 GE [49]. mCrypton and DESXL are also competitive since they are close to the 2000 GE barrier. HIGHT is less attractive since its area in GE is over 3000 GE, which is less competitive to the best AES implementations by Moradi *et al.* [40] (with 2400 GE), Hamalainen *et al.* [24] (with 3100 GE) and Feldhofer *et al.* [20] (with 3400 GE). PRINTCipher

[27], GOST [48], KATAN and KTANTAN [6] are among the most hardware-efficient, requiring less than 1000 GE.

Usually, sensors have better power and hardware capabilities than RFID tags. Since software implementations incur zero hardware manufacturing cost and are flexible to maintain, it is believed that software-efficient block ciphers are more practical for sensors. In this paper, a new family of block ciphers called *KLEIN* is designed for resource-constrained devices. Compared to related proposals, KLEIN has the advantage of the software performance on legacy sensor platforms and at the same time its hardware implementation can also be compact. Our security analysis shows that KLEIN has a conservative security margin against various cryptanalyses.

The remainder of this paper is organized as follows. Section 2 describes the design rationale and the specification of the KLEIN family. In Section 3, the security of KLEIN is analyzed by considering known attacks. Compared to related lightweight proposals, a detailed performance of KLEIN is discussed in Section 4. Section 5 concludes the paper.

2   Specification of KLEIN

In this section we specify the cipher structure of KLEIN. Also the design principles will be discussed, which are followed during the design process of KLEIN. For each of the components of KLEIN, our choices will be motivated to achieve the well balanced trade-off between performance and security. The test vectors of KLEIN can be found in Appendix A.

2.1   Structure of KLEIN

The structure of KLEIN is a typical Substitution-Permutation Network (SPN), which is also used in many advanced block ciphers, e.g. AES and PRESENT. In our first estimation for obtaining a reasonable security margin and asymmetric iteration, we choose the number of rounds N_R as 12/16/20 for KLEIN-64/80/96 respectively. A high-level description of the KLEIN encryption routine is described in Figure 1.

$sk^1 \leftarrow$ KEY;
STATE $\leftarrow$ PLAINTEXT;
for $i = 1$ *to* N_R do
   $AddRoundKey(\text{STATE}, sk^i)$;
   $SubNibbles(\text{STATE})$;
   $RotateNibbles(\text{STATE})$;
   $MixNibbles(\text{STATE})$;
   $sk^{i+1} = KeySchedule(sk^i, i)$;
end for
CIPHERTEXT $\leftarrow AddRoundKey(\text{STATE}, sk^{N_R+1})$;

Fig. 1. The encryption routine of KLEIN

Note that many lightweight block ciphers are proposed to use only the counter mode and hence, the implementation costs of decryptions can be avoided. In the design of KLEIN, its lightweight property should also take the decryption algorithm into consideration without fixing on any cipher mode.

2.2   The Round Transformation

The input and output of KLEIN are considered to be one-dimensional byte arrays. During the round transformation, all the operations can be optimized with byte-oriented algorithms.

The SubNibbles Step. Since the $AddRoundKey(x, y)$ step in the round transformation is simply $x \oplus y$, the input text will be XORed with the i-th round key sk^i (where $i \in [1, N_R]$) before the SubNibbles step. In the SubNibbles step, the XORed results will be divided into 16 of 4-bit nibbles and input to the same 16 S-boxes. The KLEIN S-box S is a 4×4 involutive permutation. The non-linear permutation executed by S is described in Table 1. The implementation costs of such a 4-bit S-box is much lower than that of an 8-bit S-box either by hardware or by software. By choosing an involutive S-box, we can also save the implementation costs for its inverse. Since the same S-boxes are used in the SubNibbles step, it allows a serialization of the design for an extremely small footprint. Moreover, we just need to provide one single side-channel protection for the S-box. Thus the overhead of an extra protection on its inverse is unnecessary.

Table 1. The 4-Bit S-box used in KLEIN

Input	0	1	2	3	4	5	6	7	8	9	A	B	C	D	E	F
Output	7	4	A	9	1	F	B	0	C	3	2	6	8	E	D	5

Since the SubNibbles step is the only non-linear layer in KLEIN, a natural requirement is an optimal resistance against linear and differential cryptanalyses. Therefore the choice of the S-box S fulfills the following conditions.

1. The S-box satisfies $\mathsf{S}(\mathsf{S}(x)) = x, x \in \mathbb{F}_2^4$, thus it can be used both in the encryption and in the decryption.
2. The S-box has no fixed points, i.e. $\mathsf{S}(x) \neq x, x \in \mathbb{F}_2^4$.
3. For any non-zero input difference $\Delta_I \in \mathbb{F}_2^4$ and output difference $\Delta_O \in \mathbb{F}_2^4$, it holds that

$$\sharp\{x \in \mathbb{F}_2^4 | \mathsf{S}(x) + \mathsf{S}(x + \Delta_I) = \Delta_O\} \leq 4. \tag{1}$$

Furthermore, if $wt(\Delta_I) = wt(\Delta_O) = 1$, we have

$$\sharp\{x \in \mathbb{F}_2^4 | \mathsf{S}(x) + \mathsf{S}(x + \Delta_I) = \Delta_O\} \leq 2. \tag{2}$$

4. For any non-zero $a, b \in \mathbb{F}_2^4$, it holds that

$$|S_b^W(a)| = |\sum_{x \in \mathbb{F}_2^4} (-1)^{b \cdot \mathsf{S}(x) + a \cdot x}| \leq 8. \tag{3}$$

Furthermore, if $wt(a) = wt(b) = 1$, we have

$$|S_b^W(a)| = |\sum_{x \in \mathbb{F}_2^4} (-1)^{b \cdot S(x) + a \cdot x}| \le 4. \tag{4}$$

The 4-bit S-box used in PRESENT satisfies $\sharp\{x \in \mathbb{F}_2^4 | S(x) + S(x + \Delta_I) = \Delta_O\} = 0$ if $wt(\Delta_I) = wt(\Delta_O) = 1$, which assures a better avalanche effect [3]. However, the PRESENT S-box is not an involution. According to our exhaustive search result, there is no such an involutive 4-bit S-box that can satisfy this additional property.

For each input differential Δ_I, the maximum probability of any output differential Δ_O is up to $4/16 = 2^{-2}$. Let p be the probability of a linear characteristic. The correlation of the linear characteristic over S is given by $q = (2p - 1)^2$ [38]. From the input-output correlation of S, it is straightforward that any linear characteristic over S has a correlation of at most $(2 \times \frac{4}{16} - 1)^2 = 2^{-2}$.

The RotateNibbles Step. After the SubNibbles step, 16 nibbles $b_0^i, b_1^i, \cdots, b_{15}^i$ will be rotated left two bytes during the i-th round where $i \in [1, N_R]$. The RotateNibbles step is illustrated in Figure 2. The inverse operation will be simply rotate right two bytes per round. Nevertheless, the RotateNibbles step can also be combined with the MixNibbles step to avoid the hardware or software costs.

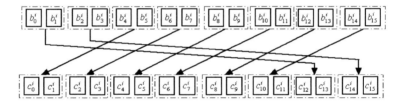

Fig. 2. The RotateNibbles step

The MixNibbles Step. The MixNibbles step is a bricklayer permutation of the state. The i-th round input nibbles $\{c_0^i, c_1^i, \cdots, c_{15}^i\}$ will be divided into 2 tuples, which will be proceeded the same as the MixColumns step in Rijndael. The tuples of the state are considered as polynomials over $\mathbb{F}_2^8$ and multiplied modulo $x^4 + 1$ with a fixed polynomial $c(x) = 03 \cdot x^3 + 01 \cdot x^2 + 01 \cdot x + 02$. The inverse is also a fixed multiplication polynomial $d(x) = 0B \cdot x^3 + 0D \cdot x^2 + 09 \cdot x + 0E$. The output of the MixNibbles step will be the intermediate state s^{i+1} for the next round transformation.

Note that the balance between the diffusion property and the software performance let us make this choice. Although bit-shifting operations are often used in the diffusion layer of many lightweight block ciphers (e.g. PRESENT and NOEKEON), efficiency is lost in software implementations. From the number of active Sboxes, it seems a better choice that the MixNibbles step chooses a matrix multiplication in $GF(2^4)$. However, a byte-oriented matrix multiplication has advantages in the software implementations for 8-bit processors (e.g. Skipjack). By using the similar implementation of the

MixColumns step for 8-bit processors [14], we can use just one 256-byte look-up table to optimize the MixNibbles step. Also the same look-up table can be used to optimize its inverse. After the 12/16/20 rounds of KLEIN-64/80/96, the MixNibbles step can still provide a high number of active Sboxes for the security of KLEIN. The property of the MixColumns step of Rijndael has been well analyzed, the details can be found in the literature [12,14,16].

Key schedule. For round transformations, all practical block ciphers use varied key schedules to expand a relative small master key to a series of dependent round keys. Since KLEIN will be used to construct block-cipher-based hash functions and message authentication codes, the key schedule should be agile even if keys are frequently changed. On the other hand, the key schedule should also consider a proper complexity for the security. To avoid the potential related-key weakness whilst balancing the performance, the key schedule of KLEIN is designed as follows.

1. Input: a 64/80/96-bit master key mk for KLEIN-64/80/96.
2. Key scheduling: Let i be the round counter of KLEIN-64/80/96. In the first round so that $i = 1$, the initial subkey $sk^1 = mk = sk_0^1||sk_1^1||\cdots||sk_t^1$ where $t = 7/9/11$ for KLEIN-64/80/96. For KLEIN-64, the $(i + 1)$-th subkey sk^{i+1} can be derived from the i-th subkey sk^i as follows.
    (a) Divide the i-th subkey sk^i into two byte-oriented tuples (a, b), such that $a = (sk_0^i, sk_1^i, \cdots, sk_{\lfloor \frac{t}{2} \rfloor}^i)$ and $b = (sk_{\lceil \frac{t}{2} \rceil}^i, sk_{\lceil \frac{t}{2} \rceil+1}^i, \cdots, sk_t^i)$. For KLEIN-64, we have $a = (sk_0^i, sk_1^i, sk_2^i, sk_3^i)$ and $b = (sk_4^i, sk_5^i, sk_6^i, sk_7^i)$.
    (b) Cycling left shift one byte position in (a, b), obtain $a' = (sk_1^i, \cdots, sk_{\lfloor \frac{t}{2} \rfloor}^i, sk_0^i)$ and $b' = (sk_{\lceil \frac{t}{2} \rceil+1}^i, \cdots, sk_t^i, sk_{\lceil \frac{t}{2} \rceil}^i)$ for the next step. For KLEIN-64, we have $a' = (sk_1^i, sk_2^i, sk_3^i, sk_0^i)$ and $b' = (sk_5^i, sk_6^i, sk_7^i, sk_4^i)$.
    (c) Swap the tuple (a', b') with a Feistel-like structure, such that $a'' = b'$ becomes the left tuple, whilst $b'' = a' \oplus b'$ becomes the right tuple.
    (d) XOR round counter i with the third byte in the left tuple a'', and substitute the second and the third bytes of the right tuple b'' by using the KLEIN S-box **S**.
3. Output: iteratively execute the above step for different key lengths, truncate the leftmost 64 bits of subkey sk^i for the i-th round transformation.

Figure 3 illustrates the KeySchedule algorithm of KLEIN-64. The key schedule of KLEIN is feasible for different key sizes. To save the memory for storing intermediate values, the subkeys of KLEIN can be generated during each round transformation. During the performance tuning on sensors, we observed that the on-the-fly key schedule of KLEIN is more resource-efficient than the traditional optimization such that all subkeys are computed in advance. Also the Feistel-like structure provides more complexities to resist weak key attacks, which was found on the PRESENT block cipher recently [8,43]. For simplicity, we only use an incremental round counter as the additive constant to avoid the slide attack. Like some other block cipher schemes, those round counters in KLEIN can also be defined by a recursion rule or an LFSR sequence in $GF(2^8)$ to avoid the potential complementation properties.

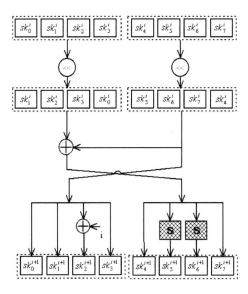

Fig. 3. The KeySchedule algorithm of 64-bit key length

3 Security Analysis

In this section we will present a security analysis of KLEIN, showing its resistance against various cryptanalytic attacks.

3.1 Linear and Differential Attacks

The resistance of linear and differential attacks of a block cipher is mainly based on the branch number, i.e. the number of active S-boxes in a certain number of rounds. In Rijndael, the authors use the Maximum Distance Separable (MDS) code to achieve the maximal branch number in a small number of rounds. By combining the RotateNibbles and MixNibbles steps, KLEIN can achieve a balance between the minimum number of active S-boxes and the software performance for resource-constrained devices.

Theorem 1. *Any four-round differential characteristic of KLEIN has a minimum of 15 active S-boxes.*

Proof. The MixColumns step in Rijndael is based on a Maximum Distance Separable code and the distance between any two distinct words called branch number is 5 [14]. Since we use the same matrix multiplication in the MixNibbles step of KLEIN, the branch number of MixNibbles is also 5. Since MixNibbles is computed with multiplications in $GF(2^8)$, an active byte in the diffusion layer of KLEIN implies one or two nibbles (i.e. the leftmost and the rightmost 4 bits) are active. For simplicity, we assume every active byte only has one active nibbles. Let $\Delta_i = L_i \| R_i$ be the i-th round input difference characteristic, where L_i and R_i denote the left and the right 4-byte tuples respectively. The differential patterns of four-round KLEIN can be analyzed as follows.

- If there is 1 non-zero byte in L_1, it will be at least one active S-box in the first round. After the Rotate and MixNibbles, the difference will be propagated to 4 bytes either in the left or the right 4-byte tuple. Thus Δ_2 will have minimum 4 active S-boxes in the second round. For simplicity, we assume L_2 contains 4 active bytes while R_2 remains zero. After the RotateNibbles step, both the left and the right tuples will have 2 active bytes. Since the branch number of MixNibbles is 5, the minimum number of active bytes with the differential characteristic Δ_3 will be 6. After RotateNibbles in the third round, if the active bytes in L_3 is 2 or 3, R_3 will have 4 or 3 active bytes respectively. In either of the situations, Δ_4 will have minimum 3+1 or 2+2 active bytes. In this general case, the minimum number of active S-boxes after four rounds is $1 + 4 + 6 + 4 = 15$.
- If there is 2 non-zero bytes in L_1, the difference will be propagated to at least 3 bytes after MixNibbles. For simplicity, we assume that L_2 contains 3 active bytes while R_2 remains zero. After RotateNibbles, the active bytes in L_2 is 1 or 2, while R_2 will have 2 or 1. Since the branch number of MixNibbles is 5, the minimum number of active bytes with the differential characteristic Δ_3 will be 7. After RotateNibbles in the third round, if the active bytes in L_3 is 3 or 4, R_3 will have 4 or 3 active bytes respectively. In either of the situations, Δ_4 will have minimum 2+1 or 1+2 active bytes. In this general case, the minimum number of active S-boxes after four rounds is $2 + 3 + 7 + 3 = 15$.
- In the case of 3 (or 4) active bytes in L_1, the difference patterns of the first three rounds will be identical to the case of 2 active bytes in the last three rounds. The minimum active bytes after three rounds are $3+7+3$ (or $4+6+4$). In the third round, first we choose all 3 (or 4) active bytes to be moved to L_3 after RotateNibbles. After MixNibbles, the active bytes will be at least 2 (or 1) since the branch number is 5. In any other choice, the active bytes in the forth round will be no less than 2 (or 1). Thus the minimum number of active S-boxes after four rounds is $3+7+3+2 = 15$ (or $4 + 6 + 4 + 1 = 15$) in this general case.

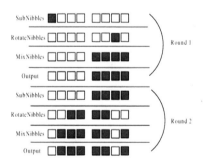

Fig. 4. A typical differential pattern of KLEIN

Figure 4 describes a typical differential pattern of KLEIN, where the colored boxes denote the active bytes in a trial. Without loss of generality, the same differential patterns will be followed where all active bytes are in R_1. If both L_1 and R_1 have one or more active bytes, it is straightforward that the minimum number of active S-boxes will be no less than 15. Thus any four-round differential characteristic of KLEIN has a minimum of 15 active S-boxes.   □

In RotateNibbles and MixNibbles, if we choose operations over $GF(2^4)$ for the MDS code, the active S-boxes in a four-round differential characteristic can be lower bounded by 25. Although a higher number of active S-boxes means KLEIN can use less rounds to be secure, our tuning experiments in sensors show that the software performance will be sacrificed by operations over $GF(2^4)$ (e.g. bit-shifting from leftmost to rightmost). However, it always requires a trade-off between the performance and the security. For ultra-lightweight in hardware, any differential characteristic of PRESENT has only 10 active S-boxes after 5 rounds.

In Rijndael, the coefficients of the MixColumns step are selected for assuring that both the differential branch number and the linear branch number are equal to 5. Based on the combination of RotateNibbles and MixNibbles, KLEIN also has the same property on the branch numbers. Therefore the minimum number of active S-boxes in a four-round linear approximation can be derived from the four-round differential propagation result of KLEIN. For brevity, the proof is omitted here.

Theorem 2. *Any four-round linear approximation of KLEIN has a minimum of 15 active S-boxes.*

The strength of a cipher against differential attacks is reflected by the maximum probability of differential , i.e. a collection of characteristics. However, in cryptanalysis we often assume that one characteristic has a much larger probability than the other characteristics of the differential. Thus a characteristic with the maximum probability is taken as an estimate of the probability of the differential. Similar assumptions can be found in linear attacks as well. Based on the minimum active S-boxes of characteristics in certain rounds, we can also derive the resistance of the differential and linear attacks on KLEIN. Since any differential characteristic over the KLEIN S-box has a maximum 2^{-2} possibility, the security against differential attacks of KLEIN-64 can be estimated as follows.

Lemma 1. *Let ϵ_{12R}^d be the maximum probability of a differential characteristic of 12 rounds of KLEIN-64. Then $\epsilon_{12R}^d \leq (2^{-2})^{12 \times 15/4} \approx 2^{-90}$.*

Since any linear characteristic over the KLEIN S-box has a correlation 2^{-2}, the security against linear attacks of the full-round KLEIN-64 is described as follows.

Lemma 2. *Let ϵ_{12R}^l be the maximal bias of a linear approximation of 12 rounds of KLEIN-64. Then $\epsilon_{12R}^l \leq (2^{-2})^{12 \times 15/4} \approx 2^{-90}$.*

By following the similar analysis, we note that the security of KLEIN-80/96 against linear and differential attacks can be gauged with 16/20 rounds.

Lemma 3. *Let ϵ_{16R}^d be the maximum probability of a differential characteristic of 16 rounds of KLEIN-80. Then $\epsilon_{16R}^d \leq (2^{-2})^{16 \times 15/4} \approx 2^{-120}$.*

Lemma 4. *Let ϵ_{16R}^l be the maximum bias of a linear approximation of 16 rounds of KLEIN-80. Then $\epsilon_{16R}^l \leq (2^{-2})^{16 \times 16/4} \approx 2^{-120}$.*

Lemma 5. *Let ϵ_{20R}^d be the maximum probability of a differential characteristic of 20 rounds of KLEIN-96. Then $\epsilon_{20R}^d \leq (2^{-2})^{20 \times 15/4} \approx 2^{-150}$.*

Lemma 6. *Let ϵ_{20R}^l be the maximum bias of a linear approximation of 20 rounds of KLEIN-96. Then $\epsilon_{20R}^l \leq (2^{-2})^{20 \times 15/4} \approx 2^{-150}$.*

Based on the above results, the KLEIN family of ciphers have a good security margin in the full rounds. The extra security margin of a block cipher may benefit the lightweight design of block-cipher-based hash functions or message authentication codes [15,21].

3.2   Key Schedule Attacks

Since there are no established guidelines for the design of key schedules, both a wide variety of designs and a wide variety of schedule-specific attacks have been proposed. The most effective attacks come under the general heading of related-key attacks and slide attacks, and both rely on the build-up of identifiable relationships between different sets of subkeys. To counter this threat, we use a round-dependent counter so that the subkey sets cannot easily be symmetric. We also use the same KLEIN S-box to provide the non-linearity of the subkeys whilst saving the implementation costs. For related-key attacks, we have the following properties for protection.

- For KLEIN-64/80/96, each bit in the key register depends on at least 4 user-supplied bits after 4/5/6 rounds.
- For KLEIN-64/80/96, all the bits in the key register are a non-linear function of the 64/80/96-bit user-supplied key by 8/10/12 rounds.

3.3   Integral Attack

Integral cryptanalysis are usually applied to exploit vulnerabilities in byte-oriented block ciphers, such as AES [14]. An integral attack will investigate the propagation of sums of many values, whilst a differential attack will consider the propagation of differences between pairs. In a byte-oriented cipher, the sum of a group differences might be a predictable value after certain rounds. For better software performance, the design of KLEIN also adopts a byte-oriented structure like AES. Thus it also faces a similar vulnerability on integral attacks [30].

First we consider a five-round integral attack on KLEIN, which is based on the attack given by Knudsen and Wagner on AES [30]. The attacker chooses a group of 256 plaintexts, which have equal values in all bytes except one. According to the mathematic properties of the RotateNibbles and MixNibbles steps, the sum of 256 bytes will be zero after three rounds of encryption. Then the attacker will guess 4 key bytes in the fourth round and 1 key bytes in the fifth round. If the $4 + 1 = 5$ key bytes are right, the sum of all 256 values should also be zero after five rounds. For KLEIN-80/96, we can extend the above attack to six rounds. Thus we need a collection of 2^{32} plaintexts in the first round and guess $4 + 5 = 9$ bytes in total. To the best of our knowledge, any integral attack on KLEIN over eight rounds will be more complicated than exhaustive key searches or requires the complete code book. Except byte-oriented integral attacks, One could try nibble-oriented attacks with 16 plaintexts which have equal values except one nibble. However, since the MixNibbles step is fully based on multiplications in $GF(2^8)$, the sum of 16 nibbles is unpredictable after three rounds. Therefore nibble-oriented integral attacks will not be more feasible than byte-oriented ones.

3.4 Algebraic Attack

The algebraic attack as well as the *Cube Attack* [17], requires the algebraic form describing the output bits has a relatively small degree in terms of the input bits being processed. To exploit the algebraic relations between input and output bits of a block cipher, attackers may consider a subset of input bits whilst leave the other fixed. In the S-box of KLEIN, every output bit can be represented by a 3-degree polynomial with 4 input variables in ANF. For total 64 input bits, the complexity of finding the polynomials for the entire cipher soon becomes too large. In the full-round KLEIN-64, the number of S-boxes in the encryption and the key schedule equals $n = 12 \times 16 + 12 \times 4 = 240$. It is well-known that any 4-bit S-box can be represented by at least 21 quadratic equations over $GF(2)$. Thus in KLEIN-64, we have the number of quadratic equations $n \times 21 = 5040$ in $n \times 8 = 1920$ variables. By changing the number of rounds, similar results can easily be extended to KLEIN-80 and KLEIN-96. In our experiment, we were unable to transform three-round KLEIN-64 to the ANF equations in a reasonable time.

3.5 Side-Channel Attack

Since it is easy to add noises and loops in the software implementation of a block cipher to avoid side-channel attacks, here we will discuss on how to secure the hardware implementation of KLEIN. Except for the SubNibbles step, KLEIN is completely linear. The S-box of KLEIN can be implemented to resist side-channel attacks even in the presence of glitches using the secret sharing method proposed by Nikova *et al.* [41]. Also the linear part of KLEIN can be securely processed by using independent shares. A survey of lightweight cryptography and DPA countermeasures [39] estimates that the masking based on secret sharing will increase the hardware overhead with a factor of 3, which is still promising because it has a moderate area overhead and was theoretically proven to be secure against DPA attacks [41].

4 Performance

Here we analyze the performance of KLEIN. Based on legacy low-resource sensors TelosB (with 16-bit TI MSP430 microcontroller) and IRIS with (8-bit ATmega128L microcontroller), a detailed comparison of KLEIN and other related ciphers is given in Table 2. These two platforms are chosen because of their opposing characteristics: TelosB has more RAM than IRIS (10 KB vs 8 KB) but IRIS has a larger Flash memory than TelosB (128 KB vs 48 KB); TelosB's transceiver CC2420 supports hardware AES encryption but IRIS does not. For resource-constrained devices, a lower RAM cost would be beneficial for power consumptions and manufactory expenses. Since the

CC2420 chip on TelosB also supports AES hardware encryption, we also test its performance by implementing the standalone AES encryption of CC2420 [53]. The result shows AES hardware implementation has a great improvement on RAM and ROM costs, while the processing speed is even lower than the software implementation. We attribute this latency to the fact that the hardware AES encryption function must power up the CC2420 chip on TelosB in advance. The latency might be improved by setting CC2420 in the standby mode, but at the expense of increased power consumptions.

From a wide range of block ciphers, PRESENT is chosen because it is ultra-lightweight for highly resource-constrained [4], while Skipjack is proven to be software-efficient for 8-bit processors [32]. Both of them have similar block and key sizes as KLEIN. For Hummingbird encryption, Engels *et al.* [18] shows that the speed optimized implementation on 8-bit microcontrollers is about 28.9% slower than PRESENT encryption when the message length is 64 bits. On 16-bit microcontrollers Hummingbird achieves around $50\% \sim 78\%$ performance improvements for different message blocks [18]. The KATAN family ciphers and PRINTCipher, while space-efficient for hardware implementation, are problematic in software performance. This is because KATAN ciphers utilize bit manipulations extensively, whereas PRINTCipher operates on 3 bits at a time, which is at odds with existing 8/16/32-bit architectures.

The ciphers are written in nesC for the TinyOS 2.1.1 platform. This version of TinyOS does provide support for CC2420's AES encryption, but only in conjunction with radio operations. Support for the so-called standalone AES encryption is provided by Zhu's code [53]. The default optimization strategy of TinyOS ("-Os", which minimizes size but not at the expense of speed) is applied to all ciphers except software AES and DESXL on IRIS. For these exceptions, "-O1" and "-O0" are used respectively to bypass compilation errors. The maximum stack size on TelosB is measured using MSPsim [19]. There is no known tool for the same purpose on IRIS. The processing speeds are measured in encryption/decryption, whilst the storage costs are calculated in together. Since there is no such an instruction in TelosB or IRIS which can measure the processing speed by cycles per byte, the speed is compared by using the results of processing the same 16-byte message in milliseconds. All software implementations are optimized using look-up tables. On IRIS, the tables are specifically programmed to be stored in Flash memory. The performance comparison in Table 2 shows that KLEIN is competitive for low-resource applications and especially suitable for sensors. Although the block processing speeds of KLEIN are lower than Skipjack, it is a reasonable trade-off considering the security margin of KLEIN.

In KLEIN, the MixNibbles step will be a non-straightforward part of hardware design. Since it is the same as the MixColumns step of AES, we may simply borrow the idea from AES hardware implementations. Feldhofer *et al.* [20] shows a hardware-efficient implementation of the MixColumns step, which only costs about 340 GE with a 32-bit width. Because the MixNibbles step can be paralleled by two 32-bit tuples, Feldhofer *et al.*'s implementation can also be used in KLEIN families. The RotateNibbles step is simple byte-shift operations, which can be implemented with a minimum hardware.

For a hardware implementation, a low-cost RFID tag might have between 1,000 and 10,000 GE in total, while its security components may occupy up to 2,000 GE only

Table 2. The software performance of KLEIN and related block ciphers

Algorithm	Performance on IRIS				
	Key length (bit)	Block size (bit)	RAM (byte)	ROM (byte)	Processing speed (ms per 16-byte message)
AES-128 (software implementation)	128	128	295	14216	1.32/1.29
NOEKEON (indirect encryption)	128	128	111	4472	3.33/3.33
NOEKEON (direct encryption)	128	128	111	4424	3.33/3.33
DESXL	184	64	306	32186	6.43/5.68
GOST	256	64	233	14342	1.93/1.89
SEA	96	96	249	1904	3.76/3.67
HIGHT	128	64	117	2510	1.84/1.46
Hummingbird	128	16	159	2646	4.30/9.14
PRESENT-80	80	64	365	6866	4.06/9.34
PRINTCipher-48	80	48	125	6184	21.6/14.9
KATAN-64	80	64	625	3260	80.5/43.5
mCrypton-64	64	64	355	9768	5.20/4.41
mCrypton-96	96	64	355	10252	5.37/4.41
mCrypton-128	128	64	355	11160	5.49/4.51
Skipjack	80	64	133	2566	0.90/0.90
KLEIN-64	64	64	105	2582	0.96/1.25
KLEIN-80	80	64	107	2672	1.21/1.70
KLEIN-96	96	64	109	2782	1.52/2.11

Algorithm	Performance on TelosB					
	Key length (bit)	Block size (bit)	RAM (byte)	ROM (byte)	Max stack (byte)	Processing speed (ms per 16-byte message)
AES-128 (software implementation)	128	128	218	10898	230	1.71/1.68
AES-128 (hardware encryption)	128	128	60	900	116	2.29
NOEKEON (indirect encryption)	128	128	56	3544	258	2.38/2.43
NOEKEON (direct encryption)	128	128	56	4224	242	2.38/2.42
DESXL	184	64	186	6966	144	1.86/1.86
GOST	256	64	190	4748	120	2.56/2.52
SEA	96	96	204	2754	120	7.3/6.89
HIGHT	128	64	40	2050	132	2.15/2.15
Hummingbird	128	16	82	1822	116	4.61/9.69
PRESENT-80	80	64	288	6424	128	6.6/11.1
PRINTCipher-48	80	48	48	6210	128	28.3/21.3
KATAN-64	80	64	548	2628	202	120/121
mCrypton-64	64	64	248	7816	182	3.4/3.91
mCrypton-96	96	64	248	8026	158	3.4/3.91
mCrypton-128	128	64	248	8748	158	3.4/3.91
Skipjack	80	64	56	1542	130	1.37/1.33
KLEIN-64	64	64	50	2980	186	1.97/2.5
KLEIN-80	80	64	52	3112	178	2.62/3.4
KLEIN-96	96	64	54	3266	182	3.32/4.55

[26,47]. The area restriction could be looser on sensors. By using VeriSilicon GSMC 0.13um low-power process high-density standard cell library, Yalcin et al. implemented KLEIN-64 for an ultra-lightweight crypto processor [2]. Based on their results and synthesized with TSMC 0.18 μm Process 1.8-Volt SAGE-X Standard Cell Library, the hardware implementation results of KLEIN families are compared to the related block ciphers in Table 3.

Table 3. Hardware implementation results comparison of KLEIN and related block ciphers

Algorithm	Implementation	Hardware Encryption			
		Logic process (μm)	Datapath (bits)	Area in GE	Cycle per block
AES-128	[51]	0.11	32	5400	54
	[24]	0.13	8	3100	160
	[40]	0.18	8	2400	226
HIGHT	[22]	0.25	64	3048	34
PRESENT-80	[4]	0.18	64	1570	32
			4	1075	563
KLEIN-64	[2]	0.13	8	1365	96
KLEIN-64	this paper	0.18	64	2475	13
			8	1397	103
			4	1220	207
KLEIN-80	this paper	0.18	64	2629	17
			8	1630	135
			4	1478	271
KLEIN-96	this paper	0.18	64	2769	21
			8	1696	167
			4	1528	335

5   Conclusion

In this paper, we have proposed a new family of block ciphers called KLEIN. The goal of our design is to provide a practical and secure cipher for low-resource applications, especially for RFIDs and wireless sensor networks. Although KLEIN mainly focuses on software implementations, it also enjoys hardware efficiency resulting from its simple structure with an involutive S-box. The various key lengths of KLEIN offer a flexibility and a moderate security level for ubiquitous applications. Therefore, our design increases the available options for lightweight block ciphers in low-resource applications.

Acknowledgement. We would like to thank Begül Bilgin for her helpful results on the hardware implementations of KLEIN. And we also thank Hongjun Wu and many anonymous reviewers for their valuable comments. We are grateful to Xinxin Fan, Chae Hoon Lim, Axel Poschmann, Eric Smith, Francois-Xavier Standaert for sharing their test vectors and reference source code with us. The work described in this paper has been supported [in part] by the European Commission through the ICT program under contract ICT-2007-216676 ECRYPT II. The authors acknowledge the financial support of SenterNovem for the ALwEN project, grant PNE07007. Yee Wei Law is partly supported by the Australian Research Council under contract number DP1095452, and the European Commission under contract number FP7-257992 (SmartSantander). The authors also thank the support of NSFC Grant 61100201.

References

1. Biham, E., Biryukov, A., Shamir, A.: Cryptanalysis of Skipjack Reduced to 31 Rounds Using Impossible Differentials. In: Stern, J. (ed.) EUROCRYPT 1999. LNCS, vol. 1592, pp. 12–23. Springer, Heidelberg (1999)
2. Bilgin, B., Kavun, E.B., Yalcin, T.: Towards an Ultra Lightweight Crypto Processor. In: Workshop on Lightweight Security & Privacy: Devices, Protocols, and Applications (Lightsec 2011), pp. 76–83. IEEE CS, Los Alamitos (2011)
3. Bogdanov, A., Knudsen, L.R., Leander, G., Paar, C., Poschmann, A., Robshaw, M.J.B., Seurin, Y., Vikkelsoe, C.: PRESENT: An Ultra-Lightweight Block Cipher. In: Paillier, P., Verbauwhede, I. (eds.) CHES 2007. LNCS, vol. 4727, pp. 450–466. Springer, Heidelberg (2007)
4. Bogdanov, A., Leander, G., Paar, C., Poschmann, A., Robshaw, M.J.B., Seurin, Y.: Hash Functions and RFID tags: Mind the Gap. In: Oswald, E., Rohatgi, P. (eds.) CHES 2008. LNCS, vol. 5154, pp. 283–299. Springer, Heidelberg (2008)
5. Bogdanov, A., Rechberger, C.: A 3-Subset Meet-in-the-Middle Attack: Cryptanalysis of the Lightweight Block Cipher KTANTAN. In: Biryukov, A., Gong, G., Stinson, D.R. (eds.) SAC 2010. LNCS, vol. 6544, pp. 229–240. Springer, Heidelberg (2011)
6. De Cannière, C., Dunkelman, O., Knežević, M.: KATAN and KTANTAN — A family of Small and Efficient Hardware-Oriented Block Ciphers. In: Clavier, C., Gaj, K. (eds.) CHES 2009. LNCS, vol. 5747, pp. 272–288. Springer, Heidelberg (2009)
7. Chipcon: CC2420: 2.4 GHz IEEE 802.15.4/Zigbee-ready RF transceiver, http://focus.ti.com/lit/ds/symlink/cc2420.pdf
8. Cho, J.Y.: Linear Cryptanalysis of Reduced-Round PRESENT. In: Pieprzyk, J. (ed.) CT-RSA 2010. LNCS, vol. 5985, pp. 302–317. Springer, Heidelberg (2010)
9. Collard, B., Standaert, F.-X.: A Statistical Saturation Attack Against The Block Cipher PRESENT. In: Fischlin, M. (ed.) CT-RSA 2009. LNCS, vol. 5473, pp. 195–210. Springer, Heidelberg (2009)
10. Crossbow: IRIS wireless measurement system, http://www.xbow.com/Products/Product_pdf_files/ Wireless_pdf/IRIS_Datasheet.pdf
11. Crossbow: TelosB mote platform, http://www.xbow.com/Products/Product_pdf_files/ Wireless_pdf/TelosB_Datasheet.pdf
12. Daemen, J., Knudsen, L.R., Rijmen, V.: Linear Frameworks for Block Ciphers. Designs, Codes and Cryptography 22(1), 65–87 (2001)
13. Daemen, J., Peeters, M., Van Assche, G., Rijmen, V.: The NOEKEON Block Cipher. The NESSIE Proposal (2000)
14. Daemen, J., Rijmen, V.: The Design of Rijndael: AES - The Advanced Encryption Standard. Springer, Heidelberg (2002)
15. Daemen, J., Rijmen, V.: A New MAC Construction ALRED and A Specific Instance ALPHA-MAC. In: Gilbert, H., Handschuh, H. (eds.) FSE 2005. LNCS, vol. 3557, pp. 1–17. Springer, Heidelberg (2005)
16. Daemen, J., Rijmen, V.: New Criteria for Linear Maps in AES-Like Ciphers. Cryptography and Communications 1(1), 47–69 (2009)
17. Dinur, I., Shamir, A.: Cube Attacks on Tweakable Black Box Polynomials. In: Joux, A. (ed.) EUROCRYPT 2009. LNCS, vol. 5479, pp. 278–299. Springer, Heidelberg (2009)
18. Engels, D., Fan, X., Gong, G., Hu, H., Smith, E.M.: Hummingbird: Ultra-Lightweight Cryptography for Resource-Constrained Devices. In: Sion, R., Curtmola, R., Dietrich, S., Kiayias, A., Miret, J.M., Sako, K., Sebé, F. (eds.) RLCPS, WECSR, and WLC 2010. LNCS, vol. 6054, pp. 3–18. Springer, Heidelberg (2010)

19. Eriksson, J., Dunkels, A., Finne, N., Österlind, F., Voigt, T.: MSPsim - An Extensible Simulator for MSP430-Equipped Sensor Boards. In: Proceedings of the European Conference on Wireless Sensor Networks (EWSN), Poster/Demo Session, Delft, The Netherlands (January 2007)
20. Feldhofer, M., Wolkerstorfer, J., Rijmen, V.: AES Implementation on a Grain of Sand. IEEE Proceedings on Information Security 152(1), 13–20 (2005)
21. Gong, Z., Hartel, P., Nikova, S., Zhu, B.: Towards Secure and Practical MACs for Body Sensor Networks. In: Roy, B.K., Sendrier, N. (eds.) INDOCRYPT 2009. LNCS, vol. 5922, pp. 182–198. Springer, Heidelberg (2009)
22. Hong, D., Sung, J., Hong, S., Lim, J., Lee, S., Koo, B., Lee, C., Chang, D., Lee, J., Jeong, K., Kim, H., Kim, J., Chee, S.: HIGHT: A New Block Cipher Suitable for Low-Resource Device. In: Goubin, L., Matsui, M. (eds.) CHES 2006. LNCS, vol. 4249, pp. 46–59. Springer, Heidelberg (2006)
23. Granboulan, L.: Flaws in Differential Cryptanalysis of Skipjack. In: Matsui, M. (ed.) FSE 2001. LNCS, vol. 2355, pp. 328–335. Springer, Heidelberg (2002)
24. Hamalainen, P., Alho, T., Hannikainen, M., Hamalainen, T.D.: Design and Implementation of Low-Area and Low-Power AES Encryption Hardware Core. In: DSD 2006: Proceedings of the 9th EUROMICRO Conference on Digital System Design, pp. 577–583. IEEE Computer Society, Washington, DC, USA (2006)
25. Healy, M., Newe, T., Lewis, E.: Analysis of Hardware Encryption Versus Software Encryption on Wireless Sensor Network Motes. In: Mukhopadhyay, S.C., Gupta, G.S. (eds.) Smart Sensors and Sensing Technology 2008. LNEE, vol. 20, pp. 3–14. Springer, Heidelberg (2008)
26. Juels, A., Weis, S.A.: Authenticating Pervasive Devices with Human Protocols. In: Shoup, V. (ed.) CRYPTO 2005. LNCS, vol. 3621, pp. 293–308. Springer, Heidelberg (2005)
27. Knudsen, L.R., Leander, G., Poschmann, A., Robshaw, M.J.B.: PRINTCipher: A Block Cipher for IC-Printing. In: Mangard and Standaert [37], pp. 16–32
28. Knudsen, L.R., Raddum, H.: On NOEKEON. The NESSIE Report (April 2001)
29. Knudsen, L.R., Robshaw, M.J.B., Wagner, D.: Truncated Differentials and Skipjack. In: Wiener, M. (ed.) CRYPTO 1999. LNCS, vol. 1666, pp. 165–180. Springer, Heidelberg (1999)
30. Knudsen, L.R., Wagner, D.: Integral Cryptanalysis. In: Daemen, J., Rijmen, V. (eds.) FSE 2002. LNCS, vol. 2365, pp. 112–127. Springer, Heidelberg (2002)
31. Könighofer, R.: A Fast and Cache-Timing Resistant Implementation of the AES. In: Malkin, T. (ed.) CT-RSA 2008. LNCS, vol. 4964, pp. 187–202. Springer, Heidelberg (2008)
32. Law, Y.W., Doumen, J., Hartel, P.H.: Survey and Benchmark of Block Ciphers for Wireless Sensor Networks. ACM Trans. Sen. Netw. 2(1), 65–93 (2006)
33. Leander, G., Paar, C., Poschmann, A., Schramm, K.: New Lightweight DES Variants. In: Biryukov, A. (ed.) FSE 2007. LNCS, vol. 4593, pp. 196–210. Springer, Heidelberg (2007)
34. Lim, C.H.: A Revised Version of CRYPTON - CRYPTON V1.0. In: Knudsen, L.R. (ed.) FSE 1999. LNCS, vol. 1636, pp. 31–45. Springer, Heidelberg (1999)
35. Lim, C.H., Korkishko, T.: mCrypton – A Lightweight Block Cipher for Security of Low-Cost RFID Tags and Sensors. In: Song, J., Kwon, T., Yung, M. (eds.) WISA 2005. LNCS, vol. 3786, pp. 243–258. Springer, Heidelberg (2006)
36. Mangard, S., Popp, T., Gammel, B.M.: Side-Channel Leakage of Masked CMOS Gates. In: Menezes, A.J. (ed.) CT-RSA 2005. LNCS, vol. 3376, pp. 351–365. Springer, Heidelberg (2005)
37. Mangard, S., Standaert, F.X. (eds.): CHES 2010. LNCS, vol. 6225. Springer, Heidelberg (2010)
38. Matsui, M.: New Structure of Block Ciphers with Provable Security against Differential and Linear Cryptanalysis. In: Gollmann, D. (ed.) FSE 1996. LNCS, vol. 1039, pp. 205–218. Springer, Heidelberg (1996)

39. Moradi, A., Poschmann, A.: Lightweight Cryptography and DPA Countermeasures: A Survey. In: Sion, R., Curtmola, R., Dietrich, S., Kiayias, A., Miret, J.M., Sako, K., Sebé, F. (eds.) RLCPS, WECSR, and WLC 2010. LNCS, vol. 6054, pp. 68–79. Springer, Heidelberg (2010)
40. Moradi, A., Poschmann, A., Ling, S., Paar, C., Wang, H.: Pushing the Limits: A Very Compact and a Threshold Implementation of AES. In: Paterson, K.G. (ed.) EUROCRYPT 2011. LNCS, vol. 6632, pp. 69–88. Springer, Heidelberg (2011)
41. Nikova, S., Rijmen, V., Schläffer, M.: Secure Hardware Implementation of Non-Linear Functions in the Presence of Glitches. In: Lee, P.J., Cheon, J.H. (eds.) ICISC 2008. LNCS, vol. 5461, pp. 218–234. Springer, Heidelberg (2009)
42. NIST. Skipjack and KEA algorithm Specifications (version 2.0). NIST online document (May 1998), http://csrc.nist.gov/groups/ST/toolkit/documents/skipjack/skipjack.pdf
43. Ohkuma, K.: Weak Keys of Reduced-Round PRESENT for Linear Cryptanalysis, pp. 249–265. Springer, Heidelberg (2009)
44. Özen, O., Varıcı, K., Tezcan, C., Kocair, Ç.: Lightweight Block Ciphers Revisited: Cryptanalysis of Reduced Round PRESENT and HIGHT. In: Boyd, C., González Nieto, J. (eds.) ACISP 2009. LNCS, vol. 5594, pp. 90–107. Springer, Heidelberg (2009)
45. Paar, C., Poschmann, A., Robshaw, M.: New Designs in Lightweight Symmetric Encryption. In: Kitsos, P., Zhang, Y. (eds.) RFID Security: Techniques, Protocols and System-on-Chip Design, pp. 349–371. Springer, Heidelberg (2008)
46. Phan, R.C.W.: Cryptanalysis of Full Skipjack Block Cipher. Electronic Letters, 69–71 (2002)
47. Poschmann, A.: Lightweight Cryptography - Cryptographic Engineering for a Pervasive-World. PhD thesis, Ruhr-University Bochum, Germany (2009)
48. Poschmann, A., Ling, S., Wang, H.: 256 Bit Standardized Crypto for 650 Ge - Gost Revisited. In: Mangard and Standaert [37], pp. 219–233
49. Rolfes, C., Poschmann, A., Leander, G., Paar, C.: Ultra-Lightweight Implementations for Smart Devices – Security for 1000 Gate Equivalents. In: Grimaud, G., Standaert, F.-X. (eds.) CARDIS 2008. LNCS, vol. 5189, pp. 89–103. Springer, Heidelberg (2008)
50. Saarinen, M.J.O.: Cryptanalysis of Hummingbird-1. In: Joux, A. (ed.) FSE 2011. LNCS, vol. 6733, pp. 328–341. Springer, Heidelberg (2011)
51. Satoh, A., Morioka, S., Takano, K., Munetoh, S.: A Compact Rijndael Hardware Architecture with S-Box Optimization. In: Boyd, C. (ed.) ASIACRYPT 2001. LNCS, vol. 2248, pp. 239–254. Springer, Heidelberg (2001)
52. Standaert, F.X., Piret, G., Gershenfeld, N., Quisquater, J.J.: SEA: A Scalable Encryption Algorithm for Small Embedded Applications. In: Domingo-Ferrer, J., Posegga, J., Schreckling, D. (eds.) CARDIS 2006. LNCS, vol. 3928, pp. 222–236. Springer, Heidelberg (2006)
53. Zhu, B.: The Standalone AES Encryption of CC2420 (TinyOS 2.10 and MICAz) (December 2008), http://cis.sjtu.edu.cn/index.php/Bo_Zhu

Appendix A. Test Vectors of KLEIN

Table 4. Test vectors for KLEIN-64

Key	Message	Cipher
0000 0000 0000 0000	FFFF FFFF FFFF FFFF	CDC0 B51F 1472 2BBE
FFFF FFFF FFFF FFFF	0000 0000 0000 0000	6456 764E 8602 E154
1234 5678 90AB CDEF	FFFF FFFF FFFF FFFF	5923 56C4 9971 76C8
0000 0000 0000 0000	1234 5678 90AB CDEF	629F 9D6D FF95 800E

Table 5. Test vectors for KLEIN-80

Key	Message	Cipher
0000 0000 0000 0000 0000	FFFF FFFF FFFF FFFF	6677 E20D 1A53 A431
FFFF FFFF FFFF FFFF FFFF	0000 0000 0000 0000	8224 7502 273D CC5F
1234 5678 90AB CDEF 1234	FFFF FFFF FFFF FFFF	3F21 0F67 CB23 687A
0000 0000 0000 0000 0000	1234 5678 90AB CDEF	BA52 39E9 3E78 4366

Table 6. Test vectors for KLEIN-96

Key	Message	Cipher
0000 0000 0000 0000 0000 0000	FFFF FFFF FFFF FFFF	DB9F A7D3 3D8E 8E36
FFFF FFFF FFFF FFFF FFFF FFFF	0000 0000 0000 0000	15A3 A033 86A7 FEC6
1234 5678 90AB CDEF 1234 5678	FFFF FFFF FFFF FFFF	7968 7798 AFDA 0BC3
0000 0000 0000 0000 0000 0000	1234 5678 90AB CDEF	5006 A987 A500 BFDD

The Hummingbird-2 Lightweight Authenticated Encryption Algorithm

Daniel Engels, Markku-Juhani O. Saarinen,
Peter Schweitzer, and Eric M. Smith

REVERE SECURITY
4500 Westgrove Drive, Suite 335, Addison, TX 75001, USA
{daniel.engels,mjos,pater.schweitzer,
eric.smith}@reveresecurity.com

Abstract. Hummingbird-2 is an encryption algorithm with a 128-bit secret key and a 64-bit initialization vector. Hummingbird-2 optionally produces an authentication tag for each message processed. Like it's predecessor Hummingbird-1, Hummingbird-2 has been targeted for low-end microcontrollers and for hardware implementation in lightweight devices such as RFID tags and wireless sensors. Compared to the previous version of the cipher, and in response to extensive analysis, the internal state has been increased to 128 bits and a flow of entropy from the state to the mixing function has been improved. In this paper we present the Hummingbird-2 algorithm, its design and security arguments, performance analysis on both software and hardware platforms, and timing analysis in relation to the ISO 18000-6C protocol.

Keywords: Hummingbird cipher, constrained devices, lightweight cryptography, ISO 18000-6C.

1   Introduction

Authenticated encryption algorithms provide confidentiality and integrity protection for messages using a single processing step. This results in performance and cost advantages, especially when the algorithm is implemented in hardware.

Hummingbird-2 is an authenticating encryption primitive that has been designed particularly for resource-constrained devices such as RFID tags, wireless sensors, smart meters and industrial controllers. Hummingbird-2 can be implemented with very small hardware or software footprint and is therefore suitable for providing security in low-cost ubiquitous devices.

The design described in this paper is an evolutionary step from Hummingbird-1 [8,10,11] and was developed in part as a response to the cryptanalysis of the cipher presented in [20]. Hummingbird-2 is resistant to all previously known cryptanalytic attacks.

The Hummingbird-2 does not directly fall to either traditional stream cipher or block cipher categories as it inherits properties from both. In this sense Hummingbird-2 resembles the Helix and Phelix proposals [9,16,22]. Since Hummingbird-2 operates on 16-bit blocks, more efficiency can be realized in applications that chirp small messages,

A. Juels and C. Paar (Eds.): RFIDSec 2011, LNCS 7055, pp. 19–31, 2012.

Table 1. S-Boxes used in Hummingbird-2

x	0	1	2	3	4	5	6	7	8	9	10	11	12	13	14	15
$S_1(x)$	7	12	14	9	2	1	5	15	11	6	13	0	4	8	10	3
$S_2(x)$	4	10	1	6	8	15	7	12	3	0	14	13	5	9	11	2
$S_3(x)$	2	15	12	1	5	6	10	13	14	8	3	4	0	11	9	7
$S_4(x)$	15	4	5	8	9	7	2	1	10	3	0	14	6	12	13	11

such as RFID devices or wireless sensors. This also makes it easy to layer in security in various protocol schemes.

This paper is structured as follows: A formal description of Hummingbird-2 is contained in Section 2. Section 3 has the preliminary results of cryptanalysis of the cipher. Software and hardware implementations are described in Section 4, together with ISO 18000-6C timing information and comparison in Section 5. Conclusions can be found in Section 6. Appendix A contains a set of implementation test vectors for Hummingbird-2.

2   Description of Hummingbird-2

The Hummingbird-2 cipher has a 128-bit secret key K and a 128-bit internal state R which is initialized using a 64-bit Initialization Vector IV. These variables are accessed as vectors of 16-bit words:

$$K = (K_1, K_2, K_3, K_4, K_5, K_6, K_7, K_8),$$
$$R = (R_1, R_2, R_3, R_4, R_5, R_6, R_7, R_8),$$
$$IV = (IV_1, IV_2, IV_3, IV_4).$$

Hummingbird-2 is entirely built from operations on 16-bit words: the exclusive-or operation on words ($\oplus$), addition modulo 65536 ($\boxplus$) and a nonlinear mixing function $f(x)$.

2.1   Nonlinear Functions $f(x)$ and $WD16(x, a, b, c, d)$

The nonlinear mixing function f consists of four-bit S-Box permutation lookups on each nibble of the word, followed by a linear mix.

The Hummingbird-2 S-Boxes S_1, S_2, S_3 and S_4 are given Table 1.[1] Let $S(x)$ denote the computation of four S-Boxes and $L(x)$ the linear transformation which is expressed using the left circular shift (rotation) operator ($\lll$). We may write the f component as

$$S(x) = S_1(x_0) \mid S_2(x_1) \mid S_3(x_2) \mid S_4(x_3)$$
$$L(x) = x \oplus (x \lll 6) \oplus (x \lll 10)$$
$$f(x) = L(S(x)).$$

---

[1] Some early versions of Hummingbird-2 used a different set of S-Boxes from Serpent [1]. Hummingbird-2 was tweaked in May 2011 to use these S-Boxes.

We further define a 16-bit keyed permutation WD16 using f as

$$\text{WD16}(x, a, b, c, d) = f(f(f(f(x \oplus a) \oplus b) \oplus c) \oplus d). \tag{1}$$

The inverse of $f(x)$ and WD16 can be derived in straightforward fashion.

2.2 Initialization

The internal state of Hummingbird-2 is initialized with a four-round procedure using the 64-bit nonce IV. We first set

$$R^{(0)} = (IV_1, IV_2, IV_3, IV_4, IV_1, IV_2, IV_3, IV_4) \tag{2}$$

and then iterate for $i = 0, 1, 2, 3$ the following:

$$t_1 = \text{WD16}(R_1^{(i)} \boxplus \langle i \rangle, K_1, K_2, K_3, K_4)$$

$$t_2 = \text{WD16}(R_2^{(i)} \boxplus t_1, K_5, K_6, K_7, K_8)$$

$$t_3 = \text{WD16}(R_3^{(i)} \boxplus t_2, K_1, K_2, K_3, K_4)$$

$$t_4 = \text{WD16}(R_4^{(i)} \boxplus t_3, K_5, K_6, K_7, K_8)$$

$$R_1^{(i+1)} = (R_1^{(i)} \boxplus t_4) \lll 3$$

$$R_2^{(i+1)} = (R_2^{(i)} \boxplus t_1) \ggg 1$$

$$R_3^{(i+1)} = (R_3^{(i)} \boxplus t_2) \lll 8$$

$$R_4^{(i+1)} = (R_4^{(i)} \boxplus t_3) \lll 1$$

$$R_5^{(i+1)} = R_5^{(i)} \oplus R_1^{(i+1)}$$

$$R_6^{(i+1)} = R_6^{(i)} \oplus R_2^{(i+1)}$$

$$R_7^{(i+1)} = R_7^{(i)} \oplus R_3^{(i+1)}$$

$$R_8^{(i+1)} = R_8^{(i)} \oplus R_4^{(i+1)}.$$

The initial state for encrypting the first plaintext word is $R^{(4)}$. Note that the two's complement numerical value of $i = 0 \ldots 3$ is used in computation of t_1.

2.3 Encryption

Encryption of a single word of plaintext P_i to ciphertext word C_i requires four invocations of WD16. [2]

$$t_1 = \text{WD16}(R_1^{(i)} \boxplus P_i, K_1, K_2, K_3, K_4)$$

$$t_2 = \text{WD16}(R_2^{(i)} \boxplus t_1, K_5 \oplus R_5^{(i)}, K_6 \oplus R_6^{(i)}, K_7 \oplus R_7^{(i)}, K_8 \oplus R_8^{(i)})$$

$$t_3 = \text{WD16}(R_3^{(i)} \boxplus t_2, K_1 \oplus R_5^{(i)}, K_2 \oplus R_6^{(i)}, K_3 \oplus R_7^{(i)}, K_4 \oplus R_8^{(i)})$$

$$C_i = \text{WD16}(R_4^{(i)} \boxplus t_3, K_5, K_6, K_7, K_8) \boxplus R_1^{(i)}.$$

---

[2] Some early versions of this paper had a typographic error here as the final addition of $R_1^{(i)}$ was missing. Thanks to Jean-Philippe Aumasson for spotting this.

After each encrypted / decrypted word, we perform the following state update:

$$R_1^{(i+1)} = R_1^{(i)} \boxplus t_3$$
$$R_2^{(i+1)} = R_2^{(i)} \boxplus t_1$$
$$R_3^{(i+1)} = R_3^{(i)} \boxplus t_2$$
$$R_4^{(i+1)} = R_4^{(i)} \boxplus R_1^{(i)} \boxplus t_3 \boxplus t_1$$
$$R_5^{(i+1)} = R_5^{(i)} \oplus (R_1^{(i)} \boxplus t_3)$$
$$R_6^{(i+1)} = R_6^{(i)} \oplus (R_2^{(i)} \boxplus t_1)$$
$$R_7^{(i+1)} = R_7^{(i)} \oplus (R_3^{(i)} \boxplus t_2)$$
$$R_8^{(i+1)} = R_8^{(i)} \oplus (R_4^{(i)} \boxplus R_1^{(i)} \boxplus t_3 \boxplus t_1).$$

A shorthand of this is $C = E(P)$. The state variable R is stepped by one iteration for each invocation of E. Note that the update function can be simplified since certain terms are re-used.

2.4 Authenticating Fixed-Length Unencrypted Associated Data

Authenticated Encryption with Associated Data (AEAD) is a method of using Hummingbird that encrypts / decrypts a payload and also authenticates any associated data (AD) that travels alongside the ciphertext such as the nonce and a packet header. AD processing is optional in implementations.

AD processing occurs after the entire encrypted payload has processed. We simply compute $E(A_i)$ but transmit A_i itself instead. Note that the size of the AD must be fixed (known by the recipient).

2.5 Stream Cipher Mode: A Technique for Encoding Short Fixed-Length Fields

Sometimes it is desirable to communicate, without message expansion, datagrams which are less than 16 bits in size. We describe an encoding technique which enables this.

Let x be the short message of $1 \leq n \leq 15$ bits. The ciphertext message is derived from the n least significant bits of $x \oplus E(0)$. If message integrity is required, the state is further updated by $E(x)$. Decoding is straightforward.

Note that encrypting the two words 0 and x has exactly the same effect on state and hence special care must be taken to ensure that both parties are in sync. If a protocol requires arbitrary-length authenticated messages, this technique can be used for padding, but the total message length (in bits) must be specified and verified in an unambiguous fixed-length AD field.

2.6 Computing the Message Authentication Code

To compute a message authentication tag T of $n \leq 8$ words, we first finalize the message by first stepping the cipher three times without producing any output.

$$E(IV_1 \boxplus R_1 \boxplus R_3 \boxplus n)$$
$$E(IV_2 \boxplus R_1 \boxplus R_3)$$
$$E(IV_3 \boxplus R_1 \boxplus R_3).$$

Here R_1 and R_3 denotes the contents of those register words immediately before each invocation of E. We then construct the words of the authentication tag T as follows:

$$T_1 = E(IV_4 \boxplus R_1 \boxplus R_3)$$
$$T_i = E(R_1 \boxplus R_3) \quad \text{for i} = 2, 3, \ldots, \text{n}.$$

2.7 Uniqueness Requirement for IVs and Keys

Hummingbird-2 is an authenticated encryption primitive and may be used in similar fashion as the Galois/Counter Mode (GCM) and GMAC, which are part of NSA "Suite B" algorithms. Implementers would be wise to take similar care in ensuring that keys and IVs are never repeated. We restate the requirement from Section 8 of [7].

> The probability that the authenticated encryption function ever will be invoked with the same IV and the same key on two (or more) distinct sets of input data shall be no greater than 2^{-32}.

Generally speaking, compliance to this requirement is recommended in order to mitigate the risk of using Hummingbird-2 in certain applications, and this cipher is not as vulnerable to repeated IV attacks as AES-GCM and should be able to resist many realistic chosen-IV attacks.

Indeed Hummingbird-2 leaks very little information should the nonce be repeated. At most all you get are exact repetitions in the ciphertext where you have exact repetitions in the plaintext.

3   Development and Analysis

The main differences between Hummingbird-1 and Hummingbird-2 are:

- The key size has been set to 128 bits to be commensurable with the actual security of the cipher.
- The state size of the cipher has been increased from 80 bits to 128 bits and the LFSR has been eliminated. The last four new state registers R_5, R_6, R_7, and R_8 are called the "accumulator" registers.
- The keyed transform, called the "E Box" in [20] now only has four invocations of the S-Boxes, compared to five in Hummingbird-1. This increases the encryption speed of the cipher.
- The authentication mechanism has been improved to thwart a message extension attack.
- Support for authenticating unencrypted associated data has been introduced with the AEAD mode discussed in Section 2.4.
- Recommendations to the reuse of keys and IVs have been introduced.
- An important design criteria was compatibility with the ISO 18000-6C timing requirements as discussed in Section 5.

We note that prior to publication, Hummingbird-2 has been subjected to a significant cryptanalytic security assurance effort. For this, the services of Jim Frazer & Son Cryptography (formerly ISSI) and the U. Waterloo Centre for Applied Cryptography Research were used, in addition to input from public analysis of Hummingbird-1. After thousands of hours of cryptanalysis, no significant flaws or sub-exhaustive attacks against Hummingbird-2 have been found. We summarize the results of our analysis in the following sections.

3.1 Structure of the Cipher

Hummingbird-2 has been designed to be as lightweight as possible while still maintaining a reasonable security margin against attacks. The state size of 128 bits should not be confused with the state size of stream ciphers (where the key is usually loaded into the evolving state registers upon initialization). In Hummingbird-2 the key is kept constant and hence we could say that the state is 128+128=256 bits of which 128 bits is evolving. There is strong experimental and theoretical evidence that the cycle upon constant input words is 2^{127}.

The initialization function is one-to-one from the IV to the four state registers R_1, R_2, R_3, and R_4. Hence there are no nonce collisions. If more than 2^{64} invocations of the E function is performed under a single key, a birthday condition in the internal state may occur. The usage condition given in Section 2.7 will prevent this. Such a birthday condition has very limited cryptographic implication beyond serving as a distinguisher with that complexity. We note that this is the same bound that can be found for the AES algorithm [17].

3.2 S-Box Selection

The S-Box (Table 1 and Section 2.1) selection was based on specific research presented in more detail in [21]. The S-Boxes also belong to the optimal classes discussed in [14].

We performed an exhaustive search through 16! possible permutations. The S-Boxes specifically belong to a classes that ideally satisfy the following conditions:

- Optimal differential bound $p \leq 1/4$, linear bound $\epsilon \leq 1/4$, and branch number 3.
- There is a minimum number of differential characteristics and linear approximations at the bounds.
- All S-boxes belong to a different linear equivalence class.
- The four S-boxes have a large Hamming distance from each other and the identity permutation.
- The algebraic degree of all but one output bit is 3 and each output bit is nonlinearly dependent on a maximum number of input bits.

3.3 Differential Cryptanalysis

Hummingbird-2 has been designed to be resistant to Differential Cryptanalysis [3,4]. The most interesting findings in our research involve the high-bit differential $\Delta = 8000$ which behaves in the same way under modular addition and XOR. Much of the nonlinearity for lower bits comes from interplay of these two operations. The four rotations in the initialization phase were introduced to increase the resistance of the cipher against certain related-key attacks.

We have verified that Hummingbird-2 is provably resistant against the types of attacks described by Saarinen in [20]. This was done by performing a search of all high-bit differentials in both initialization and actual encryption phases of the cipher.

Differentials in the Encryption Function. Let $H = 8000$ denote the high bit differential and x some undefined ciphertext differential. We found the following differentials that hold with probability 1.

$$\Delta P = 0 \quad \Delta R = (0\,0\,0\,H\,0\,0\,0\,0) \;\Rightarrow\; \Delta C = x \quad \Delta R = (0\,0\,0\,H\,0\,0\,0\,H)$$
$$\Delta P = H \quad \Delta R = (H\,0\,0\,0\,0\,0\,0\,0) \;\Rightarrow\; \Delta C = H \quad \Delta R = (H\,0\,0\,H\,H\,0\,0\,H)$$
$$\Delta P = H \quad \Delta R = (H\,0\,0\,H\,0\,0\,0\,0) \;\Rightarrow\; \Delta C = x \quad \Delta R = (H\,0\,0\,0\,H\,0\,0\,0)$$
$$\Delta P = 0 \quad \Delta R = (0\,H\,H\,0\,H\,0\,0\,0) \;\Rightarrow\; \Delta C = 0 \quad \Delta R = (0\,H\,H\,0\,H\,H\,H\,0)$$
$$\Delta P = H \quad \Delta R = (H\,H\,H\,0\,H\,0\,0\,0) \;\Rightarrow\; \Delta C = H \quad \Delta R = (H\,H\,H\,H\,0\,H\,H\,H)$$
$$\Delta P = H \quad \Delta R = (H\,H\,H\,H\,H\,0\,0\,0) \;\Rightarrow\; \Delta C = x \quad \Delta R = (H\,H\,H\,0\,0\,H\,H\,0)$$
$$\Delta P = 0 \quad \Delta R = (0\,H\,H\,H\,H\,0\,0\,0) \;\Rightarrow\; \Delta C = x \quad \Delta R = (0\,H\,H\,H\,H\,H\,H\,H).$$

It can be observed that these differentials can't be used to construct an iterative differential.

Related Keys in Encryption. For two related keys we found one iterative differential which holds with probability one. When the two keys are related by $\Delta K = (H\,0\,0\,0\,H\,0\,0\,0)$ we have:

$$\Delta P = H \quad \Delta R = (0\,0\,0\,0\,H\,0\,0\,0) \;\Rightarrow\; \Delta C = x \quad \Delta R = (0\,0\,0\,0\,H\,0\,0\,0).$$

The ciphertext differential $\Delta C = x$ has some nontrivial value. We haven't found a direct way to exploit this related key property in an attack.

3.4   Linear and Algebraic Cryptanalysis

Hummingbird-2 has been designed to be resistant to Linear Cryptanalysis [15]. We performed a search for best linear masks in the mixing function f. Encryption of a single plaintext word involves sixteen invocations of f, five additions of state words (R_1, R_2, R_3, R_4, and R_1 again) and XOR keying with both static keys and dynamic accumulator variables.

We ignore the modular additions in our analysis. The search and probability calculation was performed on up to four invocations of f, which is no longer distinguishable. Our findings give significant confidence to assert that Hummingbird-2 is resistant to linear cryptanalysis up to twelve rounds of f. We have also experimented with multiple linear approximations in our analysis [2].

The algebraic degree and branch number of the S-Boxes alone thwarts most forms of algebraic distinguishing attacks such as Cube Testers [6] and d-monomial distinguisers [19]. A typical black-box chosen-IV scenario is made difficult by the rather complicated initialization routine that has a total of sixteen WD16 invocations.

4   Implementation and Performance

Hummingbird-2 has been implemented in hardware and in software for various microcontroller architectures. Functions were written in assembly language and hand-optimized for all platforms. All library functions are C-callable and many development environments are supported.

4.1   Microcontroller Software Implementations

As Hummingbird-2 algorithm allows for trade-offs between implementation speed and size, we have implemented up to three software implementation profiles for some microcontroller platforms. Table 2 gives the characteristics of these implementations.

4.2   Hardware Implementations

Three hardware implementation profiles have been produced with differing size, power and speed characteristics. Table 3 summarizes these implementations. Figure 4.2 shows the layouts of the three cores.

- High Performance Design HB2-ee4c. This 4 clock implementation of Hummingbird is targeted at fast encryption (4 clocks) and maximum throughput and bandwidth.
- Low Area and Power Design HB2-ee16c. This 16 clock implementation of Hummingbird is targeted at minimum area and power.
- Ultra Low Area and Power Design HB2-ee20c. This 20 clock implementation of Hummingbird is targeted at ultra low area and power.

The process used was TSMC 0.13 μm, operating with 1.2 V. Encryption speed can be derived by dividing the operating frequency by the number of clocks required to encrypt a single word.

Table 2. Microcontroller software implementations of Hummingbird-2. Encryption and decryption speeds are given in cycles per 16-bit word.

Target	Encr.	Decr.	Size	MAC-64	Init.	RAM $\approx$
MSP430 "Tiny"	1520	1544	770	10768	5984	50
MSP430 "Fast"	576	729	2518	4101	2187	114
MSP430 "Furious"	359	560	3648	2648	1361	114
AVR "Fast"	745	930	3600	5689	2970	114
AVR "Furious"	574	770	4178	4310	2139	114
AVR "Ultimate"	495	652	3200	3764	1800	1500
PIC24 "Fast"	319	371	2227	2248	1162	114
PIC24 "Furious"	271	362	4959	1897	912	114
ARM Cortex	332	336	2200	2525	1492	116

Table 3. Hardware implementations of Hummingbird-2. Encryption and decryption speeds are given in cycles per 16-bit word. The library used was TSMC 180nm, 6 level metal, high density. Synopsis synthesis tools were used.

Profile	Frequency	Clocks per word	Peak pwr (μW)	Leakage (μW)	Area (μm^2)	Gate Equiv.
HB2-ee4c	100 kHz	4	1.93	4.17	27381	3220
HB2-ee4c	10 MHz	4	163.1	4.17	27381	3220
HB2-ee16c	100 kHz	16	1.845	2.85	20871	2332
HB2-ee16c	10 MHz	16	156.8	2.85	20871	2332
HB2-ee20c	100 kHz	20	1.73	2.63	19383	2159
HB2-ee20c	10 MHz	20	149.1	2.63	19383	2159

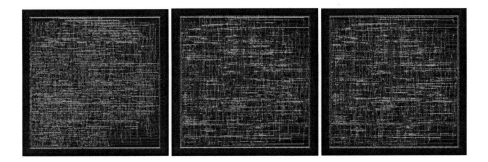

Fig. 1. From left: The layouts of HB2-ee4c, HB2-ee16c, and HB2-ee20c in 0.13 μm process

5   HB2 Timing Compatibility with ISO 18000-6C

The ISO 18000-6C protocol [12] is the leading passive UHF RFID protocol in terms of number of tags sold today. The 18000-6C protocol specifies only a 32-bit password for access control and an electronic kill function.

The primary functionality of the 18000-6C protocol is for fast and efficient tag identification across a range of operating environments. Consequently, 18000-6C supports a range of data rates at which the interrogator and the tag may communicate. Communications are controlled by the interrogator in a Reader Talks First communication scheme. The interrogator begins a communication sequence by issuing a preamble that defines the length of the logic 0 and logic 1 symbols. The length of the logic 0 symbol is referred to as Tari, which is a fundamental timing parameter for communications.

For all commands except the Write command, the Tari value determines the amount of time the tag has to begin its response to the reader after the reader has completed the last symbol in its command to the tag. This time is referred to as T1 time. Table 4 shows the T1 timing for the minimum Tari value of 6.25 μs, the maximum Tari value of 25 μs, and a commonly used Tari value of 12.5 μs.

Table 4. T1 Timing Values and Available Clock Cycles

Tari (μs)	T1 Time (μs)	Cycles 1.5 MHz	Cycles 2 MHz	Cycles 2.5 MHz
6.25	39.06	58	78	97
12.5	78.125	117	156	195
25	187.5	281	375	468

Table 5. Clocks Per Bit

Cipher	Block Size (bits)	Key Size (bits)	Clocks Per Bit
HB2	16	128	0.25
Grain-128	1	128	1
Trivium	1	128	1
Present-80	64	80	0.5
Present-128	64	128	0.5
Katan32	32	80	8
Katan48	48	80	5.31
Katan64	64	80	3.98
Iceberg	64	128	0.25
AES-128	128	128	1.25

Table 6. Comparison of Clock Cycles to Encrypt. Note that most block ciphers require initialization every time key is changed.

Cipher	Init	16 bits	32 bits	48 bits	64 bits	96 bits	128 bits
HB2	16	4	8	12	16	24	32
Grain-128	513	16	32	48	68	96	128
Trivium	1333	16	32	48	68	96	128
Present-80	0*	32	32	32	32	64	64
Present-128	0*	32	32	32	32	64	64
Katan32	0*	256	256	512	512	768	1024
Katan48	0*	255	255	255	510	510	765
Katan64	0*	255	255	255	255	510	510
Iceberg	0*	16	16	16	16	32	32
AES-128	0*	160	160	160	160	160	160

In addition to the T1 timings, Table 4 shows the number of full clock cycles available for computation within T1 for three on tag clock frequencies around 2 MHz, a common on-tag clock frequency.

Table 5 compares the clocks per bit required to encrypt a single block for various ciphers that can be implemented with up to approximately three thousand gate equivalents and are therefore fit for RFID use. The figures for Katan have been derived from [5], for Present, ICEBERG and AES from [18] and for Trivium and Grain from [13].

Based upon the clocks per bit for each cipher, in Table 6 we compare the number of clocks required to encrypt various amounts of data.

Command decode and processing overhead may be considerable. Furthermore, the mode overhead and initialization of the basic block ciphers is not considered. This additional processing will require even more overhead. While some operations may be performed in parallel, the command decode and processing must be performed prior to any cryptographic functions being performed.

In conclusion, HB2 is well suited for use in passive RFID systems due to its low power consumption, which minimally impacts range, and its high speed that enables the tag to continue normal operation within T1 timings.

6   Conclusions

We have presented Hummingbird-2, a lightweight authenticated encryption algorithm that we believe to be resistant to all standard attacks to block ciphers and stream ciphers such as differential and linear cryptanalysis, structure attacks and various algebraic attacks. Hummingbird-2 also has the further advantage of being resistant to chosen-IV attacks.

We have also presented results of software and hardware implementations of Hummingbird-2. Hummingbird-2 can be implemented with little more than 2000 gate equivalents, making it well suited for ubiquitous devices such as RFID tags and sensors. Hummingbird-2 has the additional advantage over other lightweight encryption primitives that it produces a message authentication code.

Acknowledgements. In addition to the anonymous RFIDSec '11 program committee members, we would like to thank Whitfield Diffie (who designed the original WD16 function) and the members of CACR and ISSI teams. Troy Hicks and Ken Lauffenburger were behind the hardware work on Hummingbird-2. Jared Smothermon, Stanford Hudson, and Bob Nimon did the Software implementations on various platforms.

References

1. Anderson, R., Biham, E., Knudsen, L.: Serpent: A Proposal for the Advanced Encryption Standard (1999), http://www.cl.cam.ac.uk/~rja14/Papers/serpent.pdf
2. Biryukov, A., De Cannière, C., Quisquater, M.: On Multiple Linear Approximations. In: Franklin, M. (ed.) CRYPTO 2004. LNCS, vol. 3152, pp. 1–22. Springer, Heidelberg (2004)
3. Biham, E., Shamir, A.: Differential Cryptanalysis of DES-like Cryptosystems. In: Menezes, A., Vanstone, S.A. (eds.) CRYPTO 1990. LNCS, vol. 537, pp. 2–21. Springer, Heidelberg (1991)
4. Biham, E., Shamir, A.: Differential Cryptanalysis of the Data Encryption Standard. Springer, Heidelberg (1993)
5. De Cannière, C., Dunkelman, O., Knežević, M.: KATAN and KTANTAN — A Family of Small and Efficient Hardware-Oriented Block Ciphers. In: Clavier, C., Gaj, K. (eds.) CHES 2009. LNCS, vol. 5747, pp. 272–288. Springer, Heidelberg (2009)
6. Dinur, I., Shamir, A.: Cube Attacks on Tweakable Black Box Polynomials. In: Joux, A. (ed.) EUROCRYPT 2009. LNCS, vol. 5479, pp. 278–299. Springer, Heidelberg (2009)
7. Dworkin, M.: Recommendation for Block Cipher Modes of Operation: Galois/Counter Mode (GCM) and GMAC. In: NIST Special Publication 800-38D (2007)
8. Fan, X., Hu, H., Gong, G., Smith, E.M., Engels, D.: Lightweight Implementation of Hummingbird Cryptographic Algorithm on 4-Bit Microcontroller. In: The 1st International Workshop on RFID Security and Cryptography 2009 (RISC 2009), pp. 838–884. Springer, Heidelberg (2009)

9. Ferguson, N., Whiting, D., Schneier, B., Kelsey, J., Lucks, S., Kohno, T.: Helix: Fast Encryption and Authentication in a Single Cryptographic Primitive. In: Johansson, T. (ed.) FSE 2003. LNCS, vol. 2887, pp. 330–346. Springer, Heidelberg (2003)

10. Engels, D., Fan, X., Gong, G., Hu, H., Smith, E.M.: Ultra-Lightweight Cryptography for Low-Cost RFID Tags: Hummingbird Algorithm and Protocol. Centre for Applied Cryptographic Research (CACR) Technical Reports, CACR-2009-29 (2009),
    http://www.cacr.math.uwaterloo.ca/techreports/
    2009/cacr2009-29.

11. Engels, D., Fan, X., Gong, G., Hu, H., Smith, E.M.: Hummingbird: Ultra-Lightweight Cryptography for Resource-Constrained Devices. In: Sion, R., Curtmola, R., Dietrich, S., Kiayias, A., Miret, J.M., Sako, K., Sebé, F. (eds.) RLCPS, WECSR, and WLC 2010. LNCS, vol. 6054, pp. 3–18. Springer, Heidelberg (2010)

12. International Standardization Organization. ISO/IEC 18000-6:2010. Information technology – Radio frequency identification for item management – Part 6: Parameters for air interface communications at 860 MHz to 960 MHz

13. Good, T., Benaissa, M.: Hardware results for selected stream cipher candidates. eStream, ECRYPT Stream Cipher Project Report 2007/023. In: Proceedings of SASC 2007 (2007)

14. Leander, G., Poschmann, A.: On the Classification of 4 Bit S-Boxes. In: Carlet, C., Sunar, B. (eds.) WAIFI 2007. LNCS, vol. 4547, pp. 159–176. Springer, Heidelberg (2007)

15. Matsui, M.: Linear Cryptanalysis Method for DES Cipher. In: Helleseth, T. (ed.) EUROCRYPT 1993. LNCS, vol. 765, pp. 386–397. Springer, Heidelberg (1994)

16. Muller, F.: Differential Attacks Against the Helix Stream Cipher. In: Roy, B., Meier, W. (eds.) FSE 2004. LNCS, vol. 3017, pp. 94–108. Springer, Heidelberg (2004)

17. National Institute of Standards and Technology. The Advanced Encryption Standard (AES). FIPS Publication 197, U.S. DoC/NIST (2001)

18. Poschmann, A.: Lightweight Cryptography - Cryptographic Engineering for a Pervasive World. PhD Thesis. Europaeischer Universitaetsverlag, in the IT-Security series, no 8. Also available as IACR ePrint 2009/516 (2009) ISBN 978-3899663419

19. Saarinen, M.-J.O.: d-Monomial Tests are Effective Against Stream Ciphers. In: State of the Art in Stream Ciphers (SASC) 2006. Workshop Record, K.U. Leuven (2006)

20. Saarinen, M.-J.O.: Cryptanalysis of Hummingbird-1. In: Joux, A. (ed.) FSE 2011. LNCS, vol. 6733, pp. 328–341. Springer, Heidelberg (2011)

21. Saarinen, M.-J.O.: Cryptographic Analysis of All 4×4 - Bit S-Boxes. In: Selected Areas in Cryptography (SAC) 2011, Toronto, Ontario, Canada, August 11-12 (2011)

22. Whiting, D., Schneier, B., Lucks, S., Muller, F.: Phelix – Fast Encryption and Authentication in a Single Cryptographic Primitive. In: ECRYPT Stream Cipher Project Report 2005/027 (2005), http://www.schneier.com/paper-phelix.html

A   Test Vectors

The test data is given as an array of bytes. When using these test vectors, note that Hummingbird-2 processes data in little-endian fashion (this means that the first 16-bit plaintext word in the second test vector is actually 0x1100).

```
Secret key    00 00 00 00 00 00 00 00 00 00 00 00 00 00 00 00
IV / Nonce    00 00 00 00 00 00 00 00
Plaintext     00 00 00 00 00 00 00 00 00 00 00 00 00 00 00 00
Ciphertext    C4 EF 87 A8 4F 05 A9 91 57 46 44 81 6E 25 3A CF
MAC           BA ED 40 F0 67 B0 E1 3C 76 F3 59 41 A2 B2 D1 35


Secret key    01 23 45 67 89 AB CD EF FE DC BA 98 76 54 32 10
IV / Nonce    12 34 56 78 9A BC DE F0
Plaintext     00 11 22 33 44 55 66 77 88 99 AA BB CC DD EE FF
Ciphertext    5B D1 F8 AD 23 14 20 F4 BA B1 54 C2 45 29 3D 38
MAC           C4 F6 74 C0 F6 4B 21 E7 37 24 DC 76 A6 6C 39 19
```

Elliptic Curve Cryptography on the WISP UHF RFID Tag

Christian Pendl, Markus Pelnar, and Michael Hutter

Institute for Applied Information Processing and Communications (IAIK),
Graz University of Technology, Inffeldgasse 16a, 8010 Graz, Austria
{christian.pendl,m.pelnar}@student.tugraz.at,
Michael.Hutter@iaik.tugraz.at

Abstract. The Wireless Identification and Sensing Platform (WISP) can be used to demonstrate and evaluate new RFID applications. In this paper, we present practical results of an implementation of elliptic curve cryptography (ECC) running on the WISP. Our implementation is based on the smallest recommended NIST elliptic curve over prime fields. We meet the low-resource requirements of the platform by various code-size and memory optimizations. Furthermore, we provide a cryptographic framework that allows the realization of different ECC-based protocols on the WISP. We evaluated our implementation results by considering platforms with and without a hardware multiplier. Our best implementation performs a scalar multiplication using the Montgomery powering ladder within 1.6 seconds at a frequency of 6.7 MHz.

Keywords: Public-Key Cryptography, Elliptic Curves, WISP UHF Tag, RFID, Embedded Systems, Privacy.

1 Introduction

Radio-Frequency Identification (RFID) is a wireless technology that allows the communication with passively powered devices. It is a primer for the Internet of Things where many objects are connected to each other and to the Internet to provide a more convenient life to users. With this vision in mind, several security and privacy issues arise that have to be challenged. This paper addresses the implementation of elliptic curve cryptography (ECC) on such platforms in order to overcome these concerns.

Elliptic curve cryptography (ECC) is a public-key technique that has gained much importance due to the high security level while using small key sizes. It is therefore a promising primitive for passive RFID devices to provide various public-key services. These services are for example authentication, confidentiality, non-repudiation, or data integrity. In view of RFID, privacy-preserving authentication is one of the most challenging services. In 2007, S. Vaudenay [31] provided a formal model for RFID protocols and proved that public-key cryptography is required to provide the highest level of feasible privacy in RFID

A. Juels and C. Paar (Eds.): RFIDSec 2011, LNCS 7055, pp. 32–47, 2012.

applications. ECC is a cryptographic primitive that provides a basis for such protocols.

In order to evaluate new RFID protocols and applications, Intel Research Seattle developed a common RFID platform that operates in the UHF frequency range. The Wireless Identification and Sensing Platform (WISP) consists of a tiny low-resource microcontroller that is attached to a dipole antenna. Next to the microcontroller, the tag features several sensors such as temperature, light, and 3D accelerometer which allows a broad range of RFID and sensor node applications. There already exist many publications that use the WISP as a demonstrator platform [24,25,27,32]. Only a few publications presented cryptographic implementations on the WISP such as proposed by H.-J. Chae et al. [2]. They implemented the block cipher RC5 and demonstrated the feasibility of symmetric cryptography on that platform.

In this paper, we present an implementation of elliptic curve cryptography on the WISP. To the authors' knowledge, this is the first publication that demonstrates the feasibility of ECC on that platform. First, we describe several optimizations on the arithmetic level to meet the low-resource requirements of the WISP tag. We apply a hybrid multiplication method that reduces the memory and computational requirements to a minimum. Second, we evaluate the performance of the Montgomery powering ladder based scalar multiplication over the smallest recommended NIST elliptic curve over $\mathbb{F}_{p192}$. Our results show that when running at a frequency of 6.7 MHz WISP tags that do not support a hardware multiplier need 8.3 seconds and only 1.6 seconds when a hardware multiplier is supported. As an outcome, we show that ECC-based RFID protocols can be realized on the WISP and allow the evaluation of new cryptographic implementations for RFID as a proof of concept demonstrator.

The rest of the paper is structured as follows. In Section 2, we give an introduction to elliptic curve cryptography. Section 3 describes the basic features of the WISP tag and the setup which has been used for our experiments. Afterwards, we give implementation details in Section 4. Results of our implementations are given in Section 5. Section 6 concludes the paper and describes future work.

2   Elliptic Curve Cryptography

Each cryptographic principle is based on a mathematical problem that is believed to be "hard". Elliptic curve cryptography relies on the Elliptic Curve Discrete Logarithm Problem (ECDLP) that can only be solved in exponential running time yet. This is a major advantage compared to problems based on the integer factorization or the discrete logarithm problem where subexponential algorithms exist.

An elliptic curve E over a field K is defined with the long Weierstrass equation with the restriction of the discriminant being different from zero which guarantees that the curve is smooth. By using admissible change of variables, a simplified equation can be achieved that is isomorphic to the initial equation for elliptic curves. Depending on the characteristic of the underlying field K, different cases have to be considered.

In this paper, we deal with elliptic curves over a finite field $\mathbb{F}_q$ of characteristic $\neq 2, 3$ which are defined by the short Weierstrass equation

$$y^2 = x^3 + ax + b, \tag{1}$$

with $a, b \in \mathbb{F}_q$ and the discriminant $\Delta = -16(4a^3 + 27b^2)$. The elliptic curve is defined as a set of points $P = (x, y) \in \mathbb{F}_q$ fulfilling Equation (1). With the point at infinity $\mathcal{O}$, the chord rule for point addition and the tangent rule for point doubling an additive Abelian group is formed. By using this algebraic structure and the two group operations of point addition and point doubling, a scalar multiplication can be performed. A scalar k is multiplied with a point $\boldsymbol{P}$ on the elliptic curve resulting in another point $\boldsymbol{Q} = k \cdot \boldsymbol{P}$. Due to the ECDLP, it is hard to determine k from $\boldsymbol{P}$ and $\boldsymbol{Q}$.

Elliptic-curve points can be represented in different coordinate systems. Affine representation makes use of two coordinates (x, y) to represent a point on the elliptic curve. For the group operations of point addition and point doubling, they require inversions in $\mathbb{F}_q$ which are by far the most expensive field operations. By using projective coordinates, it is possible to avoid such inversions by the costs of an additional coordinate. Homogeneous projective coordinates[1] use three coordinates (X, Y, Z) where $x = \frac{X}{Z}$ and $y = \frac{Y}{Z}$. Jacobian projective coordinates use the relation $x = \frac{X}{Z^2}$ and $y = \frac{Y}{Z^3}$. We refer the reader to e.g. [21,9] for a more detailed introduction to elliptic curves.

3   WISP UHF RFID Tag

This section gives a brief introduction to the Wireless Identification and Sensing Platform (WISP4.1DL). First, we will describe the hardware of the WISP tag. Second, we will describe the firmware and protocol implementation of the tag. Finally, the reader setup and programming tools that have been used for the implementation are described.

3.1   Hardware

The WISP tags have been developed by Intel Labs Seattle in order to provide a development platform for new RFID and sensing applications. A picture of a WISP4.1DL tag is shown in Figure 1. It is a passively powered RFID tag operating in the UHF frequency range of about 900 MHz featuring an ultra low power general-purpose microcontroller from Texas Instruments [12] (the MSP430F2132). The used microcontroller is a Reduced Instruction Set Computer (RISC) processor providing a 16-bit architecture, 8 KB of flash memory, 512 byte of RAM, and 16 working registers where only 12 can be used for general purpose.

---

[1] We write affine coordinate in lower case and projective coordinates in upper case.

In particular, the MSP430 family [13] has been especially designed for low-resource applications. It provides various operating modes that can be used to personalize the microcontroller in terms of high speed or low power. Such operating modes range from an active mode (AM) to a low-power mode (LPM4). These different modes basically differ in the number of submodules being disabled to reduce the power consumption of peripherals. In combination with the supported voltage supervisor of the WISP tag, this feature can be used to significantly extend the uptime and reading range of the tag.

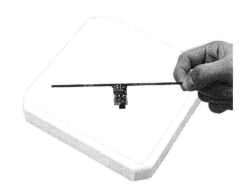

Fig. 1. WISP4.1DL in front of an UHF RFID antenna

The WISP tag includes several sensors such as a temperature sensor, a light-level detector, and a 3D accelerometer. These sensors allow the realization of a broad range of applications. A. Sample et al. [24] have been the first who reported a WISP-tag application by implementing the symmetric block cipher RC5. N. Saxena and J. Voris [25] extended the use of the accelerometer in order to generate random numbers which are important in the field of cryptography. As another example, D. Yeager et al. [32] extended the RFID antenna in order to serve as a capacitive touch sensor. Because of the combination of both computation and sensing capabilities, WISPs are perfectly suited for human-activity detection as stated by J. R. Smith et al. [27] since they can deliver motion-detection capabilities of active sensor beacons in the same battery-free form factor as RFID tags.

3.2   WISP Firmware

The communication between WISP tags and interrogators (readers) is established over the EPC Class-1 Generation-2 UHF RFID protocol [30]. It has been standardized in ISO/IEC 18000-6C, which defines the physical and logical requirements for a passive backscatter, interrogator-talks-first (ITF) RFID system.

The latest stable release of the firmware—currently the r65 (including the version HW4.1_SW6.0)—provided by Intel Labs Seattle implements main parts of the EPC Class-1 Gen-2 protocol. The firmware allows the configuration of the peripherals such as the temperature sensor or the accelerometer. The sensed data can be transmitted to the reader by either implementing custom commands of the protocol or by using simple EPC read/write commands. Additionally, data encoding can be switched between Miller-2 and Miller-4 modulation with the latter as default setting.

3.3   Reader Setup and Programming Tools

We used the Speedway Revolution R220 [11] UHF reader in our experiments. It supports the EPC Class 1 Generation 2 protocol and provides two high performance monostatic antenna ports. The communication between the reader and a PC is done over a 10/100BASE-T network. Based on this connectivity, the EPC-global Low Level Reader Protocol (LLRP) v1.0.1 is used as application interface. The transmit power is up to 32.5 dBm using an external power supply.

As a development environment, we used the IAR Embedded Workbench for the MSP430 microcontroller. The flash emulation tool MSP-FET430UIF [29] has been further used to program and debug the WISP tag over an USB interface.

4   Implementation Details

In the following, we give details about the implementation of an ECC framework that runs on the WISP4.1DL RFID tag. Since only low resources are available, several optimizations are necessary to allow the execution of ECC-based protocols on that platform.

One of the most limiting resources of the WISP4.1DL platform is the memory. In fact, the MSP430F2132 is shipped with 8 kB of flash memory where 3.2 kB is needed only for the EPC Class-1 Generation-2 protocol. Thus, implementations are limited to only 4.8 kB. In addition, the MSP430F2132 provides 512 bytes of volatile RAM. The RFID-protocol implementation needs about 200 bytes so that only 312 bytes are available for ECC. Considering these restrictions, it is important to carefully balance between speed and memory consumption. Optimizations such as unrolling of individual operations (such as it is usually the case in finite-field multiplication routines to increase the speed of execution) are therefore not always possible. Since the tag is powered passively, it is furthermore necessary to pay attention to the energy budget. Time-extensive computations need to be separated into parts after which the tag has to test if enough energy is available to continue the operation. If this is not the case, the tag gets into a sleeping mode where the capacitor of the tag can be loaded again to finish the computation.

Another limiting resource in view of ECC is the lack of a dedicated hardware multiplier on the MSP430F2132. In fact, the speed of the multiplication operation largely determines the overall ECC performance. Hardware multipliers can perform a multiplication within only a few clock cycles whereas a few hundred clock cycles are needed if no dedicated multiplier is available. However, many microcontrollers of the MSP430x2xx family feature a hardware multiplier. The work of C. Gouvêa and J. López [6], for example, made use of such a multiplier (multiply-accumulate operation) to speed up the computation on a MSP430 microcontroller. We therefore considered two different implementations for WISP tags. The first implementation provides ECC operations without a multiplier (this is the case for the available WISP4.1DL tag). The second implementation considers a dedicated hardware multiplier and provides ECC operations

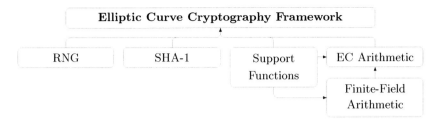

Fig. 2. Overview of the implemented ECC framework

especially optimized for that scenario (performance results have been simulated in this case).

4.1   Elliptic Curve Cryptography Framework

We implemented a general framework that provides the basic functionalities to implement ECC-based protocols on the WISP tag. Considering security and performance, we decided to base our implementation on a recommended NIST elliptic curve [23]. Due to the limiting resources, we applied the smallest recommended NIST curve over prime fields which is over $\mathbb{F}_{p192}$ where the used prime is a Mersenne-like prime defined as $p \equiv 2^{192} - 2^{64} - 1$.

The entire framework has been implemented in Assembly language to speed-up the computation. As shown in Figure 2, it consists of five main modules: a *random number generator* module, the SHA-1 *hash-function* module, a *support function* module, a *finite-field arithmetic* module, and an *elliptic-curve arithmetic* module.

As a random number generator (RNG), we implemented the algorithm proposed by G. Marsaglia [19,1]. The algorithm provides a good tradeoff between cryptographic security and computational complexity. It mainly consists of simple shift and xor operations and can therefore efficiently be implemented on the MSP430 microcontroller. For the initialization of the RNG, we used the accelerometer as also proposed by N. Saxena and J. Voris [25] in order to generate a random seed. To guarantee random initialization, the device is locked until stochastic movement of the WISP tag is detected.

We also implemented the SHA-1 hash function in our framework. In fact, hash functions are basic building blocks of cryptographic protocols. They are used, for example, in authentication protocols or digital-signature schemes. Due to memory reasons, we assume that the data which have to be hashed are shorter than the block size of the algorithm, which is 512 bits. This limits the code and memory requirements of our implementation.

The support function module is used to provide basic operations for integer arithmetics such as comparisons ($a \overset{?}{=} 0$, $a \overset{?}{=} 1$, $a \geq b$), operand copies, or initialization of array elements. These operations are needed mainly for the finite-field arithmetic and the elliptic-curve arithmetic implementation.

The finite-field arithmetic module and the elliptic-curve arithmetic module contain the main operations used to support ECC on the WISP tag. They are described in the following subsections.

4.2   Finite-Field Arithmetic

Both ECC group operations of point addition and doubling are based on underlying finite-field operations. In order to obtain an efficient performance for scalar multiplication, it is important to optimize these operations as much as possible. In fact, finite-field operations are heavily used in loops so that thousands of clock cycles can be saved for scalar multiplication by reducing only one single clock cycle in the underlying finite-field arithmetics.

The MSP430F2132 microcontroller provides a 16-bit architecture. This means that all prime-field operations are based on 16-bit operands, i.e. a 192 bit field element is stored in a 12-word array structure. In particular, we decided to represent each field element in little-endian representation. Thus, indirect autoincrement addressing can be used that is supported by the MSP430 microcontroller. This special addressing mode provides base-address incrementation after the fetch operation without any additional overhead. This allows efficient array processing and avoids additional clock cycles.

Addition and Subtraction. The addition of field elements $a + b = c$ is implemented via a loop that iterates through the twelve words of the operands starting with the least significant word. The operand words are loaded from memory and added using the *ADD* and *ADDC* instruction of the MSP430. In order to speed up the addition operation, we unrolled the loop. In addition to an out-of-place version, we also implemented an in-place version of the prime-field addition where the result overwrites one input operand, i.e. $a \leftarrow a + b$. This has the advantage that special addressing instructions can be used to save execution cycles. In fact, 34 % of the total number of clock cycles can be saved while only increasing the overall code size insignificantly. After the integer addition, the result has to be reduced modulo the prime p. This can be done by simply subtracting the prime if the result is larger than the modulus p. The prime field subtraction has been also implemented by unrolling the instructions. In contrast to modular addition, the modulus p has to be added if the result is smaller than zero.

Multiplication and Squaring. Prime-field multiplication and squaring operations consume most of the running time of a scalar multiplication. They have therefore a significant impact on the overall running time. Consequently, it is crucial to put optimization efforts into these routines. As for modular addition and subtraction, prime-field multiplication and squaring in $\mathbb{F}_p$ consist of a multiplication step (resulting in a double-precision number) and a followed reduction step modulo a prime p.

Two basic multi-precision multiplication algorithms are common: the row-wise standard schoolbook method (also called operand-scanning form) and the column-wise Comba method (also called product-scanning form) [4]. Both algorithms process the words in two loops (an outer loop and an inner loop). In 2004, N. Gura et al. [8] introduced a hybrid method that combines the row-wise and column-wise techniques. The idea behind this method is to make advantage of the two basic multi-precision multiplication algorithms to increase the performance. The Comba method is therefore used in the outer loop of the algorithm and the schoolbook method is used in the inner loop. Still, the number of required registers and needed memory accesses strongly depend on the choice of the algorithm parameter d.

If no hardware multiplier is available on the MSP430, the 16-bit operand-multiplication routine needs four of the twelve registers available. In addition to that, two registers are needed for counter variables as loops have to be used to keep the code size small. Another three registers are necessary to hold the addresses of the operands. With only three remaining registers, it is not possible to implement the hybrid method with parameter $d = 2$ as it would require seven available registers. Thus, for the WISP tag without hardware multiplier, the hybrid method has to be implemented with $d = 1$ which actually corresponds to the standard Comba method. An MSP430 with dedicated hardware multiplier can implement the hybrid method with $d = 2$. This is possible as no additional registers are needed for the 16-bit multiplication. In addition to make the hybrid method with $d = 2$ feasible, we had to use loop unrolling which makes two registers available previously needed for counter variables. As preferable side effect, loop unrolling comes with a significant performance improvement to the cost of substantial code size increase.

For squaring of a field element $c = a^2$, we decided to implement a dedicated squaring operation instead of reusing the multiplication operation. This needs additional code memory but increases the efficiency of scalar multiplication since squaring can be computed faster than multiplication. This is due to the fact that only 78 of the 144 partial products actually have to be computed in case of 192-bit operands and 16-bit wordsize. The remaining partial products can be substituted through cheap shift operations. Additionally, the number of memory accesses and thus required clock cycles can be reduced as only one operand is present. In case of no hardware multiplier the reduction of partial product calculations, which are extremely expensive, clearly outweighs the little overhead required by the squaring routine. Note that we used the squaring operation only for the implementation of the MSP430 without a hardware multiplier. For the MSP430 with a hardware multiplier, no squaring operation has been implemented. This is due to the fact that the overhead becomes more decisive as the multiplication operation of the dedicated multiplier is much faster than the software multiplication. Thus, a less significant speed improvement is obtained by a squaring operation compared to the MSP430 implementation without a hardware multiplier.

Algorithm 1. Montgomery powering ladder scalar multiplication

---

Input: $P \in E(\mathbb{F}_q)$ and $k = (k_{n-1}, \ldots, k_0)_2 \in \mathbb{N}$, with $k_{n-1} \neq 0$
Output: $Q = kP$

1: $(X_0, Z_0) \leftarrow P$; $(X_1, Z_1) \leftarrow 2P$
2: $X_0 \leftarrow X_0 \times Z_1$; $X_1 \leftarrow X_1 \times Z_0$; $Z \leftarrow Z_0 \times Z_1$;
3: **for** $i = n - 2$ downto 0 **do**
4:     $R_2 \leftarrow Z^2$, $R_3 \leftarrow R_2 + R_2$, $R_3 \leftarrow R_3 + R_2$, $R_1 \leftarrow Z \times R_2$, $R_2 \leftarrow 4b \times R_1$,
5:     $R_1 \leftarrow X_{1-k_i}{}^2$, $R_5 \leftarrow R_1 + R_3$, $R_4 \leftarrow R_5{}^2$, $R_1 \leftarrow R_1 - R_3$, $R_5 \leftarrow X_{1-k_i} \times R_1$,
6:     $R_5 \leftarrow R_5 + R_5$, $R_5 \leftarrow R_5 + R_5$, $R_5 \leftarrow R_5 + R_2$, $R_1 \leftarrow R_1 - R_3$, $R_3 \leftarrow X_{k_i}{}^2$,
7:     $R_1 \leftarrow R_1 + R_3$, $X_{k_i} \leftarrow X_{k_i} - X_{1-k_i}$, $X_{1-k_i} \leftarrow X_{1-k_i} + X_{1-k_i}$, $R_3 \leftarrow X_{1-k_i} \times R_2$,
8:     $R_4 \leftarrow R_4 - R_3$, $R_3 \leftarrow X_{k_i}{}^2$, $R_1 \leftarrow R_1 - R_3$, $X_{k_i} \leftarrow X_{k_i} + X_{1-k_i}$,
9:     $X_{1-k_i} \leftarrow X_{k_i} \times R_1$, $X_{1-k_i} \leftarrow X_{1-k_i} + R_2$, $R_2 \leftarrow Z \times R_3$, $Z \leftarrow x_P \times R_2$,
10:     $X_{1-k_i} \leftarrow X_{1-k_i} - Z$, $X_{k_i} \leftarrow R_5 \times X_{1-k_i}$, $X_{1-k_i} \leftarrow R_3 \times R_4$, $Z \leftarrow R_2 \times R_5$.
11:     $test\_power\_supply()$.
12: **end for**
13: **return** $Q = (X_0, Z)$.

To fit the final result in the underlying field $\mathbb{F}_p$, the 384-bit product or square has to be reduced modulo the prime p. As the used NIST prime p is a generalized-Mersenne prime, the reduced result can be computed by simple additions (fast NIST reduction [9]). The reduction operation can be therefore performed very efficiently.

4.3   Elliptic-Curve Arithmetic

The main operation in ECC implementations is the scalar multiplication $Q = kP$. There exist various algorithms to perform a scalar multiplication. One of the most common methods is the double-and-add (or left-to-right binary method) algorithm. It performs a double operation for every bit of the scalar but performs an addition only if the bit is 1. No addition is performed if the bit is 0. This fact makes such an implementation very efficient but provides information of the secret scalar in physical side channels [15,18]. By analyzing the running time or the power consumption of the double-and-add implementation, an adversary might identify the value of the scalar which makes an implementation weak in terms of side-channel attacks.

Another scalar-multiplication method resistant to many implementation attacks is the Montgomery powering ladder [22]. Next to the fact that it prevents many attacks due to its regular structure, it allows the computation of group operations without y-coordinates [14]. The entire scalar multiplication can be performed with x-coordinate only operations. This further reduces the memory requirements of our implementation. The Montgomery powering ladder is shown in Algorithm 1 where n denotes the bit size of the prime field, i.e. 192. The point P gets multiplied by the scalar k resulting in the point Q. All operations are performed with co-Z coordinate representation [20,16,5,10]. That means that all points on the elliptic curve share a common coordinate, i.e. Z, which requires to store only three (instead of four) variables throughout the Montgomery ladder.

We applied the formulae of M. Hutter et al. [10] to perform a scalar multiplication. The proposed formulae have been especially designed for low-resource devices and perform all operations *out-of-place* which reduces the memory requirements by one temporary register. We applied Algorithm 5 (cf. [10]), needing ten multiplications, five squarings, and sixteen additions (including subtractions)[2] to perform a (differential) addition and doubling operation. We allocated eight intermediate variables of twelve words each (thus needing 192 bytes of RAM[3] only for the scalar multiplication). In order to keep the memory requirements to a minimum, we decided to reuse four of these intermediate variables also for other operations of the framework.

Due to the high energy costs of a scalar multiplication, we decided to monitor the energy budget during this operation to increase the reading range. Therefore, after each scalar-multiplication iteration a check of the power supply is performed. Thus, the available energy is tested 190 times for one Montgomery-ladder execution. If needed the device is put into sleeping mode to recover energy.

5   Results

In the following, we present experimental results of our ECC framework suitable for WISP. All implementations have been compiled using the IAR Assembler v5.10.4 and the IAR C/C++ Compiler v5.10.6 [Kickstart LMS] that have been configured for low optimization. As stated in Section 4, we provide results of two different ECC implementations. One that has been optimized for WISP tags that feature an MSP430 with no hardware multiplier and one implementation for WISP tags with an MSP430 that supports a hardware multiplier. For a fair comparison of the two implementations, we omitted the EPC Gen-2 protocol implementation for all simulations. On the one hand we used the MSP430F233 microcontroller as a device that features a hardware multiplier, and on the other hand we used the MSP430F2132 that is assembled on the WISP4.1DL tag. To obtain practical results for the WISP4.1DL, the existing firmware has been flattened to allow a running system containing the EPC class-1 Generation-2 protocol as well as the ECC framework.

Most effort in optimizations has been put into the finite-field multiplication and squaring operation. As a multiplication method, we implemented the hybrid method as described in Subsection 4.2. Table 1 shows the amount of required clock cycles for multi-precision multiplication and squaring as a function of the

---

[2] The multiplication with the curve parameter b (or $4b$) has been realized by a normal multiplication. Multiplication with a has been realized by two additional additions.

[3] Note that the memory requirements can be further reduced to only 168 bytes (cf. Algorithm 4 in [10]). However, this would increase the runtime complexity to twelve multiplications, four squarings, and sixteen additions.

Table 1. Performance of 192-bit multi-precision multiplication and squaring

System setting	Multiplication $(a \cdot a)$ [Cycles]	Squaring (a^2) [Cycles]
WISP without HWM (d = 1)	25,350	14,361
WISP with HWM (d = 1)	5,046	3,363
WISP with HWM (d = 2)	2,581	-

different system settings. As it was expected, the worst case is the setting without hardware multiplier and the parameter $d = 1$ of the hybrid-multiplication method. The performance can be improved significantly by using a device with hardware multiplier (about 90 % improvement). We have to mention that the implementation of the hybrid-multiplication method with $d = 1$ has not been optimized for usage with hardware multiplier. So there is still a lot of room for optimizations by specially fitting the hybrid-multiplication method to devices that feature a hardware multiplier. As it can be seen in Table 1, the amount of required clock cycles for a multi-precision multiplication can roughly be halved by applying loop unrolling and using $d = 2$. Nevertheless, this optimization is not always practicable as the code size increases significantly as shown in Table 2. The increase in code size is caused by the loop unrolling when applying $d = 2$.

Another improvement can be achieved by introducing squaring (a^2) instead of multiplication $(a \cdot a)$. If no hardware multiplier is available, the number of clock cycles can be reduced roughly by the factor 1.7 to the cost of an increased code size. This enormous improvement compared to the implementation of H. Cohen et al. [3] can be explained by the high costs of partial product calculations. For the system settings with hardware multiplier the improvement is less significant as the major improvement through the use of the hardware multiplier itself. So if a computation of the partial products for a multi-precision multiplication is relatively expensive, usage of squaring is recommended because the advantage of clock-cycle reduction outweighs the drawback of an increased code size. Since squaring does not provide a major improvement in running time when compared to the hybrid-multiplication method with $d = 2$, squaring has not been implemented for this system setting.

Table 2. Flash-memory requirements of the multi-precision arithmetic implementation with and without dedicated squarer

System setting	Code size without dedicated squarer [Bytes]	Code size with dedicated squarer [Bytes]
WISP without HWM (d=1)	1,076	1,572
WISP with HWM (d=1)	1,020	1,376
WISP with HWM (d=2)	4,236	-

Table 3. Performance of one 192-bit scalar multiplication using the Montgomery ladder running on different WISP-tag settings

System setting	Without squaring [Cycles]	With squaring [Cycles]
WISP without HWM (d = 1)	63,257,925	54,630,581
WISP with HWM (d = 1)	17,376,758	15,761,884
WISP with HWM (d = 2)	10,289,883	-

The optimizations described before have been applied on the lowest implementation level. As expected and shown in Table 3, the support of a hardware multiplier provides best performance for the scalar multiplication. If no hardware multiplier is available, a squaring implementation is recommended on the WISP tag as it reduces the amount of clock cycles from 63,257,925 to 54,630,581. Thus, up to 10^7 clock cycles can be saved. Furthermore, it shows that the best performance has been obtained by using a hardware multiplier in combination with the hybrid-multiplication method with parameter $d = 2$. This setting is about six times faster than the fastest method without hardware multiplier.

We simulated the entire 192-bit scalar multiplication using the Montgomery powering ladder. It needs about $5.5 \cdot 10^7$ clock cycles on the WISP4.1DL platform. This corresponds to 8.3 seconds on the WISP running at a clock frequency of 6.7 MHz. Running at this clock frequency—which actually is the highest frequency feasible for succeeding the scalar multiplication with our hardware setup—the maximum distance to the reader is about 2 centimeters. Although the power supply is tested after each Montgomery-ladder round, the scalar multiplication will not finish at distances further than the 2 centimeters as one round

Table 4. Memory requirements of the WISP tag for different framework-level implementations

Framework level of WISP without HWM	Code [Bytes]	Const [Bytes]	Data [Bytes]
Multi-precision arithmetic	1,572	0	0
Finite-field arithmetic	2,532	0	96
ECC arithmetic	3,944	210	176
Framework level of WISP with HWM (d = 1)	**Code [Bytes]**	**Const [Bytes]**	**Data [Bytes]**
Multi-precision arithmetic	1,376	0	0
Finite-field arithmetic	2,346	0	96
ECC arithmetic	3,758	206	326
Framework level of WISP with HWM (d = 2)	**Code [Bytes]**	**Const [Bytes]**	**Data [Bytes]**
Multi-precision arithmetic	4,236	0	0
Finite-field arithmetic	5,206	0	96
ECC arithmetic	6,618	206	326

Table 5. Memory requirements on the WISP tag for additional framework modules

Module	Code [Bytes]	Const [Bytes]	Data [Bytes]
SHA-1 hash function	1,012	30	10
Random Number Generation (RNG)	218	0	4
Modified EPC Class 1 Gen 2 protocol	3,260	66	181

exceeds the number of cycles which can be processed with the power available at this distance. If reading ranges larger than the 2 centimeters are necessary, either the clock frequency can be reduced which leads to a longer computation time or an additional capacitor can be assembled on board. Reducing the clock frequency from 6.7 MHz to 6.1 MHz results in a computation time of 9.1 seconds and a maximum distance to the reader of 10 centimeters. Correspondingly, a frequency of 3.98 MHz leads to 13.9 seconds and a frequency of 0.98 MHz leads to 56.2 seconds at a maximum distance of 40 cm. If the MSP430F2132 is replaced with the MSP430F233 and the adaptions for supporting the hardware multiplier are applied, the total number of clock cycles can be reduced by the factor of 5 which results in an estimated computation time of about 1.6 seconds at 6.7 MHz.

Table 4 presents an overview of the required code size for the different system settings. All configurations except the configuration with the hardware multiplier and $d = 2$ support squaring. The code size of the additional framework modules is listed in Table 5.

5.1 Comparison with Related Work

There exist several publications about ECC implementations on the MSP430 family of microcontrollers [6,7,26,17,28]. Most of the related work makes use of the dedicated hardware multiplier that is integrated in many MSP430 architectures. The work of J. Guajardo et al. [7], for example, implemented ECC on the TI MSP430x33x microcontroller. Using an elliptic curve over $\mathbb{F}_{p128}$ they could accomplish a scalar point multiplication in 3.4 seconds at a frequency of 1 MHz. The TI MSP430x33x family features 24 KB or 32 KB of flash memory and 1,024 KB of RAM. In addition, they provide a 16×16-bit hardware multiplier. For a multiplication of two 128-bit operands, only 64 partial products instead of 144 partial products have to be calculated when multiplying two 192 bit operands. Subtraction, addition, and comparison operations also require correspondingly less cycles to complete. As a scalar multiplication method, they applied the double-and-add algorithm.

6 Conclusion

In this paper, we presented practical results of an elliptic curve cryptography (ECC) framework that runs on the Wireless Identification and Sensing Platform (WISP). In order to meet the low-resource requirements of that passively powered UHF RFID tag, we made several optimizations on arithmetic, algorithmic, and implementation level. We provided results for WISP tags with no hardware multiplier such as it is in the case for the WISP4.1DL tag and also for WISP tags which feature a dedicated hardware multiplier, e.g. the MSP430F233 microcontroller. The implementation showed that a scalar multiplication using the Montgomery powering ladder can be performed within 8.3 seconds on the WISP4.1DL tag. The same operation can be performed within 1.6 seconds on the MSP430F233 which is an increase of about 80 %. Furthermore, it showed that a dedicated squaring implementation on the WISP4.1DL improves the performance by about 14 %. Our results show the feasibility of ECC on the WISP while providing a proof of concept demonstrator for future RFID protocols and applications.

As a future work, we plan to evaluate the new generation of WISP tags which provide a Complex Logic Programmable Device (CLPD) on board. This allows to out-source individual operations which can help to reduce the memory requirements and also to improve the performance of ECC implementations. Furthermore, we plan to use the ECC-enabled WISP to evaluate new privacy-preserving authentication protocols. They can be also used to analyze the resistance of such implementations to common attacks.

Acknowledgements. The work has been supported by the IAP Programme P6/26 BCRYPT of the Belgian State (Belgian Science Policy) and by the Austrian government founded project PIT, grant no. 825743.

References

1. Brent, R.P.: Note on Marsaglia's Xorshift Random Number Generators. Journal of Statistical Software 11(4), 1–5 (2004)
2. Chae, M.-J., Yeager, D.J., Smith, J.R., Fu, K.: Maximalist cryptography and computation on the WISP UHF RFID tag. In: Proceedings of the Conference on RFID Security (2007)
3. Cohen, H., Miyaji, A., Ono, T.: Efficient elliptic curve exponentiation using mixed coordinates (1998)
4. Comba, P.G.: Exponentiation cryptosystems on the IBM PC. IBM Syst. J. 29, 526–538 (1990)
5. Goundar, R., Joye, M., Miyaji, A.: Co-Z Addition Formulae and Binary Ladders on Elliptic Curves. In: Mangard, S., Standaert, F.-X. (eds.) CHES 2010. LNCS, vol. 6225, pp. 65–79. Springer, Heidelberg (2010)
6. Gouvêa, C., López, J.: Software Implementation of Pairing-Based Cryptography on Sensor Networks Using the MSP430 Microcontroller. In: Roy, B., Sendrier, N. (eds.) INDOCRYPT 2009. LNCS, vol. 5922, pp. 248–262. Springer, Heidelberg (2009)
7. Guajardo, J., Blümel, R., Krieger, U., Paar, C.: Efficient Implementation of Elliptic Curve Cryptosystems on the TI MSP 430x33x Family of Microcontrollers. In: Kim, K.-c. (ed.) PKC 2001. LNCS, vol. 1992, pp. 365–382. Springer, Heidelberg (2001)
8. Gura, N., Patel, A., Wander, A., Eberle, H., Shantz, S.C.: Comparing Elliptic Curve Cryptography and RSA on 8-bit CPUs, pp. 119–132 (2004)

9. Hankerson, D., Menezes, A.J., Vanstone, S.: Guide to Elliptic Curve Cryptography. Springer-Verlag New York, Inc., Secaucus (2003)

10. Hutter, M., Joye, M., Sierra, Y.: Memory-Constrained Implementations of Elliptic Curve Cryptography in Co-Z Coordinate Representation. In: Nitaj, A., Pointcheval, D. (eds.) AFRICACRYPT 2011. LNCS, vol. 6737, pp. 170–187. Springer, Heidelberg (2011)

11. Impinj: Speedway Revolution - Superior Performance Made Easy (2010)

12. T. Instruments. MSP430F21x2 Mixed Signal Microcontroller, Rev. G (2009)

13. T. Instruments. MSP430x2xx Family User's Guide, Rev. F (2010)

14. Joye, M., Yen, S.-M.: The Montgomery Powering Ladder. In: Kaliski Jr., B.S., Koç, Ç.K., Paar, C. (eds.) CHES 2002. LNCS, vol. 2523, pp. 291–302. Springer, Heidelberg (2003)

15. Kocher, P.C., Jaffe, J., Jun, B.: Differential Power Analysis. In: Wiener, M. (ed.) CRYPTO 1999. LNCS, vol. 1666, pp. 388–397. Springer, Heidelberg (1999)

16. Lee, Y.K., Verbauwhede, I.: A Compact Architecture for Montgomery Elliptic Curve Scalar Multiplication Processor. In: Kim, S., Yung, M., Lee, H.-W. (eds.) WISA 2007. LNCS, vol. 4867, pp. 115–127. Springer, Heidelberg (2008)

17. Liu, A., Ning, P.: TinyECC: A Configurable Library for Elliptic Curve Cryptography in Wireless Sensor Networks. In: Proceedings of International Conference on Information Processing in Sensor Networks - IPSN 2008, St. Louis, Missouri, USA, April 22-24, pp. 245–256 (2008)

18. Mangard, S., Oswald, M.E., Popp, T.: Power Analysis Attacks - Revealing the Secrets of Smart Cards. Springer, Heidelberg (2007)

19. Marsaglia, G.: Xorshift RNGs. Journal of Statistical Software 8(14), 1–6 (2003)

20. Meloni, N.: Fast and Secure Elliptic Curve Scalar Multiplication Over Prime Fields Using Special Addition Chains. In: Cryptology ePrint Archive, Report 2006/216 (2006)

21. Menezes, A.J., van Oorschot, P.C., Vanstone, S.A.: Handbook of Applied Cryptography. CRC Press, Boca Raton (1997)

22. Montgomery, P.L.: Speeding the Pollard and Elliptic Curve Methods of Factorization. Mathematics of Computation 48(177), 243–264 (1987)

23. National Institute of Standards and Technology (NIST). FIPS-186-3: Digital Signature Standard, DSS (2009), http://www.itl.nist.gov/fipspubs/

24. Sample, A., Yeager, D., Smith, J.: WISP: A Passively Powered UHF RFID Tag with Sensing and Computation. In: RFID Handbook: Applications, Technology, Security, and Privacy (March 2008)

25. Saxena, N., Voris, J.: Accelerometer Based Random Number Generation on RFID Tags. In: 1st Workshop on Wirelessly Powered Sensor Networks and Computational RFID, WISP Summit (2009)

26. Scott, M., Szczechowiak, P.: Optimizing Multiprecision Multiplication for Public Key Cryptography. In: Cryptology ePrint Archive, Report 2007/299 (2007), http://eprint.iacr.org/

27. Smith, J.R., Fishkin, K.P., Jiang, B., Mamishev, A., Philipose, M., Rea, A.D., Roy, S., Sundara-Rajan, K.: RFID-based techniques for human-activity detection. Commun. ACM 48, 39–44 (2005)

28. Szczechowiak, P., Oliveira, L.B., Scott, M., Collier, M., Dahab, R.: NanoECC: Testing the Limits of Elliptic Curve Cryptography in Sensor Networks. In: Verdone, R. (ed.) EWSN 2008. LNCS, vol. 4913, pp. 305–320. Springer, Heidelberg (2008)

29. Texas Instruments. MSP-FET430UIF (May 2010)

30. The global language of business. EPCTM Radio-Frequency Identity Protocols Class-1 Generation-2 UHF RFID Protocol for Communications at 860 MHz 960 MHz Version 1.2.0 (October 2008)
31. Vaudenay, S.: On Privacy Models for RFID. In: Kurosawa, K. (ed.) ASIACRYPT 2007. LNCS, vol. 4833, pp. 68–87. Springer, Heidelberg (2007)
32. Yeager, D., Holleman, J., Prasad, R., Smith, J., Otis, B.: NeuralWISP: A Wirelessly Powered Neural Interface With 1-m Range. IEEE Transactions on Biomedical Circuits and Systems 3(6), 379–387 (2009)

Exploring the Feasibility of Low Cost Fault Injection Attacks on Sub-threshold Devices through an Example of a 65nm AES Implementation

Alessandro Barenghi[1], Cédric Hocquet[2], David Bol[2], François-Xavier Standaert[2], Francesco Regazzoni[2,3], and Israel Koren[4]

[1] DEI - Politecnico di Milano, Milano, Italy
barenghi@elet.polimi.it
[2] ICTEAM Institute, Université catholique de Louvain, Louvain-la-Neuve, Belgium
{first_name.last_name}@uclouvain.be
[3] ALaRI - University of Lugano, Lugano, Switzerland
regazzoni@alari.ch
[4] University of Massachusetts, Amherst, MA, USA
koren@ecs.umass.edu

Abstract. The continuous scaling of VLSI technology and the aggressive use of low power strategies (such as subthreshold voltage) make it possible to implement standard cryptographic primitives within the very limited circuit and power budget of RFID devices. On the other hand, such cryptographic implementations raise concerns regarding their vulnerability to both active and passive side channel attacks. In particular, when focusing on RFID targeted designs, it is important to evaluate their resistance to low cost physical attacks.

A common low cost fault injection attack is the one which is induced by insufficient supply voltage of the chip with the goal of causing setup time violations. This kind of fault attack relies on the possibility of gracefully degrading the performance of the chip. It is however, unclear whether this kind of low cost attack is feasible in the case of low voltage design since a reduction of the voltage may result in a catastrophic failure of the device rather than an isolated setup violation. Furthermore, the effect that process variations may have on the fault model used by the attacker and consequently the success probability of the attack, are unknown.

In this paper, we investigate these issues by evaluating the resistance to low cost fault injection attacks of chips implementing the AES cipher that were manufactured using a 65nm low power library and operate at subthreshold voltage. We show that it is possible to successfully breach the security of a custom implementation of the AES cipher. Our experiments have taken into account the expected process variations through testing of multiple samples of the chip. To the best of our knowledge, this work is the first attempt to explore the resistance against low cost fault injection attacks on devices that operate at subthreshold voltage and are very susceptible to process variations.

1 Introduction

Radio Frequency Identification (RFID) devices are nowadays used in a wide range of applications, such as health care, supply chain management, or pet identification [6].

A. Juels and C. Paar (Eds.): RFIDSec 2011, LNCS 7055, pp. 48–60, 2012.
© Springer-Verlag Berlin Heidelberg 2012

Such a pervasive diffusion raises concerns regarding the privacy of the users as the RFID tags often store sensitive information. RFID devices have a very strict power and area budget, and as a result, incorporating the necessary support needed to guarantee privacy is a challenging task since the security primitives are often too costly in terms of area and power.

A particularly appealing solution to meet the above challenges is to exploit nanometer CMOS technologies, adopt known aggressive power saving techniques, and operate the device at a subthreshold voltage (with a typical supply voltage of 0.3V to 0.5V). Using nanometer CMOS technologies, it is possible to implement standard cryptographic algorithms within the restricted available area. It is likely that future generations of RFID tags will be able to afford the cost of being manufactured in this more suitable technology [3].

By using low power cell libraries and operating the device at a subthreshold voltage, it is possible to significantly reduce the power consumption but at a price of a considerably lower speed. However, this is acceptable since although speed for RFIDs is an important design parameter, it is not the most critical one as long as it does not hinder user interaction.

A key concern for every secure cryptographic implementation is vulnerability to both active and passive physical attacks. In the case of RFID designs, it is particularly important to evaluate the resistance of new implementations to low cost physical attacks such as fault injection attacks carried out by simply decreasing the supply voltage. This kind of attacks can be brought in practice by directly feeding the chip via a tunable power supply instead of the antenna based one.

Although aggressive design techniques enable the use of standard ciphers and achieve very low power implementations, the security of the resulting circuit against such physical attacks still remains unexplored. Implementing RFIDs in nanometer technology and operating them at subthreshold voltage raises two issues that do not have to be dealt with when current off-the-shelf components are used. First, such implementations may experience functional failures if the Vdd is reduced below the reference supply voltage [3]. Thus, it is not clear whether it is practically possible to reduce the voltage in order to generate only timing faults (violations of the flip-flops' setup time) which are typically induced to mount low cost fault attacks. Second, nanometer CMOS technologies are prone to process variations. As a result, almost every chip will have its own unique timing. Thus, it is unclear to which extent fault injection attacks can be carried out in a chip independent way.

In this paper, we answer these questions by performing a practical evaluation of the susceptibility of a subthreshold voltage implementation of AES (designed to be incorporated in an RFID), to low cost fault injection attacks. The considered design has an 8-bit data path and is implemented using a 65nm low power library. In our experiments we slowly lowered the supply voltage to evaluate the susceptibility of the chip and to quantify the required precision of the power supply generator. Then, we conducted a similar set of experiments on 5 dies implementing the same functionality, to explore the effects of process variations on the susceptibility to fault attacks. To the best of our knowledge, this work is the first one that focuses on a practical evaluation of the resistance against fault injection attacks on subthreshold low power circuits.

The remainder of the paper is organized as follows. In Section 2 we briefly describe the AES algorithm and present several previously proposed fault attacks on AES. We then describe the architecture of our AES design in Section 3. Section 4 describes the attack technique chosen for our evaluation. Finally, the measurement setup and the results of our experiments are reported in Section 5.

2   Background

To practically evaluate the security level provided by a given implementation of a cipher, it is necessary to consider a number of attacks that an attacker can mount when granted physical access to the device. These attacks, commonly known as physical attacks, rely on either measuring circuit parameters during the regular functioning of the device (e.g., power consumption, Electromagnetic emissions) or actively perturbing the computation. This paper will focus on the second type of physical attacks, the so-called fault injection attacks. These attacks rely on inducing non-catastrophic faults into the computation (in order to obtain a faulty result), and analyzing the difference between the correct and wrong outputs. Since the induced faults only affect a part of the computation it is possible for the attacker to use the difference between the outputs to infer the secret key.

2.1   The AES Cipher

The cipher considered in this work is the Advanced Encryption Standard [15], due to its wide adoption and the substantial cryptanalytical scrutiny it has undergone in the last 12 years. The selected variants of the Rijndael [5] algorithm selected as AES standard support a plaintext block size of 128 bits and three key sizes of 128, 192 and 256 bits.

The AES cipher is based on the iteration of a round function composed of four primitives: SUBBYTES, SHIFTROWS, MIXCOLUMNS and ADDROUNDKEY. The number of times the round function is iterated, N_r, is 10, 12 or 14 times depending on the length of the key employed. The only exceptions to the repetition of the four primitives is the last round of the encryption where the MIXCOLUMNS primitive is missing and an extra ADDROUNDKEY performed before the first round.

The inner state of the AES cipher after each round i, denoted by S_i, can be represented as a 4×4 matrix, where each element is 8 bits wide. We denote the n-th byte, counting from left to right, from top to bottom as S_n^i.

Each primitive of the AES cipher contributes to either adding confusion or diffusion effects to the cipher, or to add a dependency on the value of the key. The SUBBYTES primitive is a non-linear mapping over $\mathbb{Z}_{2^8}$ that introduces a non-linear confusion effect. This mapping is applied to a single byte at a time and can be implemented either as a lookup table or computed on the fly. The SHIFTROWS primitive provides a row-wise diffusion effect to the inner state of the AES cipher. It rotates the four rows of the state S_i by 0,1,2 or 3 byte positions, respectively, while the values of the rotated bytes remain unaltered. The MIXCOLUMNS primitive provides column wise diffusion of the cipher state by considering the column as a vector of values over $\mathbb{Z}_{2^8}$, and multiplying the vector by a constant matrix. This operation linearly combines in an invertible way the contents of the four bytes of a column. The last operation, the ADDROUNDKEY primitive, adds the 4×4 key matrix to the state matrix of the AES cipher using a bitwise exclusive or operation.

Since the ADDROUNDKEY primitive is repeated $N_r + 1$ times, there is a need to expand the initial key provided by the user into $N_r + 1$ round keys through a key expansion routine. The AES key expansion routine manipulates the initial key through bitwise xor additions and application of the SUBBYTES primitive. The key schedule process is non-destructive, i.e., all the operations performed are bijective. As a result, if a person is in possession of 4, 6 or 8 contiguous 32 bit words of the key schedule, he is able to reconstruct the full 128, 192 or 256 bit secret key, respectively.

2.2 Related Work

A number of fault injection attacks on the AES cipher have been reported. Although some of them were not experimentally validated at the time they were presented [4,9,12,14], several other attacks were successfully mounted on real implementations. For example, in [10] the authors were able to mount a successful attack by causing temporary brown outs and glitches on the supply line of an 8-bit microcontroller. In [19], Schmidt et al. attacked an implementation of AES by blanking selectively the memory where the SBoxes are held. In [16], Peacham et al. describe a successful attack mounted, using laser induced fault injection, on an AES implementation in a commercial grade smart card, that did not include any countermeasures against fault attacks. Another technique which has proven effective in inducing controlled fault is by causing setup time violations by lowering the supply voltage below the level the circuit was designed for. In [20], Selmane et al. report the effects of attacking a commercial grade ASIC implementation of AES in a smart card, using this fault induction technique, while in [2] the authors successfully applied the technique to a full ARM9 core running a software implementation of AES. It is worthwhile to mention that passive side channel analysis techniques have also been successful in attacking implementations of RFID chips, as it is reported, for instance, in [11].

3 Target Architecture

In this section we describe the architecture of the low area and low power AES design that we have used in our experiments. Since our objective is to evaluate the effectiveness of low cost fault injection attacks mounted on RFID devices, the base architecture must satisfy strict area and power requirements.

An AES architecture that is suitable for our purposes is the one proposed by Feldhofer *et al.* [8] that has an 8-bit datapath and supports only a single key size of 128 bits. The block diagram of the considered design is shown in Figure 1. The selected design includes three components: a module for computing the non-linear transformation (S-box) that is used by the *SubBytes* operation and by the key expansion routine, a module for computing one quarter of the *MixColumn* operation per clock cycle, and a module to implement the round key addition. The *ShiftRows* operation is performed by accessing the register in an appropriate way.

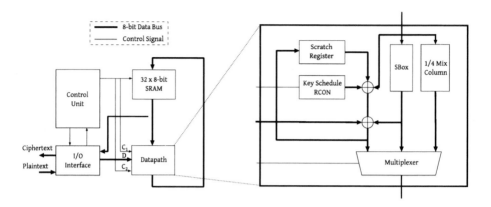

Fig. 1. Block diagram of the AES module proposed by Feldhofer *et al.* [8]

The AES design which we have implemented is similar to the one described above except for the S-Box. A lightweight S-box implementation was proposed by Satoh *et al.* [18]. It requires to transform the input data into the composite Galois field $\mathbb{Z}(((2^2)^2)^2)$, invert it there and then transform it back to $\mathbb{Z}(2^8)$. Such a design, which already resulted in a low gate count, was further optimized by Mentes *et al.* in [13]. We have therefore, selected this small footprint design for implementing the non-linear transformation in AES.

The HDL code of the described AES design was synthesized for a target clock frequency of 100 KHz using *Synopsys Design Compiler*. The target library was the ST Microelectronics 65nm LP CMOS technology with seven interconnect metal layers. Considering the fact that the device would operate in the subthreshold regime, we manually removed from the target library the cells which may not operate correctly, i.e., the ones with the longest transistor stack, such as NAND3 or NOR3. We set the timing condition to the worst-case process corner (slow NMOS and slow PMOS transistors), low temperature (-15°C), and operating supply voltage of 0.4V to achieve the desired 100 KHz clock frequency. The optimized design was then placed and routed using *Cadence SoC Encounter* and manufactured. All the dies were encapsulated in a 44 pin Ceramic Quad Flat Package (CQFP) and were tested to verify the correct execution of encryption and decryption. All the tested dies were found to operate correctly at a frequency of 1.3MHz with a power supply of 0.45V and 400KHz at 0.4V. However, by relaxing the clock frequency, it is possible to correctly operate the AES circuit at 0.25V, which is the functional limit of the design.

4   Chosen Attack Methodology

In this section we present the attack methodology we used in this work. Dusart et al. [7] have claimed that it is possible to successfully retrieve the whole secret key of an AES-128 cipher through the injection of byte-wide faults during the regular functioning of the cipher. The proposed attack relies on the injection of a single byte fault between

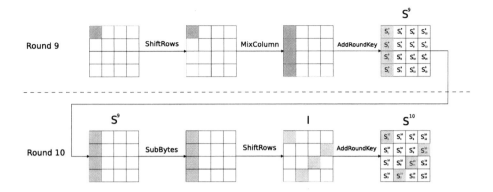

Fig. 2. Effects of the propagation of a single fault injected between the MIXCOLUMNS operations of the eight and ninth rounds

the MIXCOLUMNS step in the eighth round and the MIXCOLUMNS step in the ninth round, as depicted in Figure 2. Due to the lack of the MIXCOLUMNS operation during the tenth round, the effect of the fault is spread only over 4 of the 16 bytes of the state. Since the key addition is performed byte-wise, the values of these 4 bytes are influenced only by the 4 bytes of the last round key. Exploiting this fact and assuming that the injected fault has corrupted only one byte, the attacker may proceed to recover the 4 bytes of the key using the correct and faulty ciphertexts. The attacker makes an hypothesis on the unknown part of the key and proceeds to invert the effect of the last ADDROUNDKEY on the part of the cipher that was affected by the fault (greyed out in the figure) obtaining 4 values belonging to the state marked as I in Figure 2. This operation is performed on both the erroneous and the correct values of the ciphertext, yielding 2 groups of 4 byte values. Subsequently, the attacker proceeds to invert the effect of both the SHIFTROWS and SUBBYTES primitives, since their effect is fully known, obtaining successfully a faulty and a correct hypothetical values for four bytes of the state S^9, denoted, respectively by $\widetilde{w} = \{\widetilde{S_0^9}, \widetilde{S_1^9}, \widetilde{S_2^9}, \widetilde{S_3^9}\}$ and $w = \{S_0^9, S_1^9, S_2^9, S_3^9\}$. Bypassing the effect of the ADDROUNDKEY operation, to further roll back the cipher, the attacker computes the exclusive or of $\widetilde{w}$ and w. Doing so, the effect of the AD-DROUNDKEY function is cancelled since in computing $\delta = w \oplus \widetilde{w}$ the key values are added twice. This allows the attacker to effectively compute the difference between the correct and the erroneous state of the cipher right before the MIXCOLUMNS operation. Since the MIXCOLUMNS operation is linear with respect to the exclusive or, it is possible to map the four byte difference δ into the difference before the operation by multiplying the value by the inverse of the matrix employed in the regular MIX-COLUMNS . At this point, the attacker may check if the obtained difference is actually composed of a single byte, as the fault model required by the attack mandates, or not. Depending on whether the difference matches the fault model or not, the attacker can decide if the key hypothesis made at the beginning of this rollback procedure is a valid one or not.

The attacker iterates the same difference analysis procedure for all the possible 2^{32} values of the four unknown bytes of the key and stores only the ones which actually produce a single byte difference before the last MIXCOLUMNS operation when elaborated through the aforementioned procedure. A single sweep of this procedure yields roughly a thousand valid candidates for the 32-bit wide key slice, and may be repeated if more than one faulty ciphertext caused by a single byte fault is available to the attacker. With a second sweep of the procedure the number of key candidates is reduced to one with a reasonably high probability [17].

Since it is possible for the attacker to discern, looking at which bytes are affected by the faults, which slice of the key is the one under consideration, it is possible to reconstruct the complete last round key with 4 faults and a brute force effort of $1000^4 \sim 2^{40}$ AES encryptions, which takes about a couple of minutes on a modern desktop computer, or with 8 faults and no brute force effort at all.

Further reduction of the number of faults needed for the attack allows to employ a single fault happening between the MIXCOLUMNS operation of the seventh and the MIXCOLUMNS of the eight round as four single-byte faults happening simultaneously in each column of the state before the last MIXCOLUMNS is executed, thanks to the diffusing effect of the SHIFTROWS operation in the ninth round. This way, it is possible to retrieve the complete last round key of the cipher with a single fault and a modest brute force effort or two faults and no brute force effort. The main drawback of this method is that it is not possible to determine whether a faulty ciphertext has been originated by a fault complying with the required timing hypothesis, since the whole ciphertext value is altered. Nonetheless, if a fault which does not match the fault hypothesis is employed in the key recovery procedure, the number of valid key candidates drops to zero during the first iteration of the procedure, allowing the attacker to be aware of the issue.

After performing the aforementioned procedure, the attacker has all the bits of the last round key and is thus able to reconstruct the whole original key, if a key size of 128 bits is employed. If larger key sizes are used, it is necessary to recover more key material in order to successfully break the cipher. An extension of the above attack is reported in [2], and needs twice the number of faults in order to recover the whole AES-256 key. The fault model assumed is the same, but the attacker is required to inject faults also in the previous round.

5   Experimental Results

This section presents the measurement setup used and the experiments conducted in order to profile the behavior of the low power AES implementation and investigate the feasibility of low cost fault injection attacks based on voltage throttling.

5.1   Measurement Setup

The packaged chip was mounted on a suitable socket and a dedicated Printed Card Board (PCB) was built. The chip under test was connected to a Keithley K236 power supply, which is sufficiently precise to allow reducing the supply voltage by as little as 0.1mV, as was needed for our purposes. The power supply was connected to the power pin of the chip under test. All the tested AES circuits were clocked at a frequency of 1.3MHz by means of an external clock generator and each encryption required 1100 clock cycles (less than 1ms). Note that these characteristics are within the typical range of RFID systems.

To carry out the experiments we connected the inputs/outputs of the PCB to a logic generator/analyzer, the National Instruments NI6552. The entire acquisition system, including the scaling of the supply voltage, was controlled by a Labview 7.1 program, allowing to automate the acquisition.

5.2 Performing the Attacks

We first wanted to ascertain whether it is possible to gracefully degrade the working of the chip through lowering the supply voltage by a small amount. The key intuition behind this attack methodology is that the signal lines of the circuit representing the critical paths for a specific portion should fail first when the feeding voltage is lowered. This effect is caused by the slower rising rate of the gates, which may fail to drive the longest delay paths within the timings enforced by the clock. These experiments were repeated on different samples of the same chip in order to investigate the effects of fabrication process variations.

The first experiment with the objective of finding out whether the chip degrades gracefully, was conducted by testing how many encryptions the chip was able to perform while lowering the voltage by 0.1 mV after each test. The voltage reduction was carefully carried out in order to exactly identify the voltage level at which it was possible to have only setup time violations but no functional errors which may cause the circuit to behave differently in response to the attack. At each voltage step, we collected the results of ten thousand encryption operations and compared them to the correct one. Figure 3 depicts the results of the experiments in terms of percentage of faulty ciphertexts versus the supply voltage. As can be seen from the figure, there is a 0.8 mV interval where the fault occurrence is limited to less than 10% of the outputs and the fault occurrences gradually increase while lowering further the voltage. The 0.8 mV interval with a few fault occurrences is relevant when performing fault attacks as it maximizes the likelihood of inserting a single fault in the whole computation, as opposed to the catastrophic behavior shown when the supply voltage is considerably lowered as reported in [1,20]. The 0.8 mV interval in the supply voltage is well within the reach of the precision of the employed tunable power supply, thus we expect to be able to successfully inject exploitable faults.

To verify the impact of process variations on the position and width of the sensitive voltage range, we tested different samples of the same chip. Figure 4 reports the results of conducting the same campaign on five different sample chips implementing the same AES design. As can be clearly seen, process variations strongly affect the offset of the fault injection threshold for the sampled chip. However, it can be noticed that the rate of the degradation of the circuit performance is the same for all the samples. This in turn implies that, regardless of the different offsets in the fault onset zone, it is always possible to inject successfully single byte faults with the same low cost equipment.

After characterizing the graceful degradation of the chips, in terms of fault occurrence frequency, we moved on to investigate the actual fault pattern to discover if single

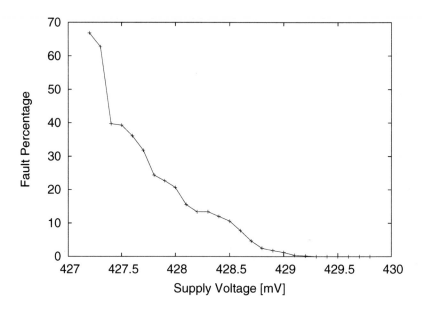

Fig. 3. Percentage of faulty outputs at different supply voltages for a single sample chip

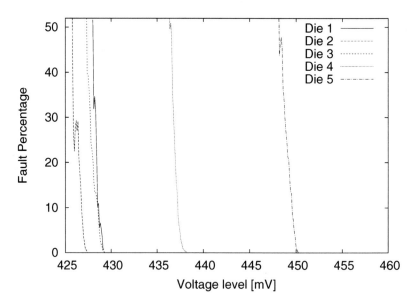

Fig. 4. Comparison of the voltage threshold of the first appearance of faults for different samples of the same chip

byte faults were present in the erroneous ciphertexts which can be collected. To this end, we collected roughly 670K faulty ciphertexts while running the chip under test within the 10% faulty ciphertext region mentioned before. In order to uniformly stress the AES implementation, the plaintexts used during this campaign were selected from the NIST standard AES test vectors. The goal of the first analysis was to understand the variance of the fault patterns. By examining the faulty ciphertexts produced by the device, we found out that the errors induced by setup time violations caused only 822 unique faults. This implies that the positions where the faults occur are very regular, since there has been an approximate repetition rate of 1000 for each fault pattern. The fault repetition rate was uniform with respect to the different plaintexts.

The last step in the characterization of attacks on this AES implementation was to find out how many faults out of the ones obtained were practically usable in order to carry out the attack. To this end, we analyzed the difference between the correct encryption process and the faulty one by rolling back the encryption process for the faulty ciphertexts. The inner states of the cipher at the beginning of each round obtained in this way were compared with the correct values and all the per-state differences were analysed. Recall that this approach does not impact the practical feasibility of the attack, since all the mentioned fault attack techniques to AES are able to successfully discard faults which do not fit the correct fault pattern.

In order to avoid possible fault pattern repetitions due to the same plaintext or key, ten thousands different plaintext and key combination were used as inputs in each experiment. We performed 10 different experiments lowering the voltage level by 0.1mV each time, while staying in the low fault rate region, to determine how wide is the actual voltage window to obtain usable single bit faults. Analysing the results we have observed that out of 39881 faulty results collected during the 10 experiments, 30386 were actually the outcome of a single byte fault, thus resulting in an average 76% of the injected faults fitting the desired fault model (single byte modification). The percentage of exploitable faults ranges from 61% (lowest voltage) to 82% (highest voltage), supporting the fact that a stronger voltage drop induces gradually more catastrophic faults in the computation. This result implies that the actual exploitable window for the fault injection is at least 1mV wide. The fault patterns in the byte indicate that the byte is actually randomly modified with no particular sensitivity of a specific bit in the byte.

The last step to confirm the feasibility of mounting fault injection attacks on the chip is to verify that the faults are hitting the specific round positions required by the attack of [7]. Figure 5 shows the distribution of the single byte faults in the state of the cipher for each voltage level employed in the measurements.

As it is possible to notice, the faults tend to hit all the rounds of the cipher, albeit with a bias for the first two. This different sensitivity to single byte faults can be ascribed to a larger number of faults hitting the control unit, with respect to the ones for a specific round. This issue may be caused by a particular sensitivity of some inner paths of the control unit to setup time violations. The very low fault rate for the first state of the cipher is to be attributed to the fact that the architecture has just loaded the values and has not performed any significant operation on the plaintext yet. These results show that it is possible to generate successfully the required faults in order to break the AES implementation under consideration. In particular, since the position of the single byte

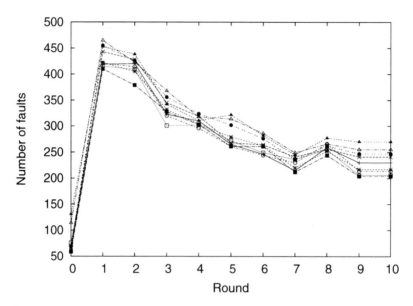

Fig. 5. Per round distribution of the single byte faults in the states of the cipher. Round 0 refers to the faults occurring before the cipher has started, allegedly during the load operations. Each line is obtained with a fixed voltage range, sweeping a 1mV interval in 0.1 mV steps.

fault in the inner state is almost uniformly distributed, the hypotheses made in [7,17] on the required number of faults hold.

The confirmation of the feasibility of an attack on the chip was obtained by executing the aforementioned attack on an ad-hoc C software implementation of the attack algorithms on a Core 2 Quad Q6600 based desktop. The observed key retrieval times were in the range of a one to two minutes, as expected from this attack technique while the memory fingerprint of the attack program stays below 1MB. Adding together the time required to acquire a sufficient amount of faulty data, which is around one day, we can state that the proposed attack is practically viable in a real world scenario, even with low resources.

6   Conclusions

In this paper, for the first time, the susceptibility to low cost fault injection attacks of a 65 nm subthreshold AES coprocessor specifically designed for RFID applications has been practically evaluated. We showed that by using a precise power supply generator which allows voltage scaling in the range of 0.1mV, it is possible to inject the faults needed to extract the secret key. We also noticed that compared to the usual situation, while attacking devices operating at subthreshold voltage, the ideal spot for the attack is located much closer to the operational voltage. Finally, we explored the effects of process variations on the ideal spot and noticed that its characteristic does not change when different chips are used. However, the exact value of the ideal voltage is different for each chip.

Acknowledgements. This work was partially supported by the Walloon Region (E-USER and S@T Skywin projects) and by the Nanotera program (SecWear project). François-Xavier Standaert is an associate researcher of the Belgian Fund for Scientific Research (FNRS-F.R.S.).

References

1. Barenghi, A., Bertoni, G., Parrinello, E., Pelosi, G.: Low Voltage Fault Attacks on the RSA Cryptosystem. In: Workshop on Fault Diagnosis and Tolerance in Cryptography, pp. 23–31 (2009)
2. Barenghi, A., Bertoni, G.M., Breveglieri, L., Pellicioli, M., Pelosi, G.: Low Voltage Fault Attacks to AES. In: Tehranipoor, M., Plusquellic, J. (eds.) HOST. IEEE Computer Society, Los Alamitos (2010)
3. Bol, D., Ambroise, R., Flandre, D., Legat, J.D.: Interests and limitations of technology scaling for subthreshold logic. IEEE Transactions on Very Large Scale Integration (VLSI) Systems 17(10), 1508–1519 (2009)
4. Chen, C.-N., Yen, S.-M.: Differential fault analysis on aes key schedule and some countermeasures. In: Proc. Information Security and Privacy, pp. 217–217 (2003)
5. Daemen, J., Rijmen, V.: The Design of Rijndael: AES - The Advanced Encryption Standard. Springer, Heidelberg (2002)
6. Das, R., Harrop, P.: RFID forecasts, players and opportunities 2011, 96, 2021. IDTechEx report (2010)
7. Dusart, P., Letourneux, G., Vivolo, O.: Differential Fault Analysis on AES. In: CoRR, cs.CR/0301020 (2003)
8. Feldhofer, M., Wolkerstorfer, J., Rijmen, V.: AES implementation on a grain of sand. IEE Proceedings on Information Security 152(1), 13–20 (2005)
9. Giraud, C.: DFA on AES. In: Dobbertin, H., Rijmen, V., Sowa, A. (eds.) AES 2005. LNCS, vol. 3373, pp. 27–41. Springer, Heidelberg (2005)
10. Hutter, M., Plos, T., Schmidt, J.-M.: Contact-Based Fault Injections and Power Analysis on RFID Tags. In: Proc. IEEE European Conference on Circuit Theory and Design, pp. 409–412 (2009)
11. Kasper, T., Silbermann, M., Paar, C.: All you can eat or breaking a real-world contactless payment system. In: Sion, R. (ed.) FC 2010. LNCS, vol. 6052, pp. 343–350. Springer, Heidelberg (2010)
12. Kim, C.H., Quisquater, J.-J.: New Differential Fault Analysis on AES Key Schedule: Two Faults Are Enough. In: Grimaud, G., Standaert, F.-X. (eds.) CARDIS 2008. LNCS, vol. 5189, pp. 48–60. Springer, Heidelberg (2008)
13. Mentens, N., Batina, L., Preneel, B., Verbauwhede, I.: A systematic evaluation of compact hardware implementations for the rijndael S-box. In: Menezes, A. (ed.) CT-RSA 2005. LNCS, vol. 3376, pp. 323–333. Springer, Heidelberg (2005)
14. Moradi, A., Shalmani, M.T.M., Salmasizadeh, M.: A generalized method of differential fault attack against AES cryptosystem. In: Goubin, L., Matsui, M. (eds.) CHES 2006. LNCS, vol. 4249, pp. 91–100. Springer, Heidelberg (2006)
15. NIST. Announcing the advanced encryption standard aes. Technical report, Federal Information Processing Standards Publication 197 (2001)
16. Peacham, D., Thomas, B.: A DFA attack against the AES key schedule. SiVenture Whitepaper (October 2006)
17. Piret, G., Quisquater, J.-J.: A Differential Fault Attack Technique against SPN Structures, with Application to the AES and KHAZAD. In: Walter, C.D., Koç, Ç.K., Paar, C. (eds.) CHES 2003. LNCS, vol. 2779, pp. 77–88. Springer, Heidelberg (2003)

18. Satoh, A., Morioka, S., Takano, K., Munetoh, S.: A Compact Rijndael Hardware Architecture with S-Box Optimization. In: Boyd, C. (ed.) ASIACRYPT 2001. LNCS, vol. 2248, pp. 239–254. Springer, Heidelberg (2001)

19. Schmidt, J.-M., Hutter, M., Plos, T.: Optical Fault Attacks on AES: A Threat in Violet. In: Proc. Workshop on Fault Diagnosis and Tolerance in Cryptography, pp. 13–22 (2009)

20. Selmane, N., Guilley, S., Danger, J.-L.: Practical Setup Time Violation Attacks on AES. In: EDCC-7 2008: Proceedings of the 2008 Seventh European Dependable Computing Conference, pp. 91–96. IEEE Computer Society, Washington, DC, USA (2008)

Side-Channel Analysis of Cryptographic RFIDs with Analog Demodulation*

Timo Kasper, David Oswald, and Christof Paar

Horst Görtz Institute for IT Security,
Ruhr-University Bochum, Germany
{timo.kasper,david.oswald,christof.paar}@rub.de

Abstract. As most modern cryptographic Radio Frequency Identification (RFID) devices are based on ciphers that are secure from a purely theoretical point of view, e.g., (Triple-)DES or AES, adversaries have been adopting new methods to extract secret information and cryptographic keys from contactless smartcards: Side-Channel Analysis (SCA) targets the physical implementation of a cipher and allows to recover secret keys by exploiting a side-channel, for instance, the electro-magnetic (EM) emanation of an Integrated Circuit (IC). In this paper we present an analog demodulator specifically designed for refining the SCA of contactless smartcards. The customized analogue hardware increases the quality of EM measurements, facilitates the processing of the side-channel leakage and can serve as a plug-in component to enhance any existing SCA laboratory. Employing it to obtain power profiles of several real-world cryptographic RFIDs, we demonstrate the effectiveness of our measurement setup and evaluate the improvement of our new analog technique compared to previously proposed approaches. Using the example of the popular Mifare DESFire MF3ICD40 contactless smartcard, we show that commercial RFID devices are susceptible to the proposed SCA methods. The security analyses presented in this paper do not require expensive equipment and demonstrate that SCA poses a severe threat to many real-world systems. This novel attack vector has to be taken into account when employing contactless smartcards in security-sensitive applications, e.g., for wireless payment or identification.

Keywords: contactless smartcards, side-channel analyis, implementation attacks, hardware security, DESFire MF3ICD40.

1 Introduction

Contactless smartcards based on RFID technology have become the basis of numerous large-scale, security-relevant applications, including amongst others public transport, wireless payment, access control, and digital identification [36].

---

* The work described in this paper has been supported in part by the European Commission through the ICT programme under contract ICT-2007-216676 ECRYPT II.

According to NXP, the vendor of the Mifare product line, more than 1 billion Mifare smartcard ICs have been sold [27]. Due to the sensitivity of the stored and transmitted data (e.g., personal information, cash balance, etc.) and the fact that accessing the wireless interface is virtually impossible to control, most RFIDs devices today comprise cryptographic mechanisms, for example to perform a mututal authentication or to encrypt the data sent over the air interface.

As a consequence of the attacks on Mifare Classic following the reverse-engineering of the proprietary cipher Crypto1 [23,11], many operators of RFID systems have migrated to contactless smartcards based on modern cryptographic primitives, such as (Triple-)DES or AES. As these ciphers are secure from a mathematical point of view and efficient theoretical attacks are currently unknown, the threat scenario is changing:

Instead of performing cryptanalytical attacks on an algorithmic level which are infeasible for modern ciphers, an adversary targets the physical hard- or software implementation. The class of *implementation attacks* includes both passive monitoring of the device during the cryptographic operation via some *side-channel*, and the active manipulation of the target by injecting permanent or transient *faults*. In this paper we focus on *non-invasive, passive* SCA exploiting the EM emanation of contactless smartcards while they execute a cryptographic primitive. This class of attacks poses a severe threat to many real-world RFID systems, as SCA may enable an adversary to extract, for instance, the secret key of a Triple-DES (3DES) or AES operation within a few hours of measurement and analysis, whereas an exhaustive search is infeasible with the currently available computational resources.

1.1   Related Work

The concept of SCA was first proposed in [20] in 1998, and the field has since then been an area of extensive research. Notable contributions include the analysis of EM leakage instead of the current consumption [2] and the method of Correlation Power Analysis (CPA) that employs the (linear) correlation coefficient during the evaluation phase to better model the behaviour of real ICs [5]. Apart from that, there is a wide variety of literature both on attack techniques and possible countermeasures — a summary can for instance be found in [22].

For SCA of RFID devices, less research has been conducted, especially with respect to attacks on real-world devices. In [28], a successful side-channel attack against a simple password-based authentication mechanism of an Ultra-High Frequency (UHF) RFID is demonstrated. Precisely monitoring the EM field during the response of the device, the authors are able to predict the password bits. However, due to the different operating principle ("backscatter") of UHF devices, the results cannot be immediately applied to contactless smartcards, which usually follow the ISO 14443 standard [13,14] employing magnetic coupling at a frequency of 13.56 MHz.

The authors of [12,31] describe several SCA attacks against a self-made implementation of the AES running on an actively powered microcontroller (μC)-based prototype RFID. As all analyses are performed in a white-box setting, i.e., with full knowledge and control of the implementation details and in the absence of countermeasures, the results do not imply a direct threat to real-world systems.

At WISA 2009, a key recovery on a commercial contactless smartcard featuring 3DES authentication and encryption was presented [17]. Working in a black-box scenario, the authors were able to profile the device, locate the encryption operation, and mount a successful non-invasive CPA on the 3DES engine. The leakage model for contactless smartcards introduced in this work forms the basis for our analysis and is outlined in Sect. 2. The authors also report that a special analog circuit (subtracting the signal of the oscillator of their reader to dampen the carrier and increase the side-channel amplitude) improves the results of their CPA, however, do not explicitly quantify the actual effect of this approach.

1.2   Contribution of This Paper

As a main contribution, we propose a novel method for isolating and amplifying the SCA leakage of cryptographic RFIDs by means of an analog demodulation circuit. We verify the validity of the leakage model introduced in [17] for real-world products by performing an analyis of the Mifare DESFire MF3ICD40 contactless smartcard. In doing so, we estimate the effectiveness of the developed circuitry by comparing the proposed analog technique to methods that are solely based on digital signal processing.

The remainder of this paper is structured as follows: in Sect. 2, we briefly summarize the leakage model put forward in [17] and explain the differences between several demodulation approaches in the context of SCA. In Sect. 3, the developed measurement environment is presented, with a focus on the special analog circuitry for extracting side-channel information. The efficiency of the setup is then practically demonstrated by analyzing the DESFire MF3ICD40 smartcard and providing power profiles of several other real-world devices in Sect. 4. Finally, we conclude in Sect. 5, suggesting aspects for future research and outlining open problems.

2   SCA of Contactless Smartcards

In contrast to their contact-based counterpart, the electrical energy for contactless smartcards is supplied wirelessly using magnetic coupling. This results in a leakage model for contactless smartcards as proposed in [17]: the side-channel signal causes an amplitude modulation of the 13.56 MHz field generated by the reader, i.e., it relates to the same physical principle as used for the data transmission from card to reader, termed *load modulation*[1]. In the time domain, an amplitude-modulated signal $s(t)$ may be written as

$$s(t) = (P_{const} + p(t)) \cdot \cos(\omega_{reader} \cdot t)$$

---

[1] Load modulation causes significantly stronger changes of the EM field compared to the side channel leakage.

where $\omega_{reader} = 2\pi\, f_{reader}$, $f_{reader} = 13.56\,\mathrm{MHz}$ denotes the carrier frequency, P_{const} the constant part of the power consumption and $p\,(t)$ the variation due to the internal operation of a smartcard, e.g., caused by different intermediate values being processed during a cryptographic operation. Note that usually $|p\,(t)| << P_{const}$, and hence the isolation and amplification of the modulating signal $p\,(t)$ is a key factor for a successful SCA. The amplitude of the strong field of the reader is several orders of magnitude greater than the side-channel leakage. When digitizing $s\,(t)$ the input range of the analog-to-digital conversion has to be set large enough to capture the full signal, resulting in a decreased accuracy of the measurements with respect to $p\,(t)$. In order to maximize the vertical resolution of the measurements and capture all relevant information it is hence beneficial to isolate the side-channel information *before* the digitizing step, so that the input range can be set corresponding to $p\,(t)$ and the accuracy of the measurements is maximized.

Basically, the problem of extracting the weak signal $p\,(t)$ from $s\,(t)$ is equivalent to that of amplitude demodulation, about which extensive research has been carried out in the context of "classical" electronic communication, cf. for instance [32]. In this paper, we focus on the principle of *incoherent* demodulation, which has the advantage that the unmodulated carrier signal is not further required.

Instead, by *rectifying* (i.e., taking the absolute value) of an amplitude-modulated signal and filtering the result, the modulating side-channel information $p\,(t)$ can directly be retreived.

The rectification may either be achieved by processing the *full wave* to obtain $|s\,(t)|$ or following the *half wave* approach, i.e., discarding the negative part of $s\,(t)^2$. The latter approach is often used in practice, as it can be realized with one diode, whereas full-wave rectification requires more complex circuits. In terms of the achievable bandwidth for receiving the modulating signal $p\,(t)$, full-wave rectification allows a maximum bandwidth of $B_{full} = f_{reader}$, whereas the half-wave method limits it to $B_{half} = \frac{f_{reader}}{2}$, for details cf. [32].

3   Measurement Setup

In this section, we present the developed measurement environment for the SCA of contactless smartcards. Fig. 1 gives an overview of the components of our setup and their interconnection. An antenna coil establishes the coupling between the contactless smartcard and an RFID reader. The latter supplies the contactless smartcard (from now on occasionally referred to as Device Under Test (DUT)) with power and sends commands by turning the EM field off for a specific amount of time. The DUT transmits its response using load modulation, i.e., it modulates the amplitude of the reader field by increasing its power consumption.

The utilized reader is a custom, freely programmable device based on the design proposed in [16]. This reader allows for sending arbitrary commands to

---

[2] The remaining half period of the sine-shaped signal can be mathematically expressed as $\frac{1}{2}\,(s\,(t) + |s\,(t)|)$.

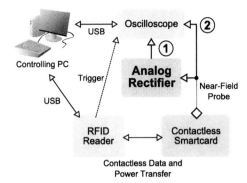

Fig. 1. Overview of measurement environment

an ISO 14443-compliant RFID and can thus be used to implement the protocols of most contactless smartcards in use today. Besides, communication according to ISO 15693 [15] is supported, however, we are not aware of any commercially available RFID complying to this standard that comprises cryptography.

For the purpose of SCA, the 13.56 MHz EM field is captured with a magnetic near-field probe manufactured by Langer EMV [21]. The resulting "raw signal" is on the one hand directly recorded by a Picoscope 5204 Digital Storage Oscilloscope (DSO) [29]. On the other hand, the same signal is further processed using the analog demodulator and filter presented in Sect. 3.2 before being captured by the second input channel of the oscilloscope. The RFID reader generates a trigger event to start a measurement when the last bit of a command has been sent to the DUT.

The overall control of the measurement process presented in Sect. 3.1 is performed by a central standard PC, which is connected to the RFID reader and the oscilloscope via a USB link. The PC prepares the commands to be sent to the DUT, transmits them to the RFID reader and initiates the acquistion of side-channel measurements. The resulting waveforms (from now on referred to as *traces*) captured by the oscilloscope are stored on the harddrive along with additional information, e.g., the input and/or output of a cryptographic operation performed by a contactless smartcard.

3.1   Measurement Process

We implemented the authentication protocols of a wide range of contactless smartcards, including Mifare Classic, Mifare DESFire MF3ICD40, Mifare DES-Fire EV1, Mifare Ultralight C, and the Basic Access Control (BAC) of the German electronic passport. All these protocols involve the execution of one or several cryptographic operations on the DUT, for which we can either control the input or obtain the output an unlimited number of times.

A side-channel trace is acquired as follows: First, the DUT is reset by switching off the field of the reader for a device-specific duration. Then, all initializations according to ISO 14443 are performed, and finally, a cryptographic operation is started by sending the appropriate command. The input data (challenge) for this operation is stored in a file so that it can be used to predict intermediate values in the analysis phase. While the device is executing this operation, side-channel traces are recorded simultaneously both for the raw field of the reader (i.e., without analog preprocessing) and for the processed signal (i.e., demodulated using the analog rectifier and filter). In case the DUT returns a relevant response (e.g., the result of an encryption), this value is also stored along with the trace. For all experiments presented in this paper, we use a sample rate of 500 MHz for digitizing the signals, which turns out to be sufficient considering the band-limiting operations performed by the analog and digital processing. This process is repeated several thousand times, depending on the characteristics of the DUT and the target for the SCA[3].

3.2   Analog Processing

According to the assumed leakage model for contactless smartcards explained in Sect. 2, the power consumption of the smartcard causes a (very weak) amplitude modulation of the field generated by the RFID reader. Hence, demodulation of this signal and isolating it from the strong carrier field of the reader can reveal the side-channel leakage and enable further analysis, e.g., key recovery by means of Simple Power Analysis (SPA) or CPA. In [17] the amplitude of the modulating signal is increased by subtracting the known, constant reader signal using analog circuitry. The actual demodulation is then performed digitally during the analysis phase. In this paper we implement a new different method by realizing the complete demodulation process with analog components, which allows to isolate and *directly* obtain the power consumption signal of an RFID smartcard.

For this purpose, we designed a custom Printed Circuit Board (PCB) comprising circuitry for amplification, rectification, and filtering of the raw analog signal. The complete schematics are given in Appendix A. The signal acquired by the EM probe is first amplified using an AD8058 Operational Amplifier (opamp) [4] and then rectified by a BAT48 Schottky diode [35]. The result is filtered using an active low-pass filter[4] with a -3 dB frequency of 6.25 MHz. The output stage is designed to drive a standard 50 Ω load, e.g., connected via a suitable coaxial cable.

In our practical experiments, it turned out that the filtering and amplification performed on the demodulation board can be further improved: the carrier signal was not suppressed as strong as desired and a slight drift of the DC component of the signal occurred during long-term measurements (e.g., due to temperature variations). Thus, we extended the demodulator with a bandpass filter circuit that further reduces the amplitude of the 13.56 MHz signal and besides provides a highpass characteristic to remove the DC shift. This second-order filter is

---

[3] For example, it turns out that a transfer on the internal data bus of a smartcard results in stronger leakage than a register update within an encryption, and hence, SCA of the latter requires significantly more traces.

[4] The filter is built with a Sallen-Key topology using an AD8045 opamp [3].

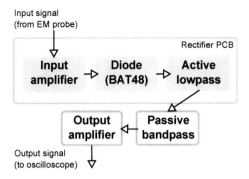

Fig. 2. Structure of the analog demodulation circuitry

built using passive components only (i.e., inductors and capacitors) and has a passband between 100 kHz and 7 MHz. Finally, the filter output is amplified to utilize the full input range of ± 100 mV of the oscilloscope. The overall structure of the demodulation system, used for the analyses presented in Sect. 4, is depicted in Fig. 2. To minimize the complexity of the board we implemented a half-wave rectification, i.e., discard the negative part of the signal. As explained in Sect. 2, this approach limits the bandwidth of the receivable signal to $\frac{13.56}{2}$ MHz.

3.3   Digital Processing

As mentioned in Sect. 3.1, side-channel traces (of the same operation) are acquired both before (raw trace, ② in Fig. 1) and after the demodulation circuitry (① in Fig. 1). For analysing the improvement provided by the analog hardware, the demodulation process thus has to be reproduced in the digital domain. For that purpose, we developed respective functions that perform half- or full-wave rectification and the necessary filtering of the raw traces. Besides, additional filtering in the evaluation phase may also be beneficial for the output of the analog demodulator, for instance, to further suppress the 13.56 MHz signal with a digital Finite Impulse Response (FIR) filter. The concrete effects of the digital processing techniques are practically evaluated in Sect. 4.1.

4   Practical Results

In this section, we demonstrate the effectiveness of our approach by analysing the side-channel leakage of several commercial contactless smartcards. As our main example we use the Mifare DESFire MF3ICD40, an ISO 14443-compliant smartcard. We briefly present the power profile of this smartcard and then compare our analog and digital processing techniques by quantifying their impact on real-world measurements. Subsequently, we perform several attacks on the 3DES encryption of the Mifare DESFire MF3ICD40 and show that the success rate of the SCA can be improved using the developed analog demodulator. Finally, we consider other contactless smartcards, including the German electronic passport and the new DESFire EV1, and present side-channel traces of these devices.

4.1   Example: Mifare DESFire MF3ICD40

Mifare DESFire MF3ICD40 [24] contactless cards feature an implementation of
3DES that can be used both for establishing a mutual authentication between
the smartcard and a reader and to ensure the confidentiality of the information
exchanged over the wireless interface. In our experiments, the device turned out
to be susceptible to SCA, and hence, we utilize it as an example to demonstrate
and evaluate the capabilities of our measurement setup. Note that all results
given in this section refer to the DESFire MF3ICD40 and do not apply to the
newer AES-based variant DESFire EV1.

Profiling. When performing an SCA in a black-box scenario (i.e., when no information about the internals of the DUT is available), the first step is usually
a profiling phase during which one attempts to map different parts of the power
trace to steps of the operation of the DUT (e.g., a data transfer or an encryption operation). We target the step in the DESFire authentication protocol (for
details on the protocol, cf. [19,9]) during which the reader sends its response
(denoted as B_2) to the challenge of the card transmits its own challenge (B_1).
To verify the response of the reader and compute its own response, the smartcard encrypts both B_1 and B_2 using 3DES with its secret symmetric key k_C, as
shown in Fig. 3.

Reader   DESFire

$$\text{Choose } B_1, B_2 \xrightarrow{\quad B_1, B_2 \quad} \begin{aligned} C_2 &= 3\text{DES}_{k_C}(B_2) \\ C_1 &= 3\text{DES}_{k_C}(B_1) \end{aligned}$$

Fig. 3. Excerpt of the Mifare DESFire authentication protocol relevant for SCA

Figure 4 shows the power trace during this operation. The depicted waveform is the result of the analog demodulation (using the hardware proposed
in Sect. 3.2) and digital filtering (using an FIR bandpass filter from 50 kHz to
8 MHz, as described in Sect. 3.3).

We performed a CPA on the plain- and ciphertext of both encryption operations using an 8-Bit hamming weight model. Note that during the profiling
stage, we are able to set the secret key k_C of the card, and can thus predict
intermediate values that are not directly output by the DUT, e.g., the resulting
ciphertexts C_1 and C_2 of the encryption of B_1 and B_2. As suggested by the
findings of [18], we were able to obtain a significant correlation result at the
correct points in time[5] using less than 1000 traces (this result is further detailed
in Sect. 4.1).

The part of the power trace that belongs to the actual 3DES encryption,
which is presumably performed by a dedicated (and protected) hardware engine

---

[5] i.e., for which eight subsequent peaks are visible in the power profile.

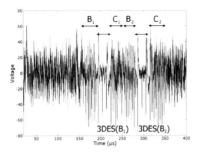

Fig. 4. Power profile of the Mifare DESFire MF3ICD40 (after analog processing)

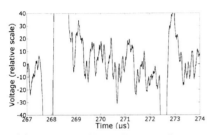

(a) Power profile in the time domain

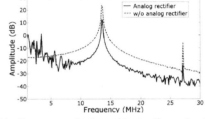

(b) Spectrum before (dashed) and after (solid) analog processing

Fig. 5. DES encryption on the Mifare DESFire MF3ICD40

on the DUT, is illustrated in Fig. 5a. In order to optimize the evaluation, we set up our environment to yield maximum amplitude for this part, and again digitally band-limited the trace with an FIR bandpass from 50 kHz to 8 MHz.

Influence of Analog Processing. To estimate the increase of the amplitude of the side-channel signal due to the analog demodulator, we focus on the part of the power trace belonging to the encryption operation and compare the power spectrum[6] before and after the analog processing.

Figure 5b compares the respective spectra (with the y-axis logarithmically scaled) for frequencies from 0 MHz to 30 MHz. For the unprocessed traces, no clear side-channel signal can be identified in the frequency domain. In contrast, the result of the analog demodulation clearly shows the spectrum of the side-channel information between 0 MHz and approx. 7 MHz.

Influence of Digital Processing. As mentioned in Sect. 3.3, further digital processing of the acquired signals is mandatory for signals recorded without analog processing to perform the demodulation. For traces already demodulated

---

[6] i.e., the squared magnitude $|DFT(s(k))|^2$ of the Discrete Fourier Transform (DFT) [33] of a signal $s(k)$.

using the proposed analog rectifier, additional digital filtering is not required — however, it can help to further improve the results of subsequent analyses. To illustrate the effect of the digital processing, Fig. 6a compares the power spectra for the filtered (blue, solid) and unfiltered (green, dashed) output of the analog demodulator. The raw signal (green, dashed) without analog filtering and its digitally demodulated variants using half-wave (blue, solid) and full-wave (red, dashed-dotted) rectification are depicted in Fig. 6b.

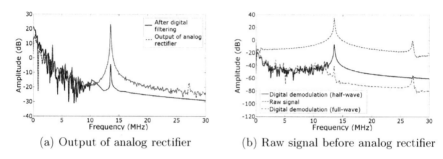

(a) Output of analog rectifier   (b) Raw signal before analog rectifier

Fig. 6. Power spectrum during DES encryption, before (dashed) and after (solid and dashed-dotted) digital processing

SCA Results. In this section, we move forward and evaluate the effect of our proposed signal processing techniques in terms of CPA results. To this end, we compare the magnitude of correlation coefficients for the analog and the digital demodulation approaches. We target the transfers on the databus of the DUT during the profiling, as detailed in Sect. 4.1. Furthermore, some CPA-relevant results of the actual hardware encryption engine are provided.

As mentioned in Sect. 4.1, a significant correlation for the bytes of the plaintext of the encryption operation can already be obtained from a small number of traces. We thus recorded 10,000 measurements and computed the correlation coefficients after (a) analog demodulation using half-wave rectification, (b) digital demodulation using half-wave rectification, and (c) digital demodulation using full-wave rectification.

The maximum value of the correlation coefficient over the number of processed traces is shown in Fig. 7 exemplarily for the fifth and the seventh byte of the plaintext B_2. To provide a measure for the significance of the correlation values, we also included the expected "noise level" of $4/\sqrt{\text{No. of traces}}$ in the diagrams (turquoise, dashed-dotted). The analog rectifier yields correlation results that are clearly distinguishable from noise after approx. 900 traces. In contrast, the digital (half-wave) equivalent of our analog processing circuit exhibits an inferior performance and displays a lower overall value for the correlation, i.e., cannot exploit the full side-channel leakage present in the measured signals. Comparing these cases using the same demodulation principle, i.e., (1) and (2) in Fig. 7, the developed analog circuitry clearly outperforms the standard digital approach. For reference, curve (3) in Fig. 7 further illustrates the results obtained for a digital full-wave rectifier,

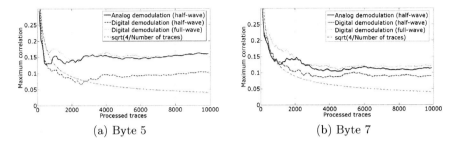

(a) Byte 5   (b) Byte 7

Fig. 7. Maximum correlation coefficient for plaintext bytes (Hamming weight) for (1) analog (blue, solid) and digital demodulation using (2) half-wave (green, dashed) and (3) full-wave rectification (red, dotted)

yielding almost equivalent correlation results compared to the half-wave analog rectifier, which indicates that realizing an analog full-wave rectifier is promising to further improve the efficiency of the measurement setup.

Focusing on the actual encryption process, beginning at approx. $270 \, \mu s$ when the last byte of B_2 has been sent, one can correlate on an intermediate value of the cipher, for instance, the output of the first round of the first DES iteration[7]. Figure 8 shows the maximum correlation coefficient for the Hamming distance between the lower 8 bit of the DES state register R before and after the first round [1]: the correlation after the analog rectification converges to a value of approx. 0.09 after 160,000 traces, while for the digital counterpart after more than 250,000 traces the correlation coefficient is just marginally distinguishable from the noise floor. Note that this analysis targets the internal cryptographic hardware and hence, as expected [22], requires more traces to detect the side-channel leakage, compared to the data bus.

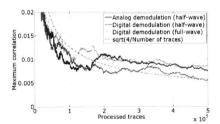

Fig. 8. Maximum correlation coefficient (8-bit Hamming distance $R_0 \rightarrow R_1$) for (a) analog (blue, solid) and digital demodulation using (b) half-wave (green, dashed) and (c) full-wave rectification (red, dotted)

4.2 Power Profiles of Different Contactless Smartcards

In order to further illustrate the capabilities of our setup and to show the general validity of the RFID leakage model used throughout this paper, we analyzed

---

[7] Knowing the key we can compute all intermediate values within the DES.

several other contactless smartcards. The selection primarily focuses on modern high-security ICs (including the new DESFire EV1 and the German electronic passport), but also comprises devices for low-cost applications, i.e., Mifare Classic and Ultralight C. Note that the results presented in this paper are not specific to RFIDs devices manufactured by NXP — in fact, we were able to reproduce similar results with products made by other vendors, but cannot disclose the results for legal reasons. In this section, we do not perform a detailed analysis of the considered DUTs as done for Mifare DESFire MF3ICD40 in Sect. 4.1, but summarize the characteristics of the respective smartcards and provide some observations made during our experiments.

Figure 9 depicts exemplary power profiles of each DUTs in this section, recorded with the analog demodulator during a particular cryptographic operation. The following paragraphs introduce the devices and give a short description of the cryptographic operations for which the side-channel traces were obtained. We highlight some particular features evident in the power profiles and try to relate them to the internal operation of the DUT.

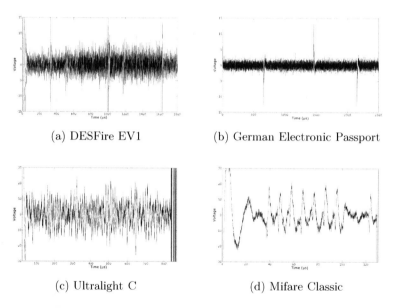

(a) DESFire EV1   (b) German Electronic Passport

(c) Ultralight C   (d) Mifare Classic

Fig. 9. Power profiles of various contactless smartcards

Mifare DESFire EV1. Mifare DESFire EV1 [26] is the successor of Mifare DESFire MF3ICD40 and was announced in 2006. Apart from authentication and encryption with 3DES, the smartcard also provides support for AES with a 128-bit key. The device is certified according to Common Criteria EAL-4+ [7] and implements special hardware countermeasures against SCA, which are, however, not further characterized in the publicly available datasheets. The authentication protocol of the DESFire EV1 is similar to that of the DESFire MF3ICD40 and was disclosed in [19]. The power profile in Fig. 9a has been recorded during the second step of the protocol which involves two AES encryptions. The noticeable peaks in the signal arise from significant shifts in the DC component that might be caused by a countermeasure involving a switching of the internal power supply of the DUT [30]. Another interesting feature is the increase in the signal amplitude from $500\,\mu s$ to $1600\,\mu s$, which might result from the AES encryption.

German Electronic Passport. The German electronic passport [6] is based on a high-security contactless smartcard either manufactured by Infineon or NXP. It comprises several levels of security and is protected by different authentication mechanisms. We implemented the BAC protocol [8] which ensures that the device can only be read with the approval of the owner by performing a 3DES-based mutual authentication based on a key derived from information printed inside the passport. SCA of the protocol itself would not provide a significant gain for an adversary (as the key is printed inside the document), however, it provides a starting point for the analysis of the DUT and allows to trigger a 3DES operation on the smartcard. As for the DESFire EV1, distinct offsets of the DC component can be observed, that again might stem from some protection mechanism.

Mifare Ultralight C. This contactless smartcard was introduced by NXP in 2009 [25] and targets cost-sensitive segments, e.g., paper tickets for public transport systems. Its cryptographic capabilities are limited, and the device only offers an authentication mechanism with 3DES (but no data encryption). Initially, we assumed that the DUT is based on a similar architecture as the Mifare DESFire MF3ICD40 analyzed in Sect. 4, however, this appears not to be the case: neither does the power profile resemble that of DESFire, nor are we currently able to reproduce the correlation results of Sect. 4.1.

Mifare Classic. Finally, we also examined the Mifare Classic, even though a successful key recovery by means of SCA would, in the light of the powerful cryptanalytical attacks [10] that allow to extract the secret key in minutes, pose little additional threat. Thus, we only performed some superficial experiments, which, however, suggest that SCA could be utilized for practical key recovery as well. The trace depicted in Fig. 9d was acquired during the verification of the reader response in the Mifare Classic authentication protocol [11]. The power profile exhibits eight characteristic peaks that appear to correspond to the eight bytes sent by the reader: in fact, we can observe a correlation with some bits of these values. Nevertheless, we will not further investigate the susceptibility of Mifare Classic to SCA in the context of this paper.

5   Conclusion

To summarize the impact of our work, we briefly outline the used methods and the results of our analyses in this section, focussing on the implications for real-world systems. We finally pinpoint directions for further improvements and research.

Summary. We present an analog demodulation circuit that is specifically designed for improving the SCA of contactless smartcards and that can be integrated into any existing EM SCA setup at a very low cost. We verify the benefits of our new methods by comparing it with a fully digital approach and practically demonstrate the effectiveness of our findings at hand of real-world targets. The developed hardware allows to directly and instantly isolate the side-channel leakage from the reader signal, before the digitizing step, and hence significantly facilitates the alignment and further profiling of SCA measurements of RFID devices.

We illustrate that modern cryptographic RFIDs devices are susceptible to (non-invasive) implementation attacks based on monitoring of the EM field. By evaluating the number of traces required for a successful CPA of the popular Mifare DESFire MF3ICD40 smartcard we quantify the advantages of using an analog demodulator compared to a digital demodulation performed in software. We identify several weaknesses in the implementation of the DESFire MF3ICD40 that enable corresponding SCA attacks to extract the secret key. Our work has severe implications for real-world systems: operators and vendors of commercial RFID systems can no longer rely on the mathematical security of the employed cryptographic algorithms, but also have to take into account that an adversary may be able to obtain secret keys by means of SCA. Thus, appropriate protective measures on the system level, e.g., ensuring that each smartcard has a unique secret key and storing sensitive data in a separate database in the backend whenever possible, are mandatory to guarantee maximum security.

Future Work. The described analog circuitry for half-wave rectification has the disadvantage that it discards half of the side-channel information, contained in the part of the reader's signal with a negative amplitude, and limits the available bandwidth of the side-channel signal. Our results indicate that using the information present in the full-wave rectified signal may enhance SCA attacks, hence a corresponding circuit is currently under development. In this context, experiments with other demodulation techniques, e.g., employing a coherent approach based on a Phase-Locked Loop (PLL), would be interesting in order to determine which method yields the best performance.

Apart from that, the technique of analog demodulation enables — due to the clear isolation of the side-channel signal from the reader signal and the noise — other signal processing methods such as resynchronization [34] that can increase the success rate of, e.g., CPA. In the context of real-world systems and especially for some of the highly protected and certified smartcards briefly presented in Sect. 4.2, these and other techniques might enable an adversary to extract secret information even in the presence of hardware countermeasures.

References

1. FIPS 46-3 Data Encryption Standard (DES),
   http://csrc.nist.gov/publications/fips/fips46-3/fips46-3.pdf
2. Agrawal, D., Archambeault, B., Rao, J.R., Rohatgi, P.: The EM side-channel(s). In: Kaliski Jr., B.S., Koç, Ç.K., Paar, C. (eds.) CHES 2002. LNCS, vol. 2523, pp. 29–45. Springer, Heidelberg (2003)

3. Analog Devices, Inc. AD8045 Voltage Feedback High Speed Amplifier Datasheet (2004)
4. Analog Devices, Inc. AD8058 Dual, High Performance Voltage Feedback 325 MHz Amplifier Datasheet (2009)
5. Brier, E., Clavier, C., Olivier, F.: Correlation Power Analysis with a Leakage Model. In: Joye, M., Quisquater, J.-J. (eds.) CHES 2004. LNCS, vol. 3156, pp. 16–29. Springer, Heidelberg (2004)
6. BSI - German Ministry of Security. Security mechanisms in electronic ID documents, http://www.bsi.de/fachthem/epass/
7. BSI - German Ministry of Security. Mifare DESFire8 MF3ICD81 Public Evaluation Documentation. Electronic resource (October 2008)
8. BSI - German Ministry of Security. Technical Guideline TR-03110 Advanced Security Mechanisms for Machine Readable Travel Documents. Electronic resource (October 2010),
   https://www.bsi.bund.de/SharedDocs/Downloads/EN/BSI/Publications/
   TechGuidelines/TR03110/TR-03110_v205_pdf.pdf?_blob=publicationFile
9. Carluccio, D.: Electromagnetic Side Channel Analysis for Embedded Crypto Devices. Master's thesis, Ruhr-University Bochum (2005)
10. Courtois, N.: The Dark Side of Security by Obscurity and Cloning Mifare Classic Rail and Building Passes, Anywhere, Anytime. In: SECRYPT 2009, pp. 331–338. INSTICC Press (2009)
11. Garcia, F.D., de Koning Gans, G., Muijrers, R., van Rossum, P., Verdult, R., Schreur, R.W., Jacobs, B.: Dismantling MIFARE Classic. In: Jajodia, S., Lopez, J. (eds.) ESORICS 2008. LNCS, vol. 5283, pp. 97–114. Springer, Heidelberg (2008)
12. Hutter, M., Mangard, S., Feldhofer, M.: Power and EM Attacks on Passive 13.56 MHz RFID Devices. In: Paillier, P., Verbauwhede, I. (eds.) CHES 2007. LNCS, vol. 4727, pp. 320–333. Springer, Heidelberg (2007)
13. International Organization for Standardization. ISO/IEC 14443-3: Identification Cards - Contactless Integrated Circuit(s) Cards - Proximity Cards - Part 3: Initialization and Anticollision (February 2001)
14. International Organization for Standardization. ISO/IEC 14443-4: Identification cards - Contactless Integrated Circuit(s) Cards - Proximity Cards - Part 4: Transmission Protocol (February 2001)
15. International Organization for Standardization. ISO/IEC 15693-3: Identification Cards - Contactless Integrated Circuit Cards - Vicinity Cards - Part 3: Anticollision and Transmission Protocol (April 2009)
16. Kasper, T., Carluccio, D., Paar, C.: An Embedded System for Practical Security Analysis of Contactless Smartcards. In: Sauveron, D., Markantonakis, K., Bilas, A., Quisquater, J.-J. (eds.) WISTP 2007. LNCS, vol. 4462, pp. 150–160. Springer, Heidelberg (2007)
17. Kasper, T., Oswald, D., Paar, C.: EM Side-Channel Attacks on Commercial Contactless Smartcards Using Low-Cost Equipment. In: Youm, H.Y., Yung, M. (eds.) WISA 2009. LNCS, vol. 5932, pp. 79–93. Springer, Heidelberg (2009)
18. Kasper, T., Oswald, D., Paar, C.: A Versatile Framework for Implementation Attacks on Cryptographic RFIDs and Embedded Devices. In: Gavrilova, M., Tan, C., Moreno, E. (eds.) Transactions on Computational Science X. LNCS, vol. 6340, pp. 100–130. Springer, Heidelberg (2010)
19. Kasper, T., von Maurich, I., Oswald, D., Paar, C.: Chameleon: A Versatile Emulator for Contactless Smartcards. In: Rhee, K.-H., Nyang, D. (eds.) ICISC 2010. LNCS, vol. 6829, pp. 189–206. Springer, Heidelberg (2011)

20. Kocher, P.C., Jaffe, J., Jun, B.: Differential Power Analysis. In: Wiener, M. (ed.) CRYPTO 1999. LNCS, vol. 1666, pp. 388–397. Springer, Heidelberg (1999)
21. Langer EMV-Technik. Details of Near Field Probe Set RF 2. Website
22. Mangard, S., Oswald, E., Popp, T.: Power Analysis Attacks: Revealing the Secrets of Smart Cards. Springer, Secaucus (2007)
23. Nohl, K., Evans, D., Starbug, Plötz, H.: Reverse-Engineering a Cryptographic RFID Tag. In: USENIX Security Symposium, pp. 185–194. USENIX Association (2008)
24. NXP. Mifare DESFire Contactless Multi-Application IC with DES and 3DES Security MF3ICD40 (April 2004)
25. NXP. Mifare Ultralight C Product Short Datasheet (May 2009)
26. NXP. Mifare DESFire EV1 Contactless Multi-Application IC Datasheet (December 2010)
27. NXP. Mifare Smart Card ICs. Website (March 2011),
    http://www.nxp.com/products/identification_and_security/
    smart_card_ics/mifare_smart_card_ics/index.html
28. Oren, Y., Shamir, A.: Remote Password Extraction from RFID Tags. IEEE Transactions on Computers 56(9), 1292–1296 (2007),
    http://iss.oy.ne.ro/RemotePowerAnalysisOfRFIDTags
29. Pico Technology. PicoScope 5200 USB PC Oscilloscopes (2008)
30. Plos, T.: Evaluation of the Detached Power Supply as Side-Channel Analysis Countermeasure for Passive UHF RFID Tags. In: Fischlin, M. (ed.) CT-RSA 2009. LNCS, vol. 5473, pp. 444–458. Springer, Heidelberg (2009)
31. Plos, T., Hutter, M., Feldhofer, M.: Evaluation of Side-Channel Preprocessing Techniques on Cryptographic-Enabled HF and UHF RFID-Tag Prototypes. In: Dominikus, S. (ed.) Workshop on RFID Security 2008, pp. 114–127 (2008)
32. Schwartz, M., Bennett, W.R., Stein, S.: Communication Systems and Techniques. Wiley (1966)
33. Smith, P.S.W.: The Scientist and Engineer's Guide to Digital Signal Processing, 1st edn. California Technical Publishing (1997)
34. van Woudenberg, J.G.J., Witteman, M.F., Bakker, B.: Improving Differential Power Analysis by Elastic Alignment. In: Kiayias, A. (ed.) CT-RSA 2011. LNCS, vol. 6558, pp. 104–119. Springer, Heidelberg (2011)
35. Vishay Semiconductors, Inc. BAT48 Schottky Diode Datasheet
36. Wikipedia. Contactless Smart Card — Wikipedia, The Free Encyclopedia (2011) (Online; accessed March 5, 2011)

A   Schematics

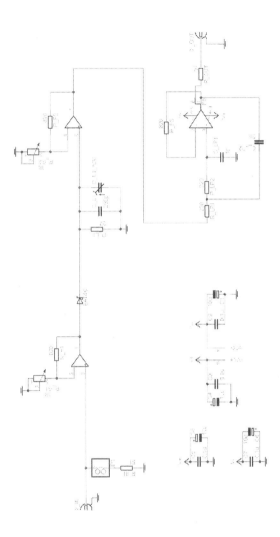

Fig. 10. Schematics of analog rectifier circuit

A Novel RFID Distance Bounding Protocol Based on Physically Unclonable Functions

Süleyman Kardaş[1,2], Mehmet Sabir Kiraz[1],
Muhammed Ali Bingöl[1,3], and Hüseyin Demirci[1]

[1] TUBITAK UEKAE, Gebze, Kocaeli, Turkey
[2] Sabanci University, Istanbul, TR-34956, Turkey
[3] Istanbul Technical University,
Institute of Science and Technology, Istanbul, Turkey

Abstract. Radio Frequency Identification (RFID) systems are vulnerable to relay attacks (i.e., mafia, terrorist and distance frauds) when they are used for authentication purposes. Distance bounding protocols are particularly designed as a countermeasure against these attacks. These protocols aim to ensure that the tags are in a distant area by measuring the round-trip delays during a rapid challenge-response exchange of short authenticated messages. Terrorist fraud is the most challenging attack to avoid, because a legitimate user (a tag owner) collaborates with an attacker to defeat the authentication system. Many RFID distance bounding protocols have been proposed recently, with encouraging results. However, none of them provides the ideal security against the terrorist fraud.

Motivated by this need, we first introduce a strong adversary model for Physically Unclonable Functions (PUFs) based authentication protocol in which the adversary has access to volatile memory of the tag. We show that the security of Sadeghi *et al.*'s PUF based authentication protocol is not secure in this model. We provide a new technique to improve the security of their protocol. Namely, in our scheme, even if an adversary has access to volatile memory she cannot obtain all long term keys to clone the tag. Next, we propose a novel RFID distance bounding protocol based on PUFs which satisfies the expected security requirements. Comparing to the previous protocols, the use of PUFs in our protocol enhances the system in terms of security, privacy and tag computational overhead. We also prove that our extended protocol with a final signature provides the ideal security against all those frauds, remarkably the terrorist fraud. Besides that, our protocols enjoy the attractive properties of PUFs, which provide the most cost efficient and reliable means to fingerprint chips based on their physical properties.

Keywords: RFID, Distance Bounding Protocol, PUF, Security, Terrorist fraud.

1 Introduction

Radio **F**requency **ID**entification (RFID) is a technology that has been widely used in daily life, such as in access control, in electronic passports, public

A. Juels and C. Paar (Eds.): RFIDSec 2011, LNCS 7055, pp. 78–93, 2012.

transportation, payment and ticketing. The reader communicates with the RFID tags using a wireless channel where the security and privacy requirements are satisfied via cryptographic building blocks (e.g, hash functions, symmetric encryptions and secure authentication protocols). However, such cryptographic mechanisms are not sufficient to enforce strong authentication in RFID systems. The seminal works of Desmedt *et al.* [8] and Beth *et al.* [3] on *mafia* and *terrorist frauds* demonstrated how an adversary can defeat such protocols by simply relaying the messages without dealing with cryptography. The *chess grandmaster attack*, which is introduced by Conway [7] in 1976, can be given as an illustration of the problem. In this problem, an unskilled player challenges two different chess grandmasters simultaneously. By only relaying the moves of the grandmasters the player finally either defeats one of the grandmasters or draws against both. Those kinds of attacks have been practically demonstrated in many different contexts and especially in RFID systems [13, 15–17, 22]. Nowadays, RFID and contactless smart card producers take relay attacks into account in the design of secure commercial products [26].

Mafia fraud is a kind of relay attack where an adversary is willing to be authenticated as if she is a legitimate prover. In order to perform this attack, the adversary relays the messages between a prover (e.g., a tag) and a verifier (e.g., a reader). Terrorist fraud is similar to mafia fraud except that the legitimate tag collaborates with an adversary to be able to authenticate her. However, the prover does not reveal his long-term private key to the adversary [6]. Finally, distance fraud is also similar to relay attacks where a fraudulent prover tries to persuade the verifier that she is within a certain authentication area whereas she is not.

In order to mitigate these frauds, two main countermeasures have been adopted. The first one is based on measuring the radio signal strength (RSS) so that the verifier can learn whether the prover is close to it. This method has a drawback that a capable adversary can regulate its signal strength to convince the verifier that it is close to the verifier [14]. The second one is measuring the round trip time of exchanged messages between the reader and the tag[8]. At *Eurocrypt'93*, Brands and Chaum [5] proposed the first distance-bounding protocol to prevent mafia fraud and distance fraud while leaving the terrorist fraud attack as an open issue. Then, several such protocols, which use the round trip time method, have been proposed to improve security levels against distance, mafia and terrorist attacks [2, 14, 20, 23, 25, 28, 30, 32, 33, 36]. However, one of the main obstacles of the existing distance bounding protocols is achieving the ideal security level (i.e., $(1/2)^n$ where n is a security parameter) against terrorist fraud. Some attempts to thwart terrorist fraud [33] yield a more serious security problem namely, the key recovery attack. This attack occurs due to the misuse of long-term key in the protocol [20].

Our Contributions. In this paper, we first analyze the security of Sadeghi *et al.*'s PUF based RFID authentication protocol [29] by our stronger adversarial model in which an adversary has access to the volatile memory of the tag. We show that their protocol is not secure in this model and we propose a new technique to avoid this attack even if the adversary has the ability to access volatile memory.

Next, we apply this technique to propose a new PUF based RFID distance bounding protocol. To the best of our knowledge, this is the first paper that introduces a PUF based RFID distance bounding protocol. It is well-known that obtaining the long-term key of a tag is crucial in order to successfully perform the terrorist and the distance frauds. One of the main problems of existing distance bounding protocols is storing the long-term key into its memory which can be obtained by a fraudulent prover. Our protocol has the advantage that the long-term key will not be stored in the memory of the tag but will be reconstructed by using a PUF circuit.

Our first PUF based distance bounding protocol is based on the well-known Hancke and Kuhn's scheme [14] which is the starting point of this work. Although their original protocol is known to be simple and efficient, the adversary's probability of success is high (namely $(3/4)^n$ for both the distance and the mafia frauds, and 1 for the terrorist fraud). By the use of PUF, the adversarial capabilities of the terrorist fraud is reduced to that of the mafia fraud. In this way, we improve the security of Hancke-Kuhn's protocol against the terrorist fraud from 1 to $(3/4)^n$.

We also propose our second distance bounding protocol which is an extension of the first one involving a hash-based final signature. To the best of our knowledge, this is the first protocol that achieves the ideal security levels $(1/2)^n$ against all frauds.

Outline of the paper. The organization of the paper is as follows: In Section 2, we briefly describe some existing distance bounding protocols. In Section 3, we illustrate the notion of PUF functions and its characteristics. Section 4 describes the adversary capabilities for both PUFs and distance bounding protocols. In Section 5, we propose our first distance bounding protocol and analyze its security. In Section 6, we present our second protocol and analyze its security. Section 7 concludes the paper.

2   Distance Bounding Protocols

Distance bounding approach was a breakthrough to thwart relay attacks by measuring the round trip time of short authenticated messages. Brands and Chaum introduced the first distance bounding protocol[5]. This protocol aims to bring a solution to mafia and distance frauds. It consists of three phases, a slow phase, followed by a fast phase and a final signature phase. The first slow phase is used to exchange the committed random bits. The proximity verification is achieved by a bitwise challenge-response during the second phase (i.e., fast phase), namely after series of n rounds where n is a security parameter. For each round of the fast phase, the verifier measures the round-trip time in order to extract the propagation time. Finally, the prover sends a final signature to the verifier and opens the commitments to complete the protocol. The success probability of mafia and distance frauds for this protocol are $(1/2)^n$, but it is not secure against terrorist fraud.

Čapkun et al. modified the Brands and Chaum's protocol to achieve mutual authentication with distance-bounding [36]. However, their protocol is also vulnerable to terrorist fraud and is not resilient to bit errors during the rapid bit exchange.

Hancke and Kuhn proposed the first use of distance bounding protocol for RFID systems [14]. The major difference from Brands and Chaum's protocol is that it does not involve a final signature phase. This protocol involves a common secret symmetric-key k between a prover and a verifier. This protocol can be briefly described as follows. The verifier first generates a nonce N_v and sends it to the prover. Similarly, the prover also generates a nonce N_p and sends it to the verifier. Two n-bit registers R^1, R^2 are computed such that $R^1 \| R^2 = f(k, N_v, N_p)$ where f is a public pseudorandom function. After that, n-round fast phase starts. For each i-th round, the verifier picks a random challenge-bit c_i and sends it to the prover. The prover replies with a response-bit r_i such that

$$r_i = \begin{cases} R_i^0 & if c_i = 0 \\ R_i^1 & if c_i = 1 \end{cases}.$$

The success probabilities against the mafia fraud and distance fraud are both equal to $(3/4)^n$ [14, 19].

Distance bounding protocols are classified into two classes depending on whether a final signature is involved (e.g., [2, 19, 20, 23, 25, 32, 33]). These papers mostly focused on improving the security against mafia and distance frauds, and in fact some of them achieved the ideal security level $(1/2)^n$ against only both frauds. Furthermore, some others achieve $(3/4)^n$ as the best security level for terrorist fraud. Unfortunately, none of these protocols achieve the ideal security against terrorist fraud.

Avoine et al. [1] introduced a unified framework for improving the analysis and the design of distance bounding protocols. The black-box and the white-box security models are introduced in the distance bounding domain, and the relation between the frauds are described with respect to these models. In the white-box model, the prover can provide more information to the adversary since the can access the internal key. We note that all the protocols in the literature are analyzed in the white-box model and therefore, the security level is worse than that can be achievable in the black-box model.

In the next section, PUFs will be described which will be later used in our protocols. We later show that the use of PUFs eliminates our protocols to be analyzed in the white-box model.

3   Physically Unclonable Functions (PUFs)

Physically Unclonable Functions (PUFs) were invented by Naccache and Fremanteau in 1992 [24]. A PUF is defined as an unclonable function that maps challenges to responses. The response r is calculated as a result of physical properties such as delays of gates and wires in a circuit, variations in the temperature and supply voltage. The unclonability of the function is guaranteed as a result of these physical processes. An ordinary PUF circuit may produce slightly different outputs to the same inputs. Using mechanisms like Fuzzy Extractors [10, 37], one can guarantee that PUF circuit produces the same response to the same challenge. For further information about other types of PUFs we refer to [31].

Since PUFs behave as a random function, it is hard to predict the inputs as given the outputs. Therefore, they can also be considered as one-way functions. In addition, a PUF circuit can easily be implemented into a small area with less than 1000 gates [34]. Besides that, their intrinsic structure yields resistance against tampering. When the adversary tries to evaluate a PUF or an IC, for instance, by using the probes to measure the wire delays, the characteristics of that particular PUF will be changed. Thus, this physical attack will not give any advantage to the adversary [21]. These features make PUF an attractive tool for authentication mechanisms in RFID systems.

In [27] the use of PUFs in RFID systems is proposed. The idea is to use a set of predetermined set of challenge-response pairs with the help of a database. The readers use the database to identify the tag. In this protocol, the possible challenge-response pairs are restricted with the database. A challenge also cannot be used for the second time, since it results to replay attacks. The proposed scheme has been implemented and analyzed in [9].

In [34], PUF is used as a secure key derivation mechanism. Instead of putting the key in memory, it is derived from the circuit each time whenever it is required. This property of PUFs mitigates the hardware-based cloning attacks. A practical illustration is RFID tags, which can easily be cloned. When equipped with a PUF, creating a clone in a reasonable time is impractical. Furthermore, the concept of SRAM-PUFs is proposed in [18]. They propose that SRAM memory cells can be used as a PUF mechanism which are readily available in the existing RFID chips.

A simple privacy preserving identification system is proposed in [4]. This protocol uses a PUF P for frequently updating the identity of tags where the reader stores the vector $(ID, P(ID), P^2(ID), \ldots, P^k(ID))$. To authenticate to a reader, a tag first sends its current ID and updates it using the PUF $P(ID)$. The reader searches the current identifier of the tag from the database. If the reader finds a tuple, it authenticates the tag and removes all the elements which have been used before in the authentication mechanism. Note that this protocol suffers from the Denial of Service Attacks since the tag must be re-initialized after at most k sessions.

Sadeghi et al. [29] suggested to deploy PUF (in a similar way as described by Tuyls and Batina in [34]) in order to develop a privacy-preserving tag authentication protocol for RFID systems. This protocol provides destructive privacy in the Vaudenay's formal framework [35].

In this paper, we will focus on an ideal PUF P such that $P : \{0,1\}^\ell \to \{0,1\}^m$ where the challenge c_i is mapped to the response r_i. P is said to be an *ideal PUF* if the following properties are satisfied.

1. If $c_i = c_j$, then we have $r_i = r_j$ for a PUF on a particular device. Presenting the same challenge to the PUF on a different device will produce a different response.
2. The mapping between c_i and r_i is unpredictable and random. For instance, if r_i and r_j differ in only a single bit, knowledge of c_i does not reveal usable information to predict c_j.
3. Any attempt to physically tamper with the device implementing P causes to change its physical characteristics. Namely, P is then destructed and can no longer be evaluated correctly.

We note that the third property of the idealized PUF can be achieved by integrating PUF circuit with the chip on the tag. To do so, Tuyls *et al.* in [34] propose *Integrated PUFs* (I-PUFs). For further information we recommend reading [29, 34]. In this work, we use the ideal PUF for distance bounding protocols and show how the security is enhanced to ideal levels.

4 Adversary Capabilities

In this section, we first present a stronger adversarial model for analysis of PUF based RFID authentication protocols which considers the accessibility to the internal state of tags. We next discuss the notion of white and black box models for distance bounding protocols. We aim to unify and express the adversarial capabilities of PUFs and distance bounding protocols.

4.1 Adversary Capabilities for PUFs

In a PUF based authentication protocol, the shared secrets are stored in its physical characteristics instead of storing them in a non-volatile memory. These keys are reconstructed whenever needed during the execution of the protocol. As soon as the keys are reconstructed, they are stored in a volatile memory of the RFID chip. In some previous articles (e.g., [29, 34]), it is assumed that the communication between a PUF circuit and a chip is not tractable by any side-channel attack.

Unlike the previous works, in this paper, we propose a more stronger adversary model where an attacker has the ability to compromise the tag and reaches the state in the volatile memory. Since the structure of the PUF circuit has been destroyed, the attacker is no longer able to re-evaluate the PUF again. Thus, a malicious tag owner can perform only one side-channel attack on the tag and access the volatile memory only once. For instance, Halderman *et al.* recently demonstrated a side-channel attack for DRAM, called *cold boot attack* [12]. In this attack, they first powered off the system and later showed how to extend the main memory persistence by 'freezing' the DRAM chips in order to maintain the memory cell state. In this way, an adversary will be able to retrieve any password or cryptographic key that was not disappeared before the system is switched off.

The protocol of Sadeghi et al. [29] is facing a similar attack described above. Their protocol is briefly described as follows (Figure 1). Let $l \in \mathbb{N}$ be a security parameter, and F:$\{0,1\}^k \times \{0,1\}^{2\alpha} \to \{0,1\}^\beta$ be a public pseudorandom (PRF) function. Each tag $\mathcal{T}$ is equipped with a PUF function P:$\{0,1\}^\gamma \to \{0,1\}^k$ and is initialized with a random state $S_1 \in_R \{0,1\}^\gamma$. The credential of each tag (ID, K), where $K \leftarrow P(S)$ and is stored in the database DB of the reader. The reader $\mathcal{R}$ first picks a random nonce a to the tag $\mathcal{T}_{ID}$. Then, $\mathcal{T}_{ID}$ picks a random nonce b and evaluates the PUF function $K = P(S)$. $\mathcal{T}_{ID}$ computes $c = F_K(a, b)$ and sends the message c along with the random nonce b and immediately erases K, a, b and c from its volatile memory. Upon receiving of b and c, $\mathcal{R}$ evaluates $c' = F_K(a, b)$ for each tuple (ID, K) in DB until there is a match. If a matching (ID, K) is found, then it accepts $\mathcal{T}_{ID}$ and returns ID; otherwise, it rejects by sending $\perp$ back.

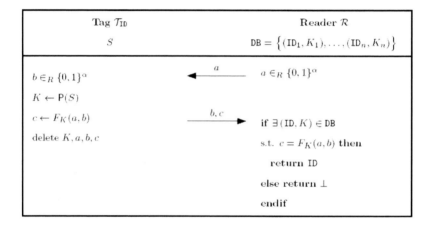

Fig. 1. Sadeghi et al.'s authentication protocol [29]

The authors claim that their protocol achieves destructive-privacy under the assumption that K is inaccessible. However, we show that their protocol suffers from the same above-mentioned cold-boot attack. Assume that an adversary sends a random nonce a to the tag $\mathcal{T}_{ID}$. $\mathcal{T}_{ID}$ then generates another random nonce b and reconstructs a secret K by evaluating the PUF with input S. The secret K is stored in the volatile memory during the computation of $c = F_K(a, b)$. The adversary compromises $\mathcal{T}_{ID}$ while $c = F_K(a, b)$ is computed and can capture the secret K. Hence, the tag can be successfully cloned although the structure of the PUF circuit has been destroyed.

In order to thwart this attack, instead of using only one key we propose to use two different keys K, L which are consecutively generated as outputs of the PUF function. Note that K and L never appear in the volatile memory at the same time. First, K is used as an input of one-way PRF function, and then completely deleted from the memory. Next, in a similar way, L is generated and used in the PRF function. Hence, whenever an adversary applies the above-mentioned attack he will be able to obtain only one of the keys, and hence will not have sufficient information to defeat the privacy. Also, since the PUF circuit has been destroyed he will not be able to perform the same attack again. Thus, applying our technique avoids the tag cloning.

4.2   Adversary Capabilities for Distance Bounding Protocols

In the analysis of our protocols, Dolev-Yao adversary model are considered [11]. In this model, the adversary can perform polynomial number of computations and cannot obtain the secret keys from the honest parties. This assumption is then relaxed with the terrorist and distance frauds, where the prover has access to the keys [1]. However, he disagrees to share these keys with any third party. The adversary may use one of the three strategies to query a prover such as pre-ask strategy, post-ask strategy and early-reply strategy. The detailed explanations of these strategies are addressed in [1].

As in the conventional distance bounding protocols, we also assume that the verifier is an honest party where it faithfully follows the protocol specifications without cheating. Mafia fraud is a kind of man-in-the-middle attack where an adversary defeats both honest parties i.e., verifier and prover. Unlike mafia fraud, in distance and terrorist frauds, the prover himself is dishonest. The previous distance bounding protocols consider that the prover has a full control on the execution of the algorithm in the device. As it is discussed in Section 3, PUFs can be used to provide resistance against side-channel attacks. Therefore, an adversary can be limited to the execution of the algorithm inside the device. In order to analyze distance bounding protocols, the generic capabilities of the adversary are addressed in [1]. The capabilities are categorized in two models, white-box model and black-box model. The following definitions of these two models are excerpted from [1].

Definition 1. *(Black-box model) In this model, the prover cannot observe or tamper with the execution of the algorithm.*

Definition 2. *(White-box model) In this model, the prover has full access to the implementation of the algorithm and has a complete control over the execution environment.*

Regarding to the white-box and the black-box models Figure 2 presents the relation between the distance, mafia and terrorist frauds. An arrow from X to Y means that, for any fraud in X that succeeds with probability p_X, then there exists an attack in Y that succeeds with probability p_Y such that $p_Y \geq p_X$. Two side arrow means that the success probabilities of two corresponding frauds are equal [1].

It is interesting to note that in the black-box model, the success probabilities of the mafia and the terrorist frauds are equal (Figure 2).

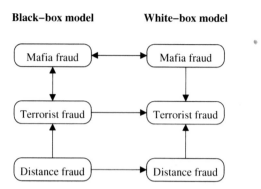

Fig. 2. Relations between the frauds in the white-box and the black-box models [1]

5   Our First Protocol

We now propose the first PUF based distance bounding protocol which is efficient for implementation in low cost devices. In the next section, we extend this protocol by adding a final signature to enhance the security against terrorist fraud. The former achieves the security level of $(3/4)^n$ against mafia, terrorist and distance frauds, where n is the number challenge/response bits during the fast phase. We show in the next section that the latter achieves the ideal security level against all the frauds (i.e., $(1/2)^n$).

5.1   Protocol Descriptions

Our first distance bounding protocol is based on Hancke and Kuhn's scheme [14], which is the starting point of this work. Although their protocol is simple and efficient the adversary's probability of success is high. The steps of our protocol are summarized below and depicted in Figure 3.

Initialization. Let $P_i : \{0,1\}^k \rightarrow \{0,1\}^\ell$ be a (unique) ideal PUF of the i-th legitimate prover $\mathcal{P}_i$. The credentials database DB of the verifier $\mathcal{V}$ stores a tuple (K_i, L_i) where $K_i = P_i(G_i^1)$ and $L_i = P_i(G_i^2)$ for random states $G_i^1, G_i^2 \in_R \{0,1\}^k$. Let also $F : \{0,1\}^\ell \times \{0,1\}^{2\ell} \rightarrow \{0,1\}^{2\ell}$ be a one-way pseudorandom function. We denote n as the main security parameter of the fast phase where $3n = 2\ell$. $|S|$ denotes the bit-length of a bit-string S.

Our protocol consists of two phases: a slow phase and a fast phase.

Slow phase:

- First of all, $\mathcal{V}$ generates a random nonce r_V and sends it to $\mathcal{P}_i$.
- Upon receiving r_V, $\mathcal{P}_i$ generates a random nonce r_P and reconstructs $K_i = P_i(G_i^1)$. $\mathcal{P}_i$ computes $T = F_{K_i}(r_P, r_V)$, then immediately deletes K_i from the memory. After that, $\mathcal{P}_i$ reconstructs the secret key $L_i = P_i(G_i^2)$ and computes the message $F_{L_i}(T)$. Similarly, $\mathcal{P}_i$ immediately deletes L_i from

the memory. The value $F_{L_i}(T)$ is divided into three registers v_1, v_2 and v_3 where $|v_1| = |v_2| = |v_3| = n$. Finally, $\mathcal{P}_i$ sends r_T and v_1 to $\mathcal{V}$.

- Upon receiving r_T and v_1, for each tuple (K_i, L_i) in DB $\mathcal{V}$ searches $v'_1, v'_2, v'_3 = F_L(F_K(r_P, r_V))$ such that $v'_1 = v_1$. If not found, $\mathcal{V}$ aborts the protocol.

Fast phase:

- The fast phase consists of n bitwise challenge-response exchange. For each round $j \in \{1, \ldots, n\}$, $\mathcal{V}$ picks a random challenge bit c_j and sends it to $\mathcal{P}_i$.
- $\mathcal{P}_i$ immediately responds $r_j = v_2^j$ if $c_j = 0$, otherwise $r_j = v_3^j$.

Verification. Whenever the fast phase is finished $\mathcal{V}$ verifies that the responses from $\mathcal{P}_i$ are correct and checks whether $\triangle t_j \leq \triangle t_{max} \ \forall \ j = 1, \ldots, n$ where $\triangle t_{max}$ is a timing bound.

5.2 Security Analysis

Mafia, terrorist, and distance frauds are the three main security concerns when considering distance bounding protocols. The following Theorem 1 indicates that no adversary (e.g., a malicious tag owner) can access to both secrets K_i and L_i. Thus, the use of PUF in the protocol makes the RFID tags as tamper proof against any malicious adversary.

Theorem 1. *Let K_i, L_i be secrets of a tag $\mathcal{T}_i$ for some i in the above-mentioned protocol (see Figure 3). Assume that there is an adversary $\mathcal{A}$ with a full side-channel capability on the tag $\mathcal{T}_i$. If P_i is an ideal PUF, then $\mathcal{A}$ can only access either the secret K_i or the secret L_i, but not both in the same tag $\mathcal{T}_i$.*

Proof. (sketch) The pre-keys G_i^1 and G_i^2 are fed into the P_i function to generate the real keys K_i and L_i. The real keys only appear during the execution of the protocol. Note that K_i and L_i never appear in the memory of $\mathcal{T}_i$ at the same time because K_i is first used as an input of a one-way PRF function, and then completely deleted from the memory. Next, in a similar way, L_i is generated and used in the PRF function. Whenever $\mathcal{A}$ applies a side channel attack to $\mathcal{T}_i$, the physical characteristics of the PUF P_i will be broken and will no longer be evaluated correctly. If $\mathcal{A}$ applies side-channel attack to extract K_i then the structure of P_i will be destroyed and L_i cannot be generated. Similarly, if $\mathcal{A}$ applies side-channel attack to extract L_i she cannot obtain K_i since it is already deleted. Therefore, $\mathcal{A}$ can access either K_i or L_i but not both. Hence, $\mathcal{A}$ will not be able to get the complete key of $\mathcal{T}_i$.

Theorem 1 indicates that a malicious prover cannot obtain the secret keys, and thus cannot evaluate the registers v_1, v_2, v_3. Unlike existing distance bounding protocols, it is not possible to apply the white-box analysis to our protocol. Therefore, we analyze our protocol according to the black-box model. In the black-box model, note that it is already proven that the capability of terrorist

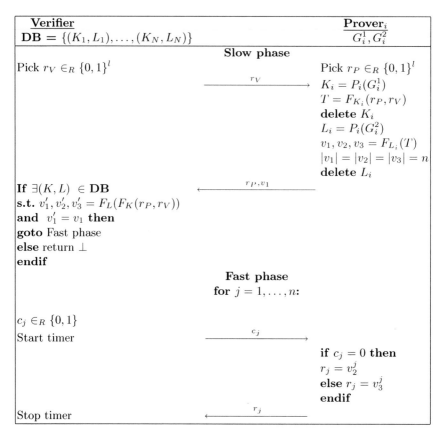

Fig. 3. Our first PUF based distance bounding protocol without a final signature

fraud is equivalent to the mafia fraud [1] (see also Figure 2). Hence, we combine the security analysis of both mafia and terrorist frauds.

Note that a malicious prover can access the registers v_1, v_2, v_3 by applying side-channel attack only once. Furthermore, he can complete only the current session successfully because of the destruction of PUF. However, since the registers v_1, v_2, v_3 are randomized this does not give any future advantage to the adversary.

For a distance bounding protocol, an adversary is able to use three different strategies to conduct her attack such that early-reply, pre-ask, and post-ask [1]. We denote by $\mathcal{A}$ a malicious adversary. Let also denote by MF, TF and DF the mafia fraud, the terrorist fraud and the distance fraud, respectively. Let F be a fraud and S be the strategy used by the adversary $\mathcal{A}$. Let $Pr_{F|S}$ be the success probability in the black-box model of the fraud F ($MF/DF/TF$) using the strategy S (*early/pre/post*). Note that the strategies can also be combined and this is denoted by an &. Next, we describe the success probability of each fraud as follows.

Mafia and terrorist fraud analysis. The adversary uses pre-ask or post-ask strategies in order to achieve mafia or terrorist fraud.

Pre-ask strategy [1]. In this strategy, $\mathcal{A}$ first relays the slow phase between $\mathcal{V}$ and $\mathcal{P}$. Then $\mathcal{A}$ executes the fast phase with $\mathcal{P}$. $\mathcal{A}$ sends predicted challenges c'_j to $\mathcal{P}$ and get the responses r'_j corresponding to her challenges. With this a strategy, $\mathcal{A}$ obtains only one of the register. Afterward, $\mathcal{A}$ executes the fast phase with $\mathcal{V}$ and receives the challenges c_js. There are two equal likely cases, (i) if $c_j = c'_j$ $\mathcal{A}$ sends the correct response with probability of 1; otherwise, (ii) $\mathcal{A}$ guess the response with probability of $1/2$. Hence, the success probability of mafia fraud and terrorist fraud for n-round fast phase is computed as follows.

$$Pr_{MF|pre} = Pr_{TF|pre} = \left(\frac{1}{2} \cdot 1 + \frac{1}{2} \cdot \frac{1}{2} \right)^n = \left(\frac{3}{4} \right)^n .$$

Post-ask strategy [1]. In pre-ask strategy, $\mathcal{A}$ first relays the slow phase, then executes the fast phase with $\mathcal{V}$. The probability of sending a correct response for a challenge is $1/2$. Then, $\mathcal{A}$ queries $\mathcal{P}$ with the correct challenges received during the fast phase to check whether she is succeed on cheating. The success probability of mafia fraud for this strategy is:

$$Pr_{MF|post} = Pr_{TF|post} = \left(\frac{1}{2} \right)^n .$$

To maximize the success probability the attacker chooses the best strategy. Hence, the success probability of both mafia and terrorist frauds are $(3/4)^n$.

Distance fraud analysis. In distance fraud, the tag owner herself is fraudulent who tries to cheat on her proximity from $\mathcal{V}$. It is important to highlight that unlike the existing protocols, the tag owner cannot control the internal executions of the tag in our protocol. The fraudulent prover can query its tag to get the responses. In distance fraud, since the prover is outside of the legal authentication region she should send the responses earlier in order to pass the proximity check (i.e., round trip time measurement). This is called *early-reply strategy* [1]. To ease our analysis, we denote the fraudulent tag owner by $\mathcal{A}$, and the tag by $\mathcal{T}$.

Pre-ask combined with early-reply strategy. In this strategy, $\mathcal{A}$ first relays the slow phase between $\mathcal{V}$ and $\mathcal{T}$, then executes the fast phase with $\mathcal{T}$. $\mathcal{A}$ can only obtain n-bit responses corresponding to her predicted challenges. Since $\mathcal{A}$ is not inside the neighborhood of $\mathcal{V}$, she sends her responses in advance. Two cases occurs for each round of the fast phase. (i) $\mathcal{A}$ predicts $\mathcal{V}$'s challenge correctly, then she sends a correct corresponding response in advance. (ii) $\mathcal{A}$ cannot not predict $\mathcal{V}$'s challenge correctly, but she sends a correct answer with probability of $1/2$. Thus, the distance fraud success probability is:

$$Pr_{DF|pre\&early} = \left(\frac{1}{2} \cdot 1 + \frac{1}{2} \cdot \frac{1}{2} \right)^n = \left(\frac{3}{4} \right)^n .$$

Post-ask combined with early-reply strategy. Similar to the mafia fraud analysis, it is clear that using the post-ask strategy is equivalent to randomly guessing the responses,

$$Pr_{DF|post\&early} = \left(\frac{1}{2}\right)^n.$$

The distance fraud attacker chooses the strategy with the maximum success probability. Consequently, the success probability of distance fraud is $(3/4)^n$.

6   Our Extended Protocol

We are now ready to propose our extended protocol which is resistant to all the frauds.

6.1   Protocol Descriptions

In what follows, we present our second protocol which is an extension of the first one by adding a final signature. This protocol consists of three phases. The first two phases are exactly the same with the previous protocol. In the third phase, the prover computes the following final signature

$$f_{sign} = h(c_1, \ldots, c_n, T, L_i).$$

where h denotes a collusion resistant and one-way hash function. To evaluate f_{sign}, first prover regenerate L_i once more and delete it from the memory as soon as f_{sign} is computed. The prover sends f_{sign} to the verifier, then the verifier checks the correctness of this message.

6.2   Security Analysis

In the first protocol, mafia and distance frauds can successfully pass the fast phase with probability of $(3/4)^n$ by predicting the challenges. However, this attack does not work in the extended protocol because the challenges received by the tag are digested in f_{sign}. In order to pass the authentication, the adversary must send a valid final signature to the verifier. Similar to the first protocol, there are two strategies for both mafia and terrorist frauds:

(i) In the pre-ask strategy, the adversary first executes the fast phase with the prover by sending $c'_1, \ldots, c'_n$ challenges, then prover replies with the corresponding responses $r'_1, \ldots, r'_n$. In the final phase, the adversary gets $f'_{sign} = h(c'_1, \ldots, c'_n, T, L_i)$. The final signature is valid if and only if all the challenges $c_1, \ldots, c_n$ sent by the verifier are equal to the ones predicted by the adversary. Thus, it is clear that the probability of $f_{sign} = f'_{sign}$ is equal to $(1/2)^n$.

(ii) In the post-ask strategy, the adversary first plays with the verifier and guesses all the responses during the fast phase. If she passes the fast phase then it is easy to get the valid final signature from the prover by forwarding the challenges of the verifier. However, the probability of guessing all the correct responses during the fast phase is equal to $(1/2)^n$. Thus,

$$Pr_{MF} = Pr_{TF} = \left(\frac{1}{2}\right)^n.$$

Similarly, the security of the extended protocol for distance fraud is also bounded by $(1/2)^n$ due to the same reasons described-above. Namely, in order to receive a valid final signature from the tag the fraudulent prover should have queried the tag with all correct challenges in advance. Hence, the use of final signature enhances the security level of our extended protocol against the distance fraud to the ideal level $(1/2)^n$.

7   Conclusion

Relay attacks are indeed practical threats for RFID systems since using only cryptographic primitives it is not easy to thwart mafia, distance and terrorist frauds. Distance bounding protocols are used to mitigate these threats. However, the existing distance bounding protocols cannot achieve ideal security level against all frauds.

In this paper, we present the first PUF based distance bounding authentication protocol. Note that the protocols based on PUFs are known to be powerful since attacks can be easily prevented and the use of expensive cryptographic primitives can be minimized. In our protocol, we use the idea of key storage mechanism based on PUFs for public-key cryptosystems presented by Tuyls and Batina [34] (which is also later used for symmetric key storage by Sadeghi et al. [29]). We modified their protocol in such a way that all the keys are not constructed at the same time. This enables us to achieve a stronger assumption and there is no way to extract the whole secret key from the tag. We show that our first protocol achieves the security level of $(3/4)^n$ against mafia, terrorist and distance frauds. We also extend our protocol by adding a final signature to enhance the security levels. Namely, we achieve the security level $(1/2)^n$ against for all mafia, terrorist and distance frauds. To the best our knowledge, this is the first paper that achieves the ideal security level $(1/2)^n$ against all frauds.

An interesting further question is whether it is possible to find an efficient protocol without a final signature having the ideal security level against all frauds.

References

1. Avoine, G., Bingöl, M.A., Kardaş, S., Lauradoux, C., Martin, B.: A Framework for Analyzing RFID Distance Bounding Protocols. Journal of Computer Security – Special Issue on RFID System Security 19(2), 289–317 (2011)
2. Avoine, G., Floerkemeier, C., Martin, B.: RFID Distance Bounding Multistate Enhancement. In: Roy, B., Sendrier, N. (eds.) INDOCRYPT 2009. LNCS, vol. 5922, pp. 290–307. Springer, Heidelberg (2009)

3. Beth, T., Desmedt, Y.: Identification Tokens – or: Solving the Chess Grandmaster Problem. In: Menezes, A., Vanstone, S.A. (eds.) CRYPTO 1990. LNCS, vol. 537, pp. 169–177. Springer, Heidelberg (1991)
4. Bolotnyy, L., Robins, G.: Physically unclonable function-based security and privacy in rfid systems. In: Proceedings of the Fifth IEEE International Conference on Pervasive Computing and Communications, pp. 211–220. IEEE Computer Society, Washington, DC, USA (2007)
5. Brands, S., Chaum, D.: Distance Bounding Protocols. In: Helleseth, T. (ed.) EUROCRYPT 1993. LNCS, vol. 765, pp. 344–359. Springer, Heidelberg (1994)
6. Bussard, L., Bagga, W.: Distance-bounding proof of knowledge to avoid real-time attacks. In: Ryoichi, S., Sihan, Q., Eiji, O. (eds.) Security and Privacy in the Age of Ubiquitous Computing, Chiba, Japan. IFIP International Federation for Information Processing, vol. 181, pp. 223–238. Springer, Heidelberg (2005)
7. Conway, J.H.: On Numbers and Games. London Mathematical Society Monographs, vol. 6. Academic Press, London (1976)
8. Desmedt, Y., Goutier, C., Bengio, S.: Special Uses and Abuses of the Fiat Shamir Passport Protocol. In: Pomerance, C. (ed.) CRYPTO 1987. LNCS, vol. 293, pp. 21–39. Springer, Heidelberg (1988)
9. Devadas, S., Suh, E., Paral, S., Sowell, R., Ziola, T., Khandelwal, V.: Design and Implementation of PUF-Based "Unclonable" RFID ICs for Anti-Counterfeiting and Security Applications. In: 2008 IEEE International Conference on RFID, pp. 58–64 (2008)
10. Dodis, Y., Ostrovsky, R., Reyzin, L., Smith, A.: Fuzzy extractors: How to generate strong keys from biometrics and other noisy data. SIAM J. Comput. 38(1), 97–139 (2008)
11. Dolev, D., Yao, A.C.-C.: On the security of public key protocols. IEEE Transactions on Information Theory 29(2), 198–207 (1983)
12. Halderman, J.A., Schoen, S.D., Heninger, N., Clarkson, W., Paul, W., Calandrino, J.A., Feldman, A.J., Appelbaum, J., Felten, E.W.: Lest we remember: cold-boot attacks on encryption keys. Commun. ACM 52, 91–98 (2009)
13. Hancke, G.: A Practical Relay Attack on ISO 14443 Proximity Cards (February 2005) (manuscript)
14. Hancke, G., Kuhn, M.: An RFID Distance Bounding Protocol. In: Conference on Security and Privacy for Emerging Areas in Communication Networks – SecureComm 2005, Athens, Greece. IEEE (2005)
15. Hancke, G.P., Mayes, K., Markantonakis, K.: Confidence in smart token proximity: Relay attacks revisited. Computers & Security 28(7), 615–627 (2009)
16. Hancke, G.P.: Practical Attacks on Proximity Identification Systems (Short Paper). In: IEEE Symposium on Security and Privacy – S&P 2006, Oakland, California, USA. IEEE, IEEE Computer Society (2006)
17. Hlaváč, M., Rosa, T.: A Note on the Relay Attacks on e-Passports: The Case of Czech e-Passports. In: Cryptology ePrint Archive, Report 2007/244 (2007)
18. Holcomb, D.E., Burleson, W.P., Fu, K.: Initial SRAM state as a fingerprint and source of true random numbers for RFID tags. In: Proceedings of the Conference on RFID Security (2007)
19. Kara, O., Kardaş, S., Bingöl, M.A., Avoine, G.: Optimal Security Limits of RFID Distance Bounding Protocols. In: Ors Yalcin, S.B. (ed.) RFIDSec 2010. LNCS, vol. 6370, pp. 220–238. Springer, Heidelberg (2010)
20. Kim, C.H., Avoine, G., Koeune, F., Standaert, F.-X., Pereira, O.: The Swiss-Knife RFID Distance Bounding Protocol. In: Lee, P.J., Cheon, J.H. (eds.) ICISC 2008. LNCS, vol. 5461, pp. 98–115. Springer, Heidelberg (2009)

21. Kulseng, L.: Lightweight mutual authentication, ownership transfer, and secure search protocols for rfid systems. Master's thesis, Electrical & Computer Engineering Department, Iowa State University (2009)
22. Markantonakis, K., Tunstall, M., Hancke, G., Askoxylakis, I., Mayes, K.: Attacking smart card systems: Theory and practice. Information Security Technical Report 14(2), 46–56 (2009); Smart Card Applications and Security
23. Munilla, J., Peinado, A.: Distance bounding protocols for RFID enhanced by using void-challenges and analysis in noisy channels. Wireless Communications and Mobile Computing 8(9), 1227–1232 (2008)
24. Naccache, D., Fremanteau, P.: Unforgeable identification device, identification device reader and method of identification. Patent-EP0583709 (1994)
25. Nikov, V., Vauclair, M.: Yet Another Secure Distance-Bounding Protocol. In: Cryptology ePrint Archive, Report 2008/319 (2008)
26. NXP. NXP mifare plus – benchmark security for mainstream applications (2009), http://mifare.net/downloads/NXP_Mifare_Plus_leaflet.pdf
27. Ranasinghe, D.C., Engels, D.W., Cole, P.H.: Security and Privacy: Modest Proposals for Low-Cost RFID Systems. In: Proc. Auto-ID Labs Research Workshop Systems (2004)
28. Reid, J., Gonzaez Neito, J., Tang, T., Senadji, B.: Detecting relay attacks with timing based protocols. In: Bao, F., Miller, S. (eds.) Proceedings of the 2nd ACM Symposium on Information, Computer and Communications Security – ASIACCS 2007, Singapore, Republic of Singapore, pp. 204–213. ACM (March 2007)
29. Sadeghi, A.-R., Visconti, I., Wachsmann, C.: PUF-Enhanced RFID Security and Privacy. In: Secure Component and System Identification – SECSI 2010, Cologne, Germany (April 2010)
30. Singelée, D., Preneel, B.: Key Establishment Using Secure Distance Bounding Protocols. In: MOBIQUITOUS 2007: Proceedings of the 2007 Fourth Annual International Conference on Mobile and Ubiquitous Systems: Networking&Services (MobiQuitous), Philadelphia, Pennsylvania, USA, pp. 1–6. IEEE Computer Society (August 2007)
31. Suh, G.E., Devadas, S.: Physical unclonable functions for device authentication and secret key generation. In: DAC 2007: Proceedings of the 44th Annual Design Automation Conference, pp. 9–14. ACM, New York (2007)
32. Trujillo-Rasua, R., Martin, B., Avoine, G.: The Poulidor Distance-Bounding Protocol. In: Ors Yalcin, S.B. (ed.) RFIDSec 2010. LNCS, vol. 6370, pp. 239–257. Springer, Heidelberg (2010)
33. Tu, Y.-J., Piramuthu, S.: RFID Distance Bounding Protocols. In: First International EURASIP Workshop on RFID Technology, Vienna, Austria (September 2007)
34. Tuyls, P., Batina, L.: RFID-Tags for Anti-counterfeiting. In: Pointcheval, D. (ed.) CT-RSA 2006. LNCS, vol. 3860, pp. 115–131. Springer, Heidelberg (2006)
35. Vaudenay, S.: On Privacy Models for RFID. In: Kurosawa, K. (ed.) ASIACRYPT 2007. LNCS, vol. 4833, pp. 68–87. Springer, Heidelberg (2007)
36. Čapkun, S., Buttyán, L., Hubaux, J.-P.: SECTOR: secure tracking of node encounters in multi-hop wireless networks. In: SASN 2003: Proceedings of the 1st ACM Workshop on Security of Ad Hoc and Sensor Networks, pp. 21–32. ACM, New York (2003)
37. Dodis, Y., Reyzin, L., Smith, A.: Fuzzy Extractors. In: Security with Noisy Data, pp. 79–99. Springer, Heidelberg (2007)

Security Analysis of Two Distance-Bounding Protocols

Mohammad Reza Sohizadeh Abyaneh

Selmer Center, University of Bergen
reza.sohizadeh@ii.uib.no

Abstract. In this paper, we analyze the security of two recently proposed distance bounding protocols called the "Hitomi" and the "NUS" protocols. Our results show that the claimed security of both protocols has been overestimated. Namely, we show that the Hitomi protocol is susceptible to a full secret key disclosure attack which not only results in violating the privacy of the protocol but also can be exploited for further attacks such as impersonation, mafia fraud and terrorist fraud attacks. Our results also demonstrates that the probability of success in a distance fraud attack against the NUS protocol can be increased up to $(\frac{3}{4})^n$ and even slightly more, if the adversary is furnished with some computational capabilities.

Keywords: RFID, Privacy, Distance bounding protocol, Distance fraud.

1 Introduction

Radio frequency identification (RFID) technology is widely being deployed today in many applications which require security, such as payment and access control applications. Although many solutions have been proposed to secure RFID systems, most of them are still susceptible to different attacks related to location such as: *distance fraud, mafia fraud* and *terrorist fraud* attacks. All of these attacks aim at suggesting a wrong assumption of the distance between a tag and a reader. In distance fraud attack, a tag operates from out of the range where it is supposed to be. Mafia fraud attack, is a kind of man-in-the-middle attack in which a rogue tag circumvents the security mechanisms by getting right answers from the legitimate tag via a rogue reader, while both legitimate entities (legitimate reader and tag) remain unaware. In the terrorist attack, a legitimate tag colludes with the adversary, giving her the necessary information to access the system by impersonating it for a limited number of times.

The described attacks require simpler technical resources than tampering or cryptanalysis, and they cannot be prevented by ordinary security protocols that operate in the high layers of the protocol stack. The main countermeasure against these attacks is the use of *distance bounding* protocols, which verify not only that the tag knows the cryptographic secret, but also that is within a certain distance. To achieve this goal, distance bounding protocols must be tightly integrated into the physical layer [1].

A. Juels and C. Paar (Eds.): RFIDSec 2011, LNCS 7055, pp. 94–107, 2012.

In 1993, Brands and Chaum proposed the first distance bounding protocol [5]. Afterward, in 2005, Hancke and Kuhn [6] proposed the first distance-bounding protocol dedicated to RFID systems. This protocol has the drawback of giving the adversary this chance to succeed with the probability of $(\frac{3}{4})^n$ rather than $(\frac{1}{2})^n$ in distance and mafia fraud attacks, where n is a security parameter. Since then, there have been many solutions proposed either similar to Hancke and Kuhn [2,7,8,10,11,12] or with different structures [5,8,9,13,14,15]. However, they mostly have something in common; they all consist of three phases, the first and the last ones called *slow phases*, and the second one called the *fast phase*. The round trip time (RTT) of a bitwise challenge and response is measured n times during the fast phase to estimate the distance, while the slow phases include all the time-consuming operations.

Recently, two distance bounding protocols have been proposed by Lopez *et al* and Gürel *et al* called Hitomi [4] and Non-Uniform Stepping (NUS) [15] distance bounding protocols respectively. These protocols are claimed to provide privacy and resistance against distance, mafia and terrorist fraud attacks.

Our Contribution. In this paper, we apply a key disclosure attack to the Hitomi protocol and a distance fraud attack on the NUS protocol. Our analysis is framed in the formal framework introduced in [16].

Outline. The remainder of this paper is organized as follows. Section 2 includes a succinct description of the framework we do our security analysis within. In Sections 3, we describe the Hitomi protocol, its security claims and our key disclosure attack on it. In Section 4, we explain the NUS protocol and explain our distance fraud attack against it, and finally, Section 5 concludes the paper.

2   Preliminaries

To lend clarity to our work, we do our security analysis on the two target distance bounding protocols within the formal framework which has been introduced by Avoine *et al* in [16]. To do so, we dedicate this section to briefly explain this framework and define the terms and models, we will utilize later.

2.1   Attack Types

There are four types of typical attacks to distance bounding protocols in the literature.

- *Impersonation Fraud*: Given a distance bounding protocol, an impersonation fraud is an attack where a lonely tag purports to be another one.
- *Distance Fraud*: Given a distance bounding protocol, a distance fraud is an attack where a dishonest and lonely tag purports to be in the neighborhood of the reader.
- *Mafia Fraud*: A mafia fraud is an attack where an adversary defeats a distance bounding protocol using a man-in-the-middle between the reader and an honest tag located outside the neighborhood.

– *Terrorist Fraud*: A terrorist fraud is an attack where an adversary defeats
a distance bounding protocol using a man-in-the-middle between the reader
and a dishonest tag located outside of the neighborhood, such that the latter actively helps the adversary to maximize her attack success probability,
without giving to her any advantage for future attacks.

2.2   Adversarial Modeling

Adversary Model

The adversary model which has been used in the framework is the Dolev-Yao
model [18]. In this model, the adversary can provoke or manipulate the communication between two parties where manipulating the communication means
relay, withhold, or insert messages and she is only limited by the constraints of
the cryptographic methods used. However, she cannot perform unbounded computations and cannot obtain the keys of honest parties. The latter assumption
is not considered for the distance fraud attacks, where the tag has access to the
keys.

Adversary's Location

In the distance fraud attack, depending on how far the adversary is from the
reader, she receives the challenges with some delay. This delay may impact the
probability of success of the attack. Considering this determining factor, we use
a modified version of the model described in [3]. In this model, the adversary
can communicate with the reader from one of the spherical zones illustrated in
Figure 1. For instance, Z_0 represents the legal authentication region with the
diameter d_0, where the adversary accesses to all the challenges and produces
valid responses on time. The distance d_0 is calculated as:

$$d_0 = c \times \frac{(\Delta t - t_d)}{2}; \quad \Delta t = 2t_p + t_d \tag{1}$$

where, c is the propagation speed of light, t_p is the one-way propagation time,
Δt is the total elapsed RTT and t_d is the processing delay of the tag.
When the adversary is located at Z_l, any response from her takes more time to
get to the reader, namely

$$t'_p = t_p + \delta_t; \quad \delta_t = \frac{\sum_{i=1}^{l} d_i}{c}. \tag{2}$$

In order to have a successful attack, the adversary should send each current
response, at least $2\delta_t$ before receiving the current challenge. Moreover, the adversary located in Z_l has access to the challenges up to l^{th} previous round before
she generates the response of the current round.

Tag Model

Considering that whether the tag has full control on the execution of the algorithm or not, we can have two different tampering capability models for the tag,
black-box and *white-box*.

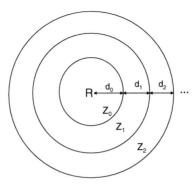

Fig. 1. Adversary's location zones

- *Black-box model*: In a black-box model, the tag cannot observe or tamper with the execution of the algorithm.
- *White-box model*: In a white-box model, the tag has full access to the implementation of the algorithm and a complete control over the execution environment.

2.3   Notations

Here, we explain the notations used hereafter.

- x: Secret key of the tag.
- $f_x(.)$: Pseudo-Random Function operation with secret key x.
- $hw(.)$: Hamming Weight calculation function.
- N_R, N_T: Random numbers generated by the reader and the tag respectively.
- n: The length of registers considered as a security parameter.

2.4   Assumptions

The protocols described in this paper are executed under following assumptions:

- The tag and the reader share a long-term secret key x.
- Each tag has a unique identifier ID.
- The tag's capabilities supports a Pseudo-Random Function (f) and can perform bitwise operations.
- The reader and the tag agree on:
  - a security parameter n.
  - a public pseudo random function f with length of n bits.
  - a timing bound t_{max}
  - a fault tolerance threshold τ.

3   The Hitomi Protocol

3.1   Description

As stated in Section 1, being a distance bounding protocol, the Hitomi protocol (Figure 2) consists of three phases, two *slow phases* which are carried out at the first and final part of the protocol called *preparation phase* and *final phase* respectively. And the fast phase which is executed in between, called *rapid bit exchange phase*.

In the preparation phase, the reader chooses a random nonce (N_R) and transmits it to the tag. In return, the tag chooses three random numbers N_{T_1}, N_{T_2} and N_{T_3} and computes two temporary keys $(k_1$ and $k_2)$ as (3) and (4).

$$k_1 = f_x(N_R, N_{T_1}, W) \tag{3}$$

$$k_2 = f_x(N_{T_2}, N_{T_3}, W') \tag{4}$$

where W and W' represent two constant parameters. By using these keys, the tag splits its permanent secret key x into two shares as *response registers*(i.e. $R^0 = k_1$ and $R^1 = k_2 \oplus x$). Finally, the tag transmits the 3-tuple $\{N_{T_1}, N_{T_2}, N_{T_3}\}$ to the reader.

The rapid bit exchange phase is a challenge and response phase with n rounds. In its ith round, the reader generates a random challenge bit c_i and sends it to the tag while initializing a clock to zero. The tag receives c_i' which may not be equal to c_i due to errors or alterations in the channel. Immediately upon receiving c_i', the tag responses with $r_i' = R_i^{c_i}$. The reader stops the clock after receiving r_i, which may not be equal to r_i' due to errors or alterations in the channel, and computes the round trip time (RTT) of this challenge and response transaction and stores it as Δt_i.

The final phase starts with computing and sending two following messages from the tag to the reader.

$$m = \{c_1', ..., c_n', r_1', ..., r_n'\} \tag{5}$$
$$t_B = f_x(m, ID, N_R, N_{T_1}, N_{T_2}, N_{T_3}) \tag{6}$$

Finally, the reader computes three kinds of errors and checks whether their summation is below a fault tolerance threshold as following.

- *errc*: the number of times that $c_i \neq c_i'$.
- *errr*: the number of times that $c_i = c_i'$ but $r_i \neq R_i^{c_i}$.
- *errt*: the number of times that $c_i = c_i'$ but the response delay Δt_i is more than a timing bound threshold $t_{max}(\Delta t_i > t_{max})$.

If the reader authentication is also demanded, the reader computes $t_A = f_x(N_R, k_2)$ and transmits it to the tag. Once the tag checks its correctness, the two entities are mutually authenticated.

The authors claim that the Hitomi protocol provides mutual authentication between the tag and the reader and also guarantees privacy protection. The authors argue that the success probability of the mafia and distance fraud attacks against their scheme is bounded by $(\frac{1}{2})^n$.

Reader	Tag
	x, ID
$N_R \in_R \{0,1\}^n$	

$$\xrightarrow{\quad N_R \quad}$$

$$N_{T_1}, N_{T_2}, N_{T_3} \in_R \{0,1\}^n$$

$$\xleftarrow{\quad N_{T_1}, N_{T_2}, N_{T_3} \quad}$$

$$k_1 = f_x(N_R, N_{T_1}, W)$$
$$k_2 = f_{k_1}(N_{T_2}, N_{T_3}, W')$$
$$\begin{cases} R^0 = k_1 \\ R^1 = k_2 \oplus x \end{cases}$$

Start of rapid bit exchange
for $i = 1...n$

$c_i \in \{0,1\}$
start clock

$$\xrightarrow{\quad c_i \quad}$$

$$r'_i = R_i^{c'_i}$$

$$\xleftarrow{\quad r_i \quad}$$

stop clock
Compute Δt_i

End of rapid bit exchange

$$m = \{c'_1, ..., c'_n, r'_1, ..., r'_n\}$$
$$t_B = f_x(m, ID, N_R, N_{T_1}, N_{T_2}, N_{T_3})$$

$$\xleftarrow{\quad m, t_B \quad}$$

Check ID in the Database
Compute R^0, R^1
$err_c = \#\{i : c_i \neq c'_i\}$
$err_r = \#\{i : c_i = c'_i, r_i \neq R_i^{c_i}\}$
$err_t = \#\{i : c_i = c'_i, \Delta t_i > t_{max}\}$
if $err_c + err_r + err_t \geq \tau$
  REJECT
else
  $t_A = f_x(N_R, k_2)$

$$\xrightarrow{\quad t_A \quad}$$

Compute and Compare t_A

Fig. 2. Hitomi RFID Distance Bounding

3.2   Key Disclosure Attack

In this section, we present an attacking scenario to the Hitomi protocol which leads to tag's secret key disclosure. Our main assumption in this attack is that the reader authentication is not demanded and so the protocol is executed without the optional message t_A. This allows an unauthorized reader(adversary) to query the tag several times without being detected.

Algorithm 1 portrays how an adversary, modeled in Section 2.2, is able to extract Δ bits of the tag's secret key by querying the tag m times.

The algorithm starts with the preparation phase in which at mth run, the adversary first generates a new random number N_R, sends it to the tag and receives the 3-tuple of $\{N_{T_1}, N_{T_2}, N_{T_3}\}$ in return.

The rapid bit exchange phase of the algorithm starts with generation of a challenge vector by the adversary which contains Δ bits of 1 and $n - \Delta$ bits of 0 ($c^{(m)}$). By sending the bits of this challenge vector to the tag in n rounds of the rapid bit exchange phase and receiving the responses, the adversary obtains $n - \Delta$ bits of $R^0 = k_1$ and Δ bits of $R^1 = k_2 \oplus x$.

We know that if the adversary is able to find k_1, she will be able to calculate k_2 by (4). Now, the adversary requires to search over all possible 2^Δ values for k_1. If we observe the output of $f_{k_1}(N_{T_2}^{(m)}, N_{T_3}^{(m)}, W')$ in the mth run of the protocol for 2^Δ times, each time with one different possible value of k_1, we will see that the number of values for the first Δ bits of k_2 ($k_{2(1)}, ..., k_{2(\Delta)}$) is less than 2^Δ. This can be calculated by a well-known problem in probability theory described in Remark 1.

Each k_2 nominates one $X_\Delta = (x_{(1)}, ..., x_{(\Delta)})$ for Δ bits of the tag's secret key (Line 16 of the Algorithm 1). So, each time the adversary queries the tag, she will obtain a set of potential candidates for X_Δ. If she continues querying the tag, each time she will obtain a set of different candidates.

These candidates can be removed from the list by further querying, unless they are nominated in the other runs. And the final candidate is the one which has been in the candidate list in all the queries. The number of times that the adversary must query the tag to be left with only one candidate is calculated by (9) and plotted in Figures 3 and 4.

Remark 1. Consider the process of tossing b balls into b bins. The tosses are uniformly at random and independent of each other. The probability of not falling any ball into a particular bin can be calculated by (7) [17].

$$\text{Pr(one particular bin remains empty)} = p_0 = \left(1 - \frac{1}{b}\right)^b \approx \frac{1}{e}, \ b \gg 1 \qquad (7)$$

Hence, the probability that a ball does not remain empty is simply $p_1 = 1 - p_0$. Due to independency, if we repeat the same experiment for m trials, the probability that one particular bin remains empty at least in one of m trials is $1 - p_1^m$. Now, we can calculate the probability that all bins experience to be empty at least in one of m trials ($Pr(Success)$) by (8).

$$Pr(Success) = (1 - p_1^m)^b = \left(1 - \left(1 - \left(1 - \frac{1}{b}\right)^b\right)^m\right)^b \qquad (8)$$

$$\approx \left[1 - \left(1 - \frac{1}{e}\right)^m\right]^b, \ b \gg 1$$

For our problem it is only required to substitute b with 2^Δ and we will have:

$$P_{Succ} = Pr(Success) = \left(1 - \left(1 - \left(1 - \frac{1}{2^\Delta}\right)^{2^\Delta}\right)^m\right)^{2^\Delta} \qquad (9)$$

Algorithm 1. Δ bit secret key disclosure

Inputs: n, Δ, W, W'

Outputs: m, Δ bits of secret key x $(x_1, ..., x_\Delta)$

1: $m \leftarrow 1$ {number of required runs of the protocol}
2: **repeat**
3:     $NumberofCandidates \leftarrow 0$
4:     $FinalCandidate \leftarrow 0$
5:     $\{counter(1), ..., counter(2^\Delta)\} \leftarrow \{0x0, ..., 0x0\}$
6:     $\{CandidateFlag(1), ..., CandidateFlag(2^\Delta)\} \leftarrow \{0x0, ..., 0x0\}$
7:     Generate $N_R^{(m)}$ and Send to the tag.
8:     Receive $N_{T_1}^{(m)}, N_{T_2}^{(m)}, N_{T_3}^{(m)}$
9:     $c^{(m)} \leftarrow (\underbrace{1, ..., 1}_{\Delta}, \underbrace{0, ..., 0}_{n-\Delta})$
10:    send the challenges to the tag in n rounds and receive the responses.
11:    $r^{(m)} \leftarrow (r_{(1)}^{(m)}, ..., r_{(n)}^{(m)})$
12:    $(k_{1(\Delta+1)}, ..., k_{1(n)}) \leftarrow (r_{(\Delta+1)}^{(m)}, ..., r_{(n)}^{(m)})$
13:    **for** $i = 0$ **to** $2^\Delta - 1$ **do**
14:        $(k_{1(1)}, ..., k_{1(\Delta)}) \leftarrow Decimal2Binary(i)^*$
15:        $(k_{2(1)}, ..., k_{2(n)}) \leftarrow f_{k_1}(N_{T_2}^{(m)}, N_{T_3}^{(m)}, W')$
16:        $(x_{(1)}, ..., x_{(\Delta)}) \leftarrow (k_{2(1)}, ..., k_{2(\Delta)}) \oplus (r_{(1)}^{(m)}, ..., r_{(\Delta)}^{(m)})$
17:        $l \leftarrow Binary2Decimal(x_{(1)}, ..., x_{(\Delta)})^{**}$
18:        **if** $CandidateFlag(l) = 0$ **then**
19:            $counter(l) \leftarrow counter(l) + 1$
20:            $CandidateFlag(l) \leftarrow 1$
21:        **end if**
22:    **end for**
23:    **for** $j = 1$ **to** 2^Δ **do**
24:        **if** $counter(j) = m$ **then**
25:            $NumberofCandidates \leftarrow NumberofCandidates + 1$
26:            $FinalCandidate \leftarrow j$
27:        **end if**
28:    **end for**
29:    $m \leftarrow m + 1$
30: **until** $NumberofCandidates = 1$
31: $(x_{(1)}, ..., x_{(\Delta)}) \leftarrow Decimal2Binary(FinalCandidate)$
32: **return** $m, (x_{(1)}, ..., x_{(\Delta)})$

* Decimal2Binary(.) outputs the binary representation of a given decimal number.
** Binary2Decimal(.) outputs the decimal representation of a given binary number.

Figure 3 illustrates the probability of success calculated in (9) while the number of protocol runs are increased. The figures have been plotted for $\Delta = 4, 8, 16$ and 32, which should be chosen according to computational constraints.

So far, we have accomplished to find the first Δ bits of the tag's secret key with a certain probability. In a similar vein, one can find other bits of the secret key

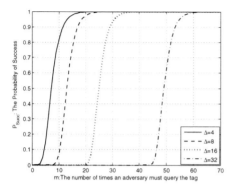 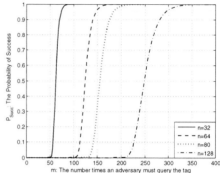

Fig. 3. Adversary success probability to find Δ bits of the secret key

Fig. 4. Adversary success probability to find the whole secret key for $\Delta = 16$

by choosing a different challenge vector (e.g. for finding $(x_{(\Delta+1)}, ..., x_{(2\Delta)})$ the challenge should be chosen like (10) and the above algorithm should be executed another time).

$$c = (\underbrace{0, ..., 0}_{\Delta}, \underbrace{1, ..., 1}_{\Delta}, \underbrace{0, ..., 0}_{n-2\Delta}) \qquad (10)$$

In this way, the adversary accomplishes to find the whole tag's secret key, if she can query the tag for enough times. Figure 4 illustrates the number of runs of the protocol which an adversary must query the tag and its probability of success to find the entirety of tags's secret key, assuming that her computational capability is limited to $2^\Delta = 2^{16}$ computations. The computations include: searching over 2^Δ values of k_1, finding k_2 for each k_1 and candidate one X_Δ.

The graphs have been plotted for four different key sizes $n = 32, 64, 80$ and 128. For instance, the adversary is required to query the tag about 70, 140, 175 and 280 times to find the tag's secret keys of size 32, 64, 80 and 128 bits with the probability of about 0.9 respectively.

It is obvious that having this attack accomplished, the adversary is able to easily either track or impersonate the tag in further interrogations. The information elicited in this attack also paves the way for performing other attacks such as mafia or terrorist fraud attacks.

4   The NUS Protocol

4.1   Description

The NUS protocol (Figure 5) also consists of three phases, two *slow phases* a fast called *rapid bit exchange phase*.

In the first slow phase, the reader chooses a random nonce(N_R) and transmits it to the tag. In return, the tag chooses another random number(N_T) and computes the response register $R = f_x(N_R, N_T)$, which is of length $2n$. The tag then initializes the variables $j1, j2, k1$ and $k2$ to $1, n, 0$ and $2n + 1$ respectively and sends back N_T to the reader.

In the ith round of the rapid bit exchange phase, the reader generates a random challenge bit c_i and sends it to the tag while initializing a clock to zero. The tag receives c_i' which may not be equal to c_i due to errors or alterations in the channel. Immediately upon receiving c_i', the tag sends the bit r_i', computed according to the procedure shown in Figure 5.

The final phase concludes with sending the message m which consists of all challenges the tag has received, from the tag to the reader and finally, the error computation which is almost the same as in the Hitomi protocol.

The authors claim that the success probability of the distance, mafia and terrorist fraud attacks against the NUS protocol is bounded by $(\frac{1}{2})^n$.

4.2 Distance Fraud Attack

In this section, we present a distance fraud attack on the NUS protocol in two different forms in white-box model: *restricted adversary* and *powerful adversary*. The main assumption we have is that the adversary is located at zone Z_1, i.e. at the ith round of the rapid bit exchange phase, the adversary accesses to the value of the challenge bit in previous round c_{i-1}, before generating current response r_i. This assumption implies that the adversary is able to update the registers $j1, j2, k1$ and $k2$ and she is aware of their correct current values, before she generates the response.

Restricted adversary
The adversary is allowed to run only once the pseudo-random function f function to compute R and observe its content before any response. The probability of success for the distance fraud attack in this model can be calculated by (11).

$$
\begin{aligned}
P_{dis} = {} & Pr(\text{Success}|x_{j1}x_{j2} = 00)Pr(x_{j1}x_{j2} = 00) \\
& + Pr(\text{Success}|x_{j1}x_{j2} = 01)Pr(x_{j1}x_{j2} = 01) \\
& + Pr(\text{Success}|x_{j1}x_{j2} = 10)Pr(x_{j1}x_{j2} = 10) \\
& + Pr(\text{Success}|x_{j1}x_{j2} = 11)Pr(x_{j1}x_{j2} = 11)
\end{aligned}
\tag{11}
$$

If $x_{j1}x_{j2} = 00$ and without knowing c_i, the adversary should anticipate the right response(r_i) between R_{k1+1} and R_{k2-1}. Let us define the probability of equality of these two bits by (12).

$$
P_{eq} = \Pr(R_{k1+1} = R_{k2-1})
\tag{12}
$$

So, we have,

$$
\begin{aligned}
Pr(\text{Success}|x_{j1}x_{j2} = 00) = {} & Pr(\text{Success}|x_{j1}x_{j2} = 00, R_{k1+1} = R_{k2-1})(P_{eq}) \\
& + Pr(\text{Success}|x_{j1}x_{j2} = 00, R_{k1+1} \neq R_{k2-1})(1 - P_{eq})
\end{aligned}
$$

Reader	Tag
	x, ID

$N_R \in_R \{0,1\}^n$

$\xrightarrow{\quad N_R \quad}$

$N_T \in_R \{0,1\}^n$
$R = f_x(N_R, N_T), |R| = 2n$
$j1 = 1, j2 = n$
$k1 = 0, k2 = 2n + 1$

$\xleftarrow{\quad N_T \quad}$

Start of rapid bit exchange
for $i = 1...n$

$c_i \in \{0,1\}$
start clock

$\xrightarrow{\quad c_i \quad}$

if $c_i' = 0$
  if $x_{j1} = 0$
    $k1 = k1 + 1, r_i' = R_{k1}$
  else
    $k2 = k2 - 2, r_i' = R_{k2}$
  $j1 = j1 + 1$
else
  if $x_{j2} = 0$
    $k2 = k2 - 1, r_i' = R_{k2}$
  else
    $k1 = k1 + 2, r_i' = R_{k1}$
  $j2 = j2 - 1$

$\xleftarrow{\quad r_i \quad}$

stop clock, Compute Δt_i

End of rapid bit exchange
$m = \{c_1', ..., c_n'\}$

$\xleftarrow{\quad m \quad}$

$err_c = \#\{i : c_i \neq c_i'\}$
Compute $(r_i')'s$ using $(c_i')'s$
$err_r = \#\{i : c_i = c_i', r_i \neq r_i''\}$
$err_t = \#\{i : c_i = c_i', \Delta t_i > t_{max}\}$
Checks $err_c + err_r + err_t \leq \tau$

Fig. 5. The NUS Distance Bounding Protocol

If $R_{k1+1} = R_{k2-1}$, the adversary can simply outputs either of these two bits and succeeds with the probability 1. Otherwise, she outputs a random bit and she will have the success probability of $\frac{1}{2}$. So,

$$Pr(\text{Success}|x_{j1}x_{j2} = 00) = 1 \times P_{eq} + \frac{1}{2} \times (1 - P_{eq}) = \frac{(1 + P_{eq})}{2} \quad (13)$$

We can do similar calculations for other three possibilities of $x_{j1}x_{j2}$. Since all four possibilities of $x_{j1}x_{j2}$ are equally likely, we have the probability of success for a distance fraud attack in one round as (14).

$$P_{dis} = \frac{(1 + P_{eq})}{2} \qquad (14)$$

In a similar vein, one can show that due to independency of the n rounds, the adversary obtains the success probability of $(\frac{1+P_{eq}}{2})^n$ for n rounds. If we assume that zeros and ones are equally likely, P_{eq} equals to $\frac{1}{2}$ and for n rounds we have:

$$P_{dis} = (\frac{3}{4})^n \qquad (15)$$

Powerful adversary

Our main assumptions in this attack are as following. We assume that, there is a 1-second latency between the preparation and rapid bit exchange phases of the protocol. It implies that the adversary can run the pseudo-random function f for c times between the preparation and the rapid bit exchange phases, where c the number of a simple random number function like a hash function that can be computed per second on a single PC [16].

In [16], Avoine et al has presented an instance of a distance fraud attack against a white-box-modeled tag in Hancke and Kuhn protocol. They have devoted the white-box modeled tag's capabilities to minimize the hamming weight difference of n-bit response registers in the Hancke and Kuhn protocol($hw(R^0 \oplus R^1)$). They have proved that if $P_i = Pr(success|(hw(R^0 \oplus R^1) = i))$, the probability of success in the distance fraud attack can be calculated by (16).

$$P_{dis} = \left(\frac{1}{2}\right)^{cn} \times \left(\sum_{i=0}^{i=n-1} (P_i) \left[\left(\sum_{j=i}^{j=n} \binom{n}{j} \right)^c - \left(\sum_{j=i+1}^{j=n} \binom{n}{j} \right)^c \right] + 1 \right) \qquad (16)$$

In order to utilize (16) for our purpose, we define $P_i = Pr(Success|hw(R) = i)$. This implies that, we devote the tag's capability to minimize the hamming weight of the response register R in the NUS protocol. Having this in mind and by using (14), we can calculate P_i for n rounds as following.

$$P_{eq} = (\frac{i}{2n})^2 + (\frac{2n - i}{2n})^2 = 1 + \frac{i^2 - 2in}{2n^2}$$
$$P_i = P_{dis} = \left[\frac{(1 + P_{eq})}{2} \right]^n = \left(1 + \frac{i^2 - 2in}{4n^2} \right)^n \qquad (17)$$

As the response register R in the NUS protocol is of length $2n$, we only need to substitute n by $2n$ and P_i by (17) in (16). Table 1 compares the claimed security of the NUS protocol and our results in restricted and powerful adversary models in terms of the probability of success of an adversary in the distance fraud attack. For example, for $n = 32$, the probability of success in the distance fraud attack in a restricted adversary model is 1.0045×10^{-4}. This probability improves to 0.0035 in a powerful adversary model for $c = 2^{23}$ which roughly represents the number of hashes that can be computed today per second on a single PC [16]. These probabilities are remarkably beyond the claimed security $(\frac{1}{2})^{32} = 2.3283 \times 10^{-10}$.

Table 1. Comparison of the probability of success for distance fraud attack against the NUS protocol for $c = 2^{23} \approx 10^6$

	n=32	n=64	n=80	n=128
Claimed Security	$2.3283{\times}10^{-10}$	5.4210×10^{-20}	$8.2718{\times}10^{-25}$	2.9387×10^{-39}
Restricted Adversary	$1.0045{\times}10^{-4}$	$1.0090{\times}10^{-8}$	$1.0113{\times}10^{-10}$	$1.0183{\times}10^{-16}$
Powerful Aadversary	0.0035	$4.5101{\times}10^{-7}$	$4.7459{\times}10^{-9}$	$5.1498{\times}10^{-15}$

5   Conclusions

The design of a secure distance bounding protocol which can resist against the existing attacks for RFID systems is still challenging. Despite of interesting proposals in the literature, this field still lacks a concrete solution.

Recently, two solutions have been proposed for this purpose called the Hitomi and the NUS distance bounding protocols. We presented a secret key disclosure attack on the former and a distance fraud attack on the latter protocol. Our results showed that the security margins which was expected to be yielded by them have been overestimated.

We showed that the Hitomi protocol is vulnerable to a full secret key disclosure attack by querying the tag several times. In addition, the probability of success in a distance fraud attack against the NUS protocol was shown to be able to be increased up to $(\frac{3}{4})^n$, if the adversary gets close enough to the reader. This probability can even be slightly improved, if the tag has some computational capabilities.

References

1. Fajarado, J.M., Peinado Dominguez, A.: Security in RFID and Sensor Networks, 1st edn. Auerbach publication (2009) ISBN:978-1-4200-6839-9
2. Avoine, G., Tchamkerten, A.: An Efficient Distance Bounding RFID Authentication Protocol: Balancing False-Acceptance Rate and Memory Requirement. In: Samarati, P., Yung, M., Martinelli, F., Ardagna, C.A. (eds.) ISC 2009. LNCS, vol. 5735, pp. 250–261. Springer, Heidelberg (2009)
3. Kara, O., Kardaş, S., Bingöl, M.A., Avoine, G.: Optimal Security Limits of RFID Distance Bounding Protocols. In: Ors Yalcin, S.B. (ed.) RFIDSec 2010. LNCS, vol. 6370, pp. 220–238. Springer, Heidelberg (2010)
4. Peris-Lopez, P., Hernandez-Castro, J.C., Estevez-Tapiador, J.M., van der Lubbe, J.C.A.: Shedding Some Light on RFID Distance Bounding Protocols and Terrorist Attacks. arXiv.org, Computer Science, Cryptography and Security (June 2010)
5. Brands, S., Chaum, D.: Distance Bounding Protocols. In: Helleseth, T. (ed.) EU-ROCRYPT 1993. LNCS, vol. 765, pp. 344–359. Springer, Heidelberg (1994)
6. Hancke, G., Kuhn, M.: An RFID Distance Bounding Protocol. In: Conference on Security and Privacy for Emerging Areas in Communication Networks SecureComm 2005, Athens, Greece, pp. 67–73 (September 2005)
7. Kim, C.H., Avoine, G.: RFID Distance Bounding Protocol with Mixed Challenges to Prevent Relay Attacks. In: Garay, J.A., Miyaji, A., Otsuka, A. (eds.) CANS 2009. LNCS, vol. 5888, pp. 119–133. Springer, Heidelberg (2009)

8. Kim, C.H., Avoine, G., Koeune, F., Standaert, F.-X., Pereira, O.: The Swiss-Knife RFID Distance Bounding Protocol. In: Lee, P.J., Cheon, J.H. (eds.) ICISC 2008. LNCS, vol. 5461, pp. 98–115. Springer, Heidelberg (2009)
9. Munilla, J., Ortiz, A., Peinado, A.: Distance Bounding Protocols with Void-Challenges for RFID. In: Workshop on RFID Security RFIDSec 2006, Graz, Austria (July 2006)
10. Munilla, J., Peinado, A.: Security Analysis of Tu and Piramuthu's Protocol. In: New Technologies, Mobility and Security NTMS 2008, Tangier, Morocco, pages 15 (November 2008)
11. Reid, J., Neito, J.G., Tang, T., Senadji, B.: Detecting relay attacks with timing based protocols. In: Bao, F., Miller, S. (eds.) Proceedings of the 2nd ACM Symposium on Information, Computer and Communications Security ASIACCS 2007, Singapore, Republic of Singapore, pp. 204–213 (March 2007)
12. Tu, Y.-J., Piramuthu, S.: RFID Distance Bounding Protocols. In: First International EURASIP Workshop on RFID Technology, Vienna, Austria (September 2007)
13. Trujillo-Rasua, R., Martin, B., Avoine, G.: The Poulidor Distance-Bounding Protocol. In: Ors Yalcin, S.B. (ed.) RFIDSec 2010. LNCS, vol. 6370, pp. 239–257. Springer, Heidelberg (2010)
14. Peris-Lopez, P., Hernandez-Castro, J.C., Tapiador, J.M.E., Palomar, E., van der Lubbe, J.C.A.: Cryptographic Puzzles and Distance-bounding Protocols: Practical Tools for RFID Security. In: IEEE International Conference on RFID, Orlando (2010)
15. Özhan Gürel, A., Arslan, A., Akgün, M.: Non-Uniform Stepping Approach to RFID Distance Bounding Problem. In: Garcia-Alfaro, J., Navarro-Arribas, G., Cavalli, A., Leneutre, J. (eds.) DPM 2010 and SETOP 2010. LNCS, vol. 6514, pp. 64–78. Springer, Heidelberg (2011)
16. Avoine, G., Bingol, M.A., Kardas, S., Lauradoux, C., Martin, B.: A Formal Framework for Cryptanalyzing RFID Distance Bounding Protocols. In: Cryptology ePrint Archive, Report 2009/543 (2009)
17. Feller, W.: An Introduction to Probability Theory and its Applications. Wiley India Pvt. Ltd. (2008)
18. Dolev, D., Yao, A.C.-C.: On the security of public key protocols. IEEE Transactions on Information Theory 29(2), 198–207 (1983)

An Automatic, Time-Based, Secure Pairing Protocol for Passive RFID

George T. Amariucai[1], Clifford Bergman[2], and Yong Guan[1]

[1] Dept. of Electrical and Comp. Engineering, Iowa State University
{gamari,guan}@iastate.edu
[2] Dept. of Mathematics, Iowa State University
cbergman@iastate.edu

Abstract. This paper introduces the Adopted-Pet (AP) protocol, an automatic (i.e. requiring no human interaction) secure pairing protocol, adequate for the pairing between a passive RFID tag and a reader. Most pairing protocols rely for their security on a certain advantage that the legitimate devices have over any malicious users. Such advantages include proximity (employing near-field communication) or secret keys that are either produced with the assistance of, or verified by, the legitimate user. The advantage exploited by our novel AP protocol is the amount of *uninterrupted time* spent by the two devices in the proximity (although not requiring near-field communication) of each-other. We discuss several implementation configurations, all based on pseudo-random bit generators, employing short-length LFSRs, and requiring no more than 2000 transistors. This makes the protocol ideally suited for low-cost passive RFID tags. For each configuration we show that the AP protocol is highly secure against occasional malicious entities.

Keywords: Automatic pairing protocol, time-based pairing, passive RFID.

1 Introduction

Recent technological advances, combined with an increasing demand for automatic inventory and tracking, provide a glimpse of a near future in which radio-frequency identification (RFID) becomes ubiquitous. From industrial platforms to home environments, from retail stores or restaurants to medical facilities, the potential use of passive RFID tags is only limited by human imagination.

Passive RFID tags are small, barely-visible, extremely cheap and hence extremely resource-limited electronic devices, which can communicate wirelessly to a more powerful device—a "reader"—usually during an automatic inventory. The typical passive RFID tag has no internal power source, and runs its internal circuitry by harvesting power from the electromagnetic waves produced by the reader during a query. Rather than producing and transmitting an electromagnetic wave of its own, the tag responds to queries from the reader by *backscattering* [1], i.e. by modulating the waveform reflected back to the reader—this can be done by varying the load impedance of the tag's antenna.

A. Juels and C. Paar (Eds.): RFIDSec 2011, LNCS 7055, pp. 108–126, 2012.
© Springer-Verlag Berlin Heidelberg 2012

Unfortunately, as with any relatively new technology, numerous controversies still surround the wide-scale deployment of RFID. In fact, consumers' fear of privacy invasion have already triggered several small-scale street protests around the world. Indeed, current RFID tags are subject to privacy attacks, which could make it feasible to track the movements of a person (the same idea is non-malevolently used to track patients in clinics or senior citizens in assisted-living facilities), or to inventory their personal possessions.

As an immediate countermeasure, pairing algorithms could be implemented to ensure that the RFID tags only respond to very few authenticated tag readers. Although device pairing protocols abound in the literature [2,3,4,5], very few of these protocols can be implemented into the cost-constrained, resource-limited passive RFID tags. Moreover, most low-complexity pairing protocols require human interaction to complete the pairing process. For example, the user is required to shake the two devices simultaneously in [3], or to push a button in [4,5]. The *Resurrecting Duckling Protocol* of [2], requires that the new tag should be "killed" by its previous owner and then "resurrected" by the new owner. The "duckling" will then trust only the the first reader that attempts to communicate with it during resurrection. The immediate drawback is that if the duckling is accidentally "killed" and then "resurrected" by a malicious user, the legitimate user looses access to the tag.

Human interaction is generally not desirable, because it is often viewed as an additional burden on the consumer, who may disregard proper protocol, leading to faulty pairings or omissions. In this paper, we are concerned with automatic pairing that would provide commercial-level privacy for recently-introduced applications like smart refrigerators [6,7], or smart wardrobes or bookshelves, which periodically inventory their contents, and are able to provide suggestions like a shopping list, a matched outfit, or the location of a book. We should note that, while human interaction may be appropriate for the pairing of highly security-sensitive devices, such as personal computers, users should not be expected to perform dozens of check-in procedures after every trip to the grocery store, in order to pair each item with their smart refrigerator or pantry.

We address the pairing between a passive RFID tag and a reader by proposing an automatic, time-based pairing protocol, which we view as an alternative to the Resurrecting Duckling protocol of [2], and which we denote the *Adopted-Pet (AP) Protocol*. As opposed to the *Resurrecting Duckling protocol*, our *Adopted Pet Protocol* provides a more natural method of secure and *transient* [2] association between the tag and the reader in the home environment. Just as when adopting a new pet from the animal shelter, in our protocol trust is earned by spending a long, quality time together. Once brought into the home environment, the new tag will start being *courted* by a home reader. After the tag and the reader spend a pre-programmed amount of time together (usually overnight), the tag starts trusting the reader, and responding to its queries.

The main advantage of our AP protocol is that it requires no human interaction. Moreover, if the tag accidentally begins to trust another reader (for example during a trip), the home reader can re-gain the tag's trust upon return.

Naturally, this has the drawback that, if the item to which the RFID tag is attached is stolen, the thief can use the tag with his own home readers. However, we believe this should be irrelevant, since the value of the RFID-enabled service is generally less than the intrinsic value of the object to which it is attached. In addition, any sensible thief would attempt to remove the RFID tags from the stolen products anyway, to destroy the evidence of the crime. Moreover, the security of most encrypted devices becomes questionable when the device is stolen, because the thief has an unlimited time for breaking the encryption.

Our contributions can be summarized as follows: (a) we introduce the novel idea of uninterrupted-time-based pairing, and define the *adopted-pet* (AP) pairing protocol; (b) we provide a robust implementation philosophy, which can tolerate interference and desynchronizations, and demands extremely limited resources; (c) we discuss four possible implementations of the protocol inside passive RFID tags, in detail, emphasizing their individual security features and resource requirements; (d) we provide an analysis of the reader's part of the protocol. The paper is organized as follows. Section 2 presents the system and threat models. The AP protocol is introduced in Section 3, along with the RFID-adequate implementation philosophy. Section 4 discusses the four practical design solutions, while Section 5 delves deeper into the protocol security. Finally, we provide some hardware-related considerations in Section 6, and some concluding remarks in Section 7. *Take-Away Points* are emphasized throughout the paper, to facilitate reading and information synthesis (nevertheless, the take-away points alone *do not* constitute a good summary of the paper).

2   System Model, Threat Model, and Challenges

We consider a ubiquitous RFID environment, in which RFID readers are mounted in most public places, such as grocery stores, bars or train stations, and are carried around by individuals, in the form of their smart phones or laptops. In our model, most products available in stores contain individual RFID tags, and cannot be individually re-programmed at checkout (for instance, to "kill" the resurrecting duckling in each product, the checkout reader would have to establish secure individual communication with each item – a simple inventory would not suffice). Moreover, we assume that most RFID tags are designed according to the same flexible RFID standard. The tags attached to various items need to be usable by the customers, inside their homes, with their smart refrigerators, bookshelves and wardrobes.

Nevertheless, the RFID tags should not allow themselves to be inventoried by illegitimate readers during their trip from the store to the customer's home, or during any subsequent times when the products to which they are attached are worn or carried around. Our threat model consists of illegitimate readers attempting to inventory the tag. Since commercial-grade RFID devices (readers and tags) are designed for close-range communication, we do not concern ourselves with illegitimate readers that might eavesdrop on the legitimate reader and impersonate the latter. This sort of attack is normally beyond the scope of pairing protocols. It is also beyond the scope of pairing protocols to deal with jamming attacks. For completeness, we should also mention that attacks where the malicious entity attempts to modify the information transmitted over the channel in a controlled fashion (as in [8]) are not practical for our protocol. This is due to the fact that, in our protocol, the only information-bearing signals are transmitted by the tag. To mount such an attack, an adversary would need to be in close proximity to the tag (to receive its query responses), achieve a certain level of synchronization with the tag (in the presence of any scattering phenomena), and transmit with power well above that of the tag's backscattered signal. Otherwise, since most modern RFID protocols use a variant of frequency-shift-keying modulation (F2F, FM0, MMS, etc.), based on detecting transitions rather than power levels, the results of such an attack would be totally unpredictable (hence categorized as *jamming*).

Our time-based trust-earning protocol raises several serious challenges. To better understand them, consider the following two real-life scenarios, which summarize the model for the environment in which our AP protocol is intended to function, and the model for the attacks that the AP protocol should be able to foil.

Scenario 1—legitimate pairing: A new tag is brought into the home environment. The tag is attached to a product, like a food or clothing item, and should be used by a home reader, such as one in a smart fridge or wardrobe [6,7]. The moment the tag enters the radius of action of a reader, the reader begins "courting" the tag. The reader needs to gather enough information about the tag, so that it will be able to prove to the tag that it has been around for a long period of time, which defines it as a *legitimate reader*.

Scenario 2—the man on the bus: A certain tag is carried around by its owner, and subjected to the owner's daily routine. The routine includes a several-hour bus ride to work. The attacker happens to also ride the same bus, and his customized reader attempts to pair with the tag. However, the attacker cannot spend more than several hours a day in the proximity of the tag, without being detected.

Take-Away Point 1. *It is important to note that passive RFID tags generally have no internal time reference. A tag's only notion of time comes from successive reader queries. This makes it unfeasible for the tag to keep track of the actual time spent in the company of a certain reader per day. If in Scenario 1 the consumer takes the tag outside the home for a short while—and while outside the home, the tag is interrogated by other readers—(or if the tag becomes inaccessible to the reader due to some form of temporary interference), then upon return, the tag does not know whether it has been a minute or a day. On the other hand, if the tag would just count the number of queries from a certain reader, and pair with the reader after a certain threshold is reached, then it would only take several days for the "man on the bus" in Scenario 2 to gain control of the tag.*

In conclusion, to differentiate between the legitimate reader and the "man on the bus", it does not suffice to consider only the quantity of time spent in the presence of the tag. Rather, we need to take advantage of the time quality:

we can expect that the time spent by the legitimate reader in the company of the tag is less likely to exhibit large interruptions than the time spent by the attacker in the proximity of the tag.

Take-Away Point 2. *To summarize, our pairing protocol should have the following characteristics:*

- *It should be automatic;*
- *It should enable the legitimate reader to pair with the tag after spending enough time in the presence of the tag;*
- *It should not allow the pairing between a tag and a reader based only on the short but many interactions between them;*
- *It should not rely on any absolute time references;*
- *It should be adequate for implementation in low-cost, resource-constrained passive RFID tags.*

3   The Adopted-Pet (AP) Protocol

Our Adopted-Pet (AP) protocol relies on the fact that a reader located inside the tag owner's home should be able to spend more *uninterrupted* time in the presence of the tag than any other reader located anywhere outside the home. By *uninterrupted* time we mean an interval of time during which the tag is not interrogated by any other reader. If the tag is interrogated by a different reader between two such uninterrupted time intervals, we say that the tag and the initial reader have become *desynchronized*. Naturally, a reader located in the tag owner's place of work might have an advantage similar to a reader located in the home environment, but we should assume that the place of work is generally a safe environment (otherwise, the tag owner has more serious problems than his RFID tag being inventoried).

The AP protocol is described in Figure 1. The reader attempts an inventory of all the tags within its reach. As soon as a tag accesses the medium, and the channel is proved to be clear (no collisions are detected) [1], the reader proves to the tag that it can be trusted. The tag will only respond with its Universal Product Code (UPC) if the reader querying it proves that it knows the tag's secret password. Otherwise (if the tag is new), the tag will assume that the reader is not legitimate, and it will respond with a *"no trust"* sequence, followed by a piece of information related to the secret password—throughout this paper we shall call this *"a clue"*. If the reader keeps querying the new tag, for long uninterrupted time intervals, it will eventually accumulate enough information to learn the tag's secret password. However, if a certain malicious reader queries the tag for many short uninterrupted time intervals, such that between any two such time intervals the tag receives an unknown number of queries from other readers, the information extracted from the tag's responses should be of little value to the malicious reader. It is important to note that our protocol integrates naturally with the current RFID singulation protocols; that is, only minor changes need to be made to both reader and tag, while the physical and medium access control

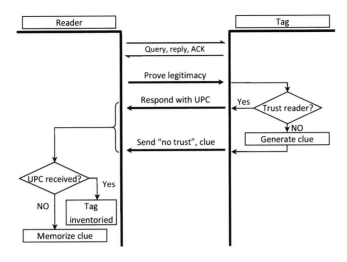

Fig. 1. An outline of the AP protocol

layers remain unchanged. Moreover, a single reader should be able to deal with large numbers of new (distrustful) tags simultaneously.

We envision a system in which a reader can gather information about the tag's secret password at a rate that starts at an initial value, and increases exponentially with every new tag response. However, if the reader and the tag become desynchronized, the rate of gathering information returns to its initial value, and starts increasing from there. Note that this does not imply that the information obtained by the reader during the first uninterrupted time interval is lost. When the gathered information reaches a certain threshold, the tag's secret key can be learned. We shall refer to such an idealized system as an *"exponential-leakage-rate system"*. The gathering of information is represented in Figure 2, for three different scenarios: (a) the information threshold is reached by a reader which queries the tag during the single uninterrupted time interval $[t_0, t_4]$, (b) the information threshold is reached by a reader that queries the tag during two distinct uninterrupted time intervals $[t_0, t_3]$ and $[t_5, t_7]$, and finally (c) an attacker queries the tag during the short uninterrupted time intervals $[t_0, t_2]$, $[t_5, t_6]$, and $[t_8, t_9]$, without reaching the information threshold. Note that our exponential-leakage-rate system also displays a time threshold $t_1 - t_0$. In order for a reader to obtain any information about the tag's secret password, the reader should query the tag for an uninterrupted time interval of at least $t_1 - t_0$. For example, no information is obtained by the attacker in the third scenario (c) during interval $[t_5, t_6]$.

In the spirit of recycling, we propose to use cryptosystems which lose information about their secret key at such an increasing rate, but only when surveyed continuously. As an intuitive (although neither practical, nor desirable) example, the password could be the title of a book from a library. The tag could transmit

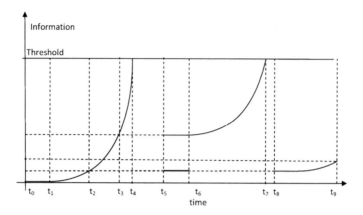

Fig. 2. Gathering information about the secret key for the AP protocol, in an exponential-leakage-rate system

one letter from the book, in order, every minute. If the reader listens continuously for a large period of time, it will obtain an entire chapter, and probably be able to identify the book. Similarly, if the reader listens for several medium-sized distinct uninterrupted time intervals, it will obtain substantial pieces of two different chapters, probably leading to the identification of the book as well. However, if an attacker can only listen over many really short uninterrupted time intervals, it will get a meaningless set of words, without even a position reference in the book. Clearly, this example does not have good security properties, since an attacker might identify the book by focusing on very peculiar words, or by looking at word frequencies.

For a more practical solution, consider the following implementation philosophy, that relies on the well-known linear-feedback shift register (LFSR).

Take-Away Point 3. *Assume that the tag contains an internal LFSR, of length L, the characteristic polynomial of which (of degree L) is programmable by an authorized reader, and constitutes the tag's secret password. If the reader proves to the tag that it knows the characteristic polynomial of its LFSR, the reader is considered authorized, and the tag responds to its queries with the UPC, and allows the reader to re-program the LFSR. On the other hand, if the RFID tag does not trust the querying reader, it generates a single bit with its internal LFSR (of length L), and responds with this bit. The reader memorizes the bit. If the reader can gather $2L$ contiguous bits, it can then solve for the coefficients of the LFSR's characteristic polynomial—a linear system of L equations with L unknowns. Note that efficient methods for solving the system may be implemented in the reader, such as the Berlekamp-Massey algorithm [9]. It is interesting to note that the legitimate reader is expected to* mount a successful linear-complexity attack *against the tag.*

The fact that an authorized reader is allowed to re-program the tag's LFSR provides a form of forward security – should the tag's secret leak at some point in time, the presence of the owner in a certain spot at a previous time should not be verifiable. Moreover, this ensures that any information about the tag's secret which leaks to an adversary (see Figure 2) becomes useless before the secret is breached.

Example 1. *Let us consider a concrete example. An RFID tag can be throttled [10] to respond only once every minute. If the tag has a built-in LFSR of length $L = 300$, any reader that spends an uninterrupted time of 10 hours in the tag's proximity can determine the characteristic polynomial. Suppose, instead, that the reader can only afford to spend 7.5 hours a day with the tag. The first equation can be written only after 5 hours of uninterrupted time (i.e. $L + 1$ queries), as discussed in more detail in Section 5.1. Hence, the characteristic polynomial can be discovered after only two days. On the other hand, if an attacker gains access to the tag for a single session of, say 5 hours (this would include any possible "man on the bus" type of attacker), he can only gain access to a contiguous bit sequence of length $L = 300$. This leaks absolutely no information about the characteristic polynomial, since any LFSR with a register length at least 300 is capable of producing any non-zero 300-bit sequence. Even if the attacker gathers a large number of such L-bit sequences, over the course of a year, the* ubiquitous RFID environment *ensures that the number of bits generated by the tag's internal LFSR between two attacker sessions is unknown and unpredictable. Hence, the attacker's information is completely useless both because the search space for the missing bits would be prohibitively large and also because there may be a great many different polynomials capable of producing each of the individual subsequences obtained.*

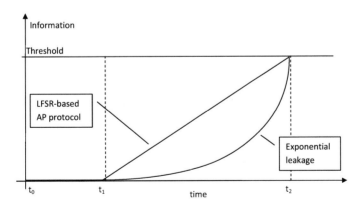

Fig. 3. The LFSR-based, vs. the exponential-leakage-rate system-based AP protocol

Note that in Example 1 above, the number of possible configurations for the tag's internal LFSR is at least equal to the number of primitive polynomials of degree 301 over $\mathbf{GF}(2)$, which is given by $\frac{\phi(2^{301}-1)}{301} \geq \frac{\sqrt{2^{301}-1}}{301} \sim 10^{42}$, where $\phi(\cdot)$ is Euler's totient function.

Take-Away Point 4. *The LFSR-based AP protocol is a first-order approximation of our exponential-leakage-rate concept, as illustrated in Figure 3.*

Take-Away Point 5. *The AP protocol has all of the desired features of Take-Away Point 2:*

- *Since the tag responds to all querying readers (although it responds with the UPC only to trusted readers), giving untrusted readers a chance to earn their trust, the protocol is fully automatic;*
- *Since it is based on the legitimate reader spending large periods of uninterrupted time in the presence of the tag, a home reader (like a smart fridge or bookshelf) would be able to pair with the tag overnight;*
- *Since no information about the tag's secret is leaked until a relatively long interval of uninterrupted time is spent with the tag, the protocol is secure and guarantees user privacy;*
- *Since the tag is only concerned with verifying whether the reader knows its secret, and with running its internal pseudo-random bit generator, the protocol does not need the tag (or the reader) to keep an absolute time reference;*
- *Since our implementation philosophy relies on a simple LFSR, we should be able to implement the protocol with very little expense of resources.*

In the following sections we provide a more complete analysis, including alternative implementation, and how to deal with tag-reader desynchronizations.

4   Design Considerations

At the heart of our proposed implementation of the adopted pet protocol is a pseudo-random bit generator implemented (as a finite-sate machine – FSM) on a passive RFID tag. The exact details of the generator are not specified in the protocol. In fact, the protocol assumes that these details are secret.

Pseudo-random bit generators are heavily used in cryptography for *stream ciphers*. When used in this way, the two parties to the communication must utilize exactly the same generating algorithm and agree on a shared secret—the encryption key. Usually this means that the details of the algorithm such as the characteristic polynomials and the filtering function or combining function, are public knowledge and the encryption key takes the form of the initial state of the generator.

However, that is not how we will be using the generator. In our context, there is no shared secret, and in fact, the state of the generator is not all that important. Instead, we treat the specific parameters of the generator as secret. Each tag will have its own set of parameters. In our realization of the AP protocol, *the RFID tag's key is the characteristic polynomial*. In order to gain the trust of the tag, the reader must prove that it knows the polynomial, either by sending it to the tag, or by predicting additional bits of the sequence and sending those to the tag. This latter "proof" is desirable if the tag is not aware of the characteristic polynomial associated with its internal FSM.

We shall discuss several implementation options in the following subsections. For now, we review some of the simple facts behind pseudo-random bit generators. Let $z_0, z_1, z_2, \ldots$ be a sequence of bits generated by the tag. As it is generated by a finite state machine, the sequence is eventually periodic. Consequently, it is possible to recreate the sequence via a linear recurrence relation such as

$$z_{j+L+1} = c_0 z_j + c_1 z_{j+1} + \cdots + c_{L-1} z_{j+L} \tag{1}$$

with $c_0, c_1, \ldots, c_{L-1} \in \{0, 1\}$. Computations are performed in the two-element field, $\mathbb{F}_2$. This is nothing but an algebraic formulation of a *linear feedback shift register*. Note that the entire sequence is determined by the coefficients $c_0, \ldots c_{L-1}$ and the initial seed $z_0, \ldots, z_{L-1}$. The smallest value of L for which a recurrence such as (1) exists is called the *linear complexity* of the sequence. The polynomial

$$f(X) = c_0 + c_1 X + c_2 X^2 + \cdots + c_{L-1} X^{L-1} + X^L \tag{2}$$

is called the *characteristic polynomial* of the sequence.

The following well-known fact is relevant to this discussion.

Lemma 1. *The characteristic polynomial of a sequence of linear complexity L can be computed from $2L$ consecutive bits of the sequence.*

Further discussion of this issue is postponed until Section 5.1 because it concerns not only the legal owner of the tag, but also an eavesdropper who may wish to inappropriately gain the trust of the tag. In the following subsections we discuss some potential designs.

4.1   The Bare Linear Feedback Shift Register

So far, in the family of finite-state machines we have discussed only the LFSR. The LFSR is a good candidate for our AP protocol, but may not be able to satisfy all foreseeable demands. Take the following example.

Example 2. *Consider a system with the same privacy characteristics as that in Example 2 (10 hours minimum uninterrupted time spent with a reader before pairing, and 5 hours minimum uninterrupted time before any information is leaked). However, assume that the tag is required to respond to interrogations at least once every second (instead of once every minute as in Example 1). The tag's internal LFSR should have length $L = 18000$.*

Such an LFSR is too long for practical purposes. As discussed in Section 6 below, the extremely stringent cost constraints characteristic of RFID technology do not allow the use of LFSRs of total length more than 150 for security purposes. This value is only half the length we used in our Example 1, and less than one hundredth of the length required by Example 2.

However, implementing the generator as a simple LFSR of length (and, for a primitive characteristic polynomial, linear complexity) $L \leq 150$ is almost surely too low for reasonable security.

Take-Away Point 6. *To conclude, our protocol calls for a pseudo-random bit generator with linear complexity L of moderate size (in the order of 10^4), involving registers with cummulated length less than 150. The bit-generation rate and linear complexity should be such that the legitimate owner can collect $2L$ consecutive bits under normal circumstances, while an eavesdropper is unlikely to collect even an L-bit subsequence in each attempt.*

Several methods are available for increasing the linear complexity of a LFSR-based pseudo-random bit generator. In what follows, we discuss three of the most popular ones.

4.2   The Nonlinear Combination Generator

A *nonlinear combination generator* is composed of N LFSR's operating in sync. At each step, each of the shift registers generates a new output bit simultaneously – let these outputs be $x_n^1, x_n^2, \ldots x_n^N$. The output of the generator is obtained by applying a nonlinear combining function f to the outputs of the component LFSR's: $z_n = f(x_n^1, x_n^2, \ldots x_n^N)$

The period of the resulting sequence $\{z_n\}$ will be the least common multiple of the periods of the component generators. If all of the component LFSR's have primitive characteristic polynomials, and if the degrees of those polynomials are pairwise distinct and approximately equal to L_0, then the linear complexity of the output sequence will be in the order of L_0^r, where r is the nonlinear order [11, 6.48] of the function f [11, 6.49].

However, while the bare LFSR was only subject to linear-complexity attacks, the more sophisticated nonlinear combination generators are also the subject of correlation attacks. In fact, their vulnerability against correlation attacks is a direct function of the correlation immunity of f [11, 6.52]. It is also known [11, 6.53] that if the nonlinear function f is m-th order correlation immune, and balanced, then its nonlinear order is bounded as $r \leq N - m - 1$. For a guide to constructing correlation-immune functions of a given order, the reader is refered to [12].

In the remainder of this section, let us consider that such a nonlinear m-th order correlation immune function f, of nonlinear order $N-m-1$ is readily available. The linear complexity L of the nonlinear combination generator employing f is $O(L_0^{N-(m+1)})$, the total register length is NL_0, and the complexity of a correlation attack is $O(2^{2L_0(m+1)})$ [11]. We consider that resistance to correlation attacks of order less than 2^{128} is adequate for our application.

Example 3. *Imposing our design constraints, we get $NL_0 < 150$ and $2L_0(m+1) > 128$, which result in $N < 150/L_0$, and $(m+1) > 64/L_0$. The linear complexity is thus $L < L_0^{86/L_0}$. To accomodate the requirements from Example 2, we can set $L_0 = 30$, yielding a linear complexity $L \simeq 17000$, and requiring a number of $N = 5$ registers (of length L_0 each), and a first-order correlation immune function f of nonlinear order $m = 3$.*

It is worth noting that the function $L(x) = x^{a/x}$ with $x > 0$ has first-order derivative

$$\frac{dL(x)}{dx} = x^{a/x} \frac{a}{x^2} \left(1 - \ln(x)\right),\tag{3}$$

which implies the existence of a single (global) maximum at $x = e$ (Euler's number). Hence, for discrete $x = L_0$, the maximum is always at $L_0 = 3$, and roughly equal to $e^{a/e}$. Since in our scenario $a = (N - m - 1)L_0$, it is possible that for certain design constraints (small total register length or high complexity of the correlation attack), the desired linear complexity is not achievable. Also, when the desired linear complexity is achievable, there will generally be two possible choices for L_0. For implementation purposes, the value larger than 3 should be desirable.

4.3   The Nonlinear Filter Generator

A *nonlinear filter generator* consists of an LFSR of length L_0 and a nonlinear filtering function F of nonlinear order r. Starting from an initial seed (or state) $x_0, x_1, \ldots, x_{L_0-1}$, the LFSR determines additional bits according to the recurrence relation

$$x_{n+k} = c_0 x_n + c_1 x_{n+1} + \cdots + c_{L_0-1} x_{n+L_0-1}.$$

The output of the generator is the sequence $z_0, z_1, \ldots$ determined by the rule $z_n = F(x_n, x_{n+1}, \ldots, x_{n+L_0-1})$.

The period of the output sequence is the same as that of the LFSR, which can be set at $2^{L_0} - 1$ by choosing the characteristic polynomial of the LFSR to be primitive. The linear complexity of the output sequence can be bounded as [13]:

$$\binom{L_0}{2} \leq L \leq \sum_{j=1}^{r} \binom{L_0}{j},\tag{4}$$

where r denotes the degree of the polynomial F (i.e. F's nonlinear order).

The nonlinear filter generator is subject to multiple types of attacks, in addition to the linear-complexity attack. In what follows, we discuss these attacks and show that none of them is a serious concern for our application. The inversion attacks of [14,15] rely on the public knowledge of the component LFSR structure and of the nonlinear filtering function (which in our AP protocol are the secrets of the tag), and can be foiled anyway by selecting a proper generator design. Another class of attacks, which also require complete knowledge of both the characteristic polynomial of the LFSR and the filtering function, are the *algebraic attacks* of [16].

Several types of correlation attacks have been investigated (see [12] for a literature review), but they all assume publicly-known LFSR connection polynomials.

It is interesting to note that some attacks, which assume that the nonlinear function is also secret, will first attempt to find an equivalent nonlinear combination generator [12,17].

For our application, the fact that the nonlinear filter generator uses a single LFSR has a certain advantage over the other multiple-LFSR pseudorandom bit generators like the nonlinear combination generator discussed in Section 4.2. To see this, note that the divide-and-conquer correlation attacks devised for the nonlinear combination generator will brute-force the initial state of one LFSR at a time. Hence, they can be easily adapted to deal with unknown LFSR characteristic polynomials by brute-forcing these polynomials, along with the initial states, one LFSR at a time. However, the single LFSR in the nonlinear filter generator can be designed with a register length of roughly $L_0 = 150$ (if we neglect the resources required for the implementation of the nonlinear function). Note that this value of L_0 guarantees a linear complexity at least in the order of 10^4, which is what was required in Example 2. However, adapting the existing attacks to an unknown characteristic polynomial is no longer practical – brute-forcing the single, longer LFSR would increase the complexity of the attack by $O(2^{150})$.

4.4   The Shrinking Generator

A *shrinking generator* [18] consists of two registers of lengths L_A (for the *A-sequence*, or the output-generating sequence) and L_S (for the *S-sequence*, or the controlling sequence), controlled by the same clock. The generator only produces an output bit at time n if the n-th bit of the control sequence is 1. In this case, the output of the generator coincides with the n-th bit of the output-generating sequence. However, if the n-th bit of the control sequence is 0, the generator does not output anything. The linear complexity L of a shrinking generator defined as above was bounded in [18] as $L_A 2^{L_S-2} \leq L \leq L_A 2^{L_S-1}$.

A variant of the shrinking generator, the "self-shrinking generator", consists of a single LFSR. The odd bits of the LFSR's output function as the *A-sequence*, while the even bits work as the *S-sequence*. The linear complexity of the self-shrinking generator with a register of length L_{SS} was shown in [19] to be bounded as $2^{\lfloor L_{SS}/2 \rfloor - 1} \leq L \leq 2^{L_{SS}-1} - (L_{SS} - 2)$.

Looking back to Example 2, a linear complexity of $L = 18000$ could be achieved by a self-shrinking generator of length only $L_{SS} = 32$, or by a shrinking generator with two registers of length $L_S = L_A = 13$.

However, it turns out that the easily-achievable high linear complexity of the shrinking generator and its variants comes at a cost. It was shown in [18] that the shrinking generator (with secret connection polynomials) is subject to a correlation attack that requires only $2L_A L_S$ contiguous bits and time at most $O(2^{2L_S} L_S L_A^2)$ [18]. If we recall that $L \geq L_A 2^{L_S-2}$, we see that in order to achieve a reasonably high computational complexity (which would render the protocol secure from an attacker)—a complexity in the order of 2^{128} would be acceptable—we need to increase the linear complexity to values much larger than our AP protocol can deal with. Recall that our protocol relies on the legitimate user to mount a successful linear-complexity attack.

Example 4. *Take $L_A = L_S = L_0$. Our design constraints can be written as $2L_0 < 150$ and $2^{2L_0}L_0^3 > 2^{128}$. The latter one implies $L_0 > 56$, which requires a total register length of $2L_0 > 112$ (this would satisfy the first constraint), but yields a linear complexity $L > L_0 2^{L_0-2} \simeq 10^{18}$. For a legitimate reader to mount a successful linear-complexity attack within 10 hours of uninterrupted time, it would need to querry the tag more than 10^{13} times per second. Note that the highest frequency band allowed for RFID applications is around $10GHz$ (UHF-RFID)[1], and hence RFID applications cannot accommodate a "baseband" signal with a bandwidth of $10GHz$.*

Take-Away Point 7. *To conclude this section, we have seen that our AP protocol can be implemented at very low cost, by using a nonlinear filter generator, or a nonlinear combination generator. While a bare LFSR could be adequate for certain low-security-risk applications (like RFID tags attached to groceries) where a small linear complexity can be tolerated, the shrinking generator increases the linear complexity more than most applications can handle (it could take years of uninterrupted UHF communication for a reader to mount a successful linear-complexity attack against a correlation-immune shrinking generator).*

5 Security Analysis

Based on the discussion in Section 4, we can state that the AP protocol implemented with properly-designed nonlinear combination generators, or nonlinear filter generators, is immune to correlation attacks. Hence, it seems that the best technique for an attacker to gain control of the tag is to follow the same process as a legitimate reader: to query the tag and collect a number of bits large enough to enable a linear-complexity attack. In this section we consider this attack from the malicious user's perspective, and show that it is not feasible under normal conditions. In addition, we discuss whether or not the attacker could extract more information from the knowledge of the tag owner's daily routine.

5.1 Linear-Complexity-Based Attacks

Suppose that a reader obtains a sequence of contiguous bits $z_0, z_1, z_2, \ldots$ created according to the recurrence (1) and wishes to determine the coefficients $c_0, c_1, \ldots, c_{L-1}$. The sequence of bits satisfies the following system of linear equations:

$$c_0 z_0 + c_1 z_1 + \cdots + c_{L-1} z_{L-1} = z_L$$
$$c_0 z_1 + c_1 z_2 + \cdots + c_{L-1} z_L = z_{L+1}$$
$$c_0 z_2 + c_1 z_3 + \cdots + c_{L-1} z_{L+1} = z_{L+2} \tag{5}$$
$$\vdots$$
$$c_0 z_{L-1} + c_1 z_L + \cdots + c_{L-1} z_{2L-2} = z_{2L-1},$$

in the unknowns $c_0, \ldots, c_{L-1}$. Such a system is easily solved for moderately-large linear complexities L. For example, using ordinary Gaussian elimination, the system is solvable in time $O(L^3)$. This observation constitutes a proof of Lemma 1.

Note that in the previous paragraph, the linear complexity of the generator is assumed known in advance. Nevertheless, even if the linear complexity is unknown, one could simply try every possible linear complexity, starting from 1. Using Gaussian elimination, the solution (and the linear complexity) would be found in time at most

$$O(1^3) + O(2^3) + \cdots + O(L^3) \leq L \cdot O(L^3) = O(L^4).$$

For very large linear complexities L, a reader could implement the Berlekamp-Massey algorithm [9] which, for every new received bit, computes the smallest-size LFSR that could have generated the currently-available sequence of bits. Moreover, the Berlekamp-Massey algorithm does not require that the linear complexity be known in advance.

However, to formulate and solve the system in (5), we implicitly made the following two assumptions: (A) $2L$ bits of the sequence are known, and (B) the known bits are consecutive. The first assumption is essential. It is not hard to find two distinct sets of coefficients which generate sequences that coincide on $2L - 1$ consecutive bits. We emphasize that in this discussion we are treating the sequence $z_0, z_1, \ldots$ as being generated by a black box.

Now we turn to the second assumption: the consecutiveness of the known bits. Suppose that instead of consecutive bits, we have obtained $2L$ bits, with k unknown bits interspersed among them. We wish to address the complexity of determining the unknown coefficients $c_0, \ldots, c_{L-1}$ in this scenario. By treating each missing bit as an additional unknown, one can still set up a system of equations as in (5), but now there will be $L + k$ equations in $L + k$ unknowns. However, the system is no longer linear: it becomes quadratic. This is because if z_j is an unknown representing a missing bit, then the system will contain quadratic terms of the form $c_i z_j$, for $i = 0, \ldots, L - 1$. In fact, of the $(L + k)^2$ terms in the system, approximately Lk of them will be quadratic.

Unlike the situation for linear systems, there is no known efficient method of solving a quadratic system over a finite field. The problem of finding one solution to a quadratic system over our field $\mathbb{F}_2$ is NP-complete [20], and known in the literature as the "MQ problem." Note that NP-completeness is a worst-case analysis, and it is entirely possible that the system that would arise in this particular application has a polynomial-time solution. However, none of the algorithms with which we are familiar seem to apply here. In particular, algorithms such as XSL [21] are not appropriate since the system is not sparse. Furthermore, the quadratic system may not have a unique solution. It may require additional equations (and therefore, additional known bits) to obtain uniqueness.

Of course, one could always find the solution through exhaustive search. Note that for each of the 2^k choices for the unknown z-bits, we are reduced to a linear system (in the unknown c_i's) that we can solve by Gaussian elimination or by the Berlekamp-Massey algorithm. Alternatively, we can try each of the 2^L

choices for the c_i's and solve the resulting linear system for the unknown bits. The running time for this approach is therefore $O(2^{\min(L,k)})$.

While this running time ensures that an exhaustive-search attack is not feasible for the man on the bus, the exhaustive-search method may be a good solution for approaching small desynchronizations between the tag and the legitimate reader (as stated in Section 3 above, such desynchronizations can appear as a result of the user taking the tag outside for a small time interval, or of temporary interference, such as a cell phone positioned close to the tag). If, for example, the tag responds to each query with a newly-generated bit, accompanied by the previous three or four bits, the reader can easily (and with good probability) identify such desynchronizations, and, as soon as it has collected enough information, proceed with an exhaustive search for the missing bits.

Take-Away Point 8. *The considerations above show that, for a legitimate reader that should have access to a large number of contiguous bits, with small interruptions, finding the secret key should be feasible, by employing a simple exhaustive-search over the missing bits, and solving the system in (5). However, if the interruptions are large and the sequences of contiguous bits small (the case of the "man on the bus"), the secret key is very likely to remain secret.*

5.2   Predictable Environments and Tag Tracking

We have already specified that our protocol will function in a *ubiquitous RFID environment*. This assumption is not at all restrictive: it is meant to create a challenging environment for the legitimate user, rather than hinder the attacker. Whether the assumption holds true or not, the tag is being interrogated numerous times throughout the day, either by various non-authenticated readers, or by the legitimate reader alone. Therefore, it is safe to assert that the number of bits produced by the tag's internal LFSR between two attacker sessions is unknown and unpredictable.

However, let us suppose that the number of bits produced by the tag's LFSR between any two attack sessions is roughly the same (a daily routine, along with a very punctual attacker might enable this scenario). A natural question is whether the attacker can synchronize his encounters with the tag owner in such a manner that would grant him access to consecutive short spans of the tag's output. For example, the attacker might be able to obtain S bits of the tag's output at each encounter. If the attacker synchronizes the encounters such that the tag has generated exactly $T+S$ bits between two encounters, where T is the period of the pseudo-random sequence generated by the tag's secret FSM, the bits obtained in two consecutive encounters would be consecutive. Even if the actual number of bits generated between two encounters a random variable R with mean $T+S$ and very small variance, the attacker can assume that $R=T+S$, and attempt to correct for the error in this assumption by using an exhaustive-search method of the type described in the previous section. We shall call this strategy a *"predictable-environment attack"*.

However, due to the fact that even small-linear-complexity FSMs display very large periods of the output sequence (for linear complexity L, if the characteristic polynomial of the equivalent LFSR is primitive, the period is $T = 2^L - 1$), it is safe to assume that all the sequences of S bits that an attacker might be able to gather in his lifetime belong to the same LFSR period.

Take-Away Point 9. *Consequently, any "predictable-environment attack" is reduced to the intractable large-desynchronization problem of Section 5.1.*

Another problem which may arise in a predictable environment is *tag tracking*. Consider a scenario where the attacker acts as the man on the bus for a while (possibly multiple encounters), and then wants to use the information gathered about the targeted tag to verify the presence of its owner in a certain spot, at a certain time. For example, gaining access to the RFID readers in a bar, the man on the bus wants to find out whether the victim was present there last night. The problem is quite complex, and is beyond the scope of this paper. However, for completeness, in the remainder of this subsection, we briefly discuss a worst-case type of scenario.

Assume that the attacker has gained access to S_1 consecutive bits (highly unlikely) of the targeted tag's output on the bus, and collects another S_2 consecutive bits from the bar's RFID reader. Let us also assume that the attacker knows that, if the S_2 bits were produced by the targeted tag, then there would be exactly r unknown bits between the bus encounter and the moment the bar RFID reader began gathering bits from the tag (that is, the tag was interrogated r times by other, unknown readers). It is clear that if $S_1 + S_2 < 2L$, the attacker can make no inference about whether the S_2 bits were produced by the targeted tag. This is due to the fact that the attacker's best strategy is to compute a system of $S_1 + S_2 + r - L$ (quadratic) equations with $L + r > S_1 + S_2 + r - L$ unknowns, as explained in Section 5.1 above. Such a system would likely admit an infinity of solutions. On the other hand, if $S_1 + S_2 \geq 2L$, the attacker can compute a system of more than $L + r$ equations, with $L + r$ unknowns. If the system has no solution, the attacker can infer that the S_2 bits obtained from the bar were not produced by the targeted tag. However, a more involved probabilistic analysis is required if the system does admit a solution. For example, if $S_1 = 1$, the fact that the system has a solution does not provide much certainty about the presence of the targeted tag in the bar. Neither does the case when S_2 is small. On the opposite end, if $S_1 \geq 2L$ and $S_2 \geq 2L$, then the attacker can verify the presence of the targeted tag in the bar with absolute certainty. Such an analysis is beyond the scope of this paper.

Nevertheless, for practical situations, the worst case scenario would still have the attacker check whether a system of $S_1 + S_2 + r - L$ quadratic equations with $L + r$ unknowns has a solution. This problem is as hard as finding the solution, and would normally prevent the attacker from attaining his goal, as discussed in Section 5.1 above.

6   RFID Hardware Constraints

In Section 4.1 we have already mentioned that we can only afford to implement the AP protocol using LFSRs of cummulated length less than 150. To see why, we outline the design limitations imposed by the passive RFID architecture. It seems to be generally accepted that a reasonable resource expense for security should not exceed 2000 transistors for a passive RFID tag. Since most pseudo-random bit generators are based on linear feedback shift registers, let us consider the implementation of an LFSR on such a tag. Each cell in an LFSR is a latch with 8 transistors (2 NAND or 2 NOR gates), and each binary addition is an XOR gate with 5 transistors. This brings the total number of transistors used by an LFSR of length L_0 to roughly $13L_0$. Based on our ceiling of 2000 transistors, this limits the number of cells to 150.

Moreover, if the AP protocol implementation dictates the use of a nonlinear function for combining the outputs of several LFSRs (or filter the state of a single LFSR), the design should consider registers of total length even less than 150, to allow for the implementation of the function.

7   Concluding Remarks

We have introduced a novel pairing protocol, ideally suited for low-cost, passive RFID devices. Our protocol is entirely automatic, and based on the two pairing devices spending large periods of uninterrupted time in the proximity of each other. Successful pairing is based on the legitimate reader mounting a liner-complexity attack on the tag's internal pseudo-random number generator (PRNG), where the tag's secret key is the internal structure of the PRNG (or more precisely, the characteristic polynomial of the equivalent LFSR). The algorithm design prevents an unauthorized user from learning the tag's secret, and hence from pairing with the tag. This level of security is ensured by the fact that any unauthorized user should not be able to spend an uninterrupted period of time larger than several hours a day in the company of the tag.

The examples provided throughout the paper show that practical implementation of the tag's PRNG should consider either nonlinear combination generators or nonlinear filter generators. We have shown that, while simple LFSRs may be considered for certain applications, more powerful linear-complexity-enhancing designs, like the shrinking generators, could render the linear-complexity attacks (on which the legitimate user relies) unfeasible.

The Adopted Pet protocol is a first step towards a paradigm where authentication and security is based on the legitimate parties mounting successful attacks on each-other's cryptographic protocols, and where the work of anonymous attackers and hackers can serve as the basis for faster authentication and legitimate decryption.

Acknowledgements. This work was partially supported by NSF under grants No. CNS-0644238, CNS-0831470, and DUE-0911708. We appreciate Adi Shamir, Ari Juels, Kevin Fu, and anonymous reviewers for their valuable suggestions and comments made at the workshop and in the paper reviews.

References

1. Dobkin, D.M.: The RF in RFID: passive UHF RFID in Practice. Elsevier Inc. (2008)

2. Stajano, F., Anderson, R.: The resurrecting duckling: security issues for ad-hoc wireless networks. In: AT&T Software Symposium (1999)
3. Mayrhofer, R., Gellersen, H.: Shake Well Before Use: Authentication Based on Accelerometer Data. In: LaMarca, A., Langheinrich, M., Truong, K.N. (eds.) Pervasive 2007. LNCS, vol. 4480, pp. 144–161. Springer, Heidelberg (2007)
4. Oshiba, T., Nebayashi, H.: Device pairing based on adaptive channel fluctuation control for large-scale organizations. In: IEEE Symposium on Computers and Communications, ISCC 2009, pp. 901–906 (2009)
5. Soriente, C., Tsudik, G., Uzun, E.: BEDA: button-enabled device association. In: International Workshop on Security for Spontaneous Interaction, IWSSI 2007 (2007)
6. Luo, S., Xia, H., Gao, Y., Jin, J., Athauda, R.: Smart fridges with multimedia capability for better nutrition and health. In: International Symposium on Ubiquitous Multimedia Computing, UMC 2008, pp. 39–44 (2008)
7. Gu, H., Wang, D.: A content-aware fridge based on RFID in smart home for home-healthcare. In: 11th International Conference on Advanced Communication Technology, ICACT 2009, vol. 2, pp. 987–990 (2009)
8. Hopper, N.J., Blum, M.: Secure human identification protocols. In: Boyd, C. (ed.) ASIACRYPT 2001. LNCS, vol. 2248, pp. 52–66. Springer, Heidelberg (2001)
9. Massey, J.L.: Shift-register synthesis and BCH decoding. IEEE Trans. Information Theory 15, 122–127 (1969)
10. Juels, A.: Minimalist Cryptography for Low-Cost RFID Tags (Extended abstract). In: Blundo, C., Cimato, S. (eds.) SCN 2004. LNCS, vol. 3352, pp. 149–164. Springer, Heidelberg (2005)
11. Menezes, A., van Oorschot, P., Vanstone, S.: Handbook of Applied Cryptography. CRC Press (1996)
12. Cusick, T.V., Stanica, P.: Cryptographic Boolean Functions and Applications. Elsevier Inc. (2009)
13. Lhlein, B.: Attacks based on conditional correlations against the nonlinear filter generator. In: Cryptology ePrint Archive, Report 2003/020 (2003)
14. Golic, J.D., Clark, A., Dawson, E.: Generalized inversion attack on nonlinear filter generators. IEEE Trans. Computers 49, 1100–1109 (2000)
15. Golic, D.: On the security of nonlinear filter generators. In: Proc. Fast Software Encryption – Cambridge 1996, pp. 173–188 (1996)
16. Courtois, N.T., Meier, W.: Algebraic Attacks on Stream Ciphers with Linear Feedback. In: Biham, E. (ed.) EUROCRYPT 2003. LNCS, vol. 2656, pp. 345–359. Springer, Heidelberg (2003)
17. Siegenthaler, T.: Cryptanalysts Representation of Nonlinearly Filtered ML-Sequences. In: Pichler, F. (ed.) EUROCRYPT 1985. LNCS, vol. 219, pp. 103–110. Springer, Heidelberg (1986)
18. Coppersmith, D., Krawczyk, H., Mansour, Y.: The Shrinking Generator. In: Stinson, D.R. (ed.) CRYPTO 1993. LNCS, vol. 773, pp. 22–39. Springer, Heidelberg (1994)
19. Blackburn, S.R.: The complexity of the self-shrinking generator. IEEE Transactions on Information Theory 45, 2073–2077 (1999)
20. Fraenkel, A.S., Yesha, Y.: Complexity of problems in games, graphs and algebraic equations. Discrete Applied Mathematics 1, 15–30 (1979)
21. Courtois, N.T., Pieprzyk, J.: Cryptanalysis of Block Ciphers with Overdefined Systems of Equations. In: Zheng, Y. (ed.) ASIACRYPT 2002. LNCS, vol. 2501, pp. 267–287. Springer, Heidelberg (2002), Updated version: http://eprint.iacr.org/2002/044

BUPLE: Securing Passive RFID Communication through Physical Layer Enhancements

Qi Chai and Guang Gong

Department of Electrical and Computer Engineering
University of Waterloo
Waterloo, Ontario, N2L 3G1, Canada
{q3chai,ggong}@uwaterloo.ca

Abstract. Although RFID systems offer many noteworthy characteristics, security and privacy issues associated with them are not easy
to address. In this paper, we investigate how to solve the eavesdropping, modification and one particular type of relay attacks toward the
tag-to-reader communication in passive RFID systems without requiring lightweight ciphers or secret credentials shared by legitimate parties using a physical layer approach. To this end, we propose a novel
physical layer scheme, called *Backscatter modulation- and Uncoordinated
frequency hopping-assisted Physical Layer Enhancement* (BUPLE). The
idea behind it is to use the amplitude of the carrier to transmit messages as normal, while to utilize its periodically varied frequency to hide
the transmission from the eavesdropper/relayer and to exploit a random
sequence modulated to the carrier's phase to defeat malicious modifications. We further improve its eavesdropping resistance through the coding in the physical layer as BUPLE ensures that the tag-to-eavesdropper
channel is strictly noisier than the tag-to-reader channel. Three practical
Wiretap Channel Codes (WCCs) for passive tags are then proposed: two
of them are constructed from linear error correcting codes, and the other
one is constructed, for the first time to the best of our knowledge, from
resilient vector Boolean functions. The security and usability of BUPLE
in conjunction with WCCs are further confirmed by our proof of concept
implementation and testing on the software defined radio platform with
a programmable WISP tag.

Keywords: RFID security, eavesdropping, backscatter, frequency hopping, wiretap channel.

1 Introduction

Radio Frequency Identification (RFID), which allows remote identification of objects automatically, is one of the most promising technologies to enable ubiquitous computing and Internet of Things (IoT). The modest computation/storage
capabilities of passive or battery-free tags and the necessity to keep their prices
low constitute a challenging problem that goes beyond the well-studied problems

A. Juels and C. Paar (Eds.): RFIDSec 2011, LNCS 7055, pp. 127–146, 2012.

of modern cryptography. Typical risks are (1) the reader-tag communication via a radio channel is susceptible to *eavesdropping, modification* and *relay*, which are the concerns in this paper; (2) each RFID tag has a unique or fixed identity, which, once it has been captured by a malicious reader, leaks the geometric location of the tag, and invades the privacy of the tag holder; moreover, (3) the lack of tamper-resistant memory makes fabricating or counterfeiting a tag effortless.

To mitigate attacks in (1), this work presents a marked departure from the existing paradigm such as *lightweight cryptography* [8,2,19,14] – we focus on defeating eavesdropping, modification and one particular type of relay attacks toward the tag-to-reader communication in passive RFID systems without requiring on-tag ciphers or secret credentials to be shared by legitimate parties. Our solution exploits the physical layer resources of passive RFID systems, i.e., backscatter modulation, uncoordinated frequency hopping and the coding for the wiretap channel, exhibiting a promising way to provide security functions while keeping the hardware cost of the reader and the tag almost unchanged, as expected in many RFID applications.

1.1   Problem Statement and Security Model

Assuming that a powerful RFID reader shares a common RF channel with a passive tag which is computation and storage-constrained, no secrets or authentication materials are shared by these two entities. We address the following problem: *how could confidentiality, authenticity and integrity of the tag-to-reader communication be preserved in the presence of a budget-limited adversary A?* Here, by "confidentiality", we mean that given an eavesdropped version of the raw signal, to A, the entropy of the message from the tag does not decrease. By "authenticity", we mean that the reader should be clear who the sender of the message is. By "integrity", we mean that malicious modifications to the message can be detected by the reader. By "budget-limited", we mean that A's RF devices are effective in a narrow frequency band.

We assume that the two communicating entities are legitimate and are not compromised; otherwise, little can be done from the physical layer (issues caused by a malicious reader or an impersonated tag are beyond the scope of this paper). We adopt a Dolev-Yao-alike model that A controls the communication which allows him to conduct the following actions:

- **Eavesdropping:** A intercepts tag-to-reader signals, demodulates and decodes to get communicated messages.
- **Modification:** A either adds to the channel a signal, which converts bit "0" into "1" (called *bit flipping* [7]), or adds to the channel a signal representing a bit string different from the one sent by the tag with a significantly higher power than that of the original signal (called *signal overshadowing* [7]). However, A is unable to eliminate energy from any channel.
- **Relay:** A places an active radio device in between a valid reader and a victim tag, e.g., [11], which generates new signals in a narrow frequency band to

answer the valid reader according to the format of backscatter modulation after querying the victim tag.[1]

1.2   Our Contributions

To thwart the aforementioned threats, we present the following contributions:

1. We propose a novel physical layer scheme, called *Backscatter modulation-and Uncoordinated frequency hopping-assisted Physical Layer Enhancement* (BUPLE), for passive RF communication. The idea is to use the amplitude of the carrier wave to transmit messages as normal, while to utilize its periodically varied frequency to hide the transmission from the eavesdropper/relayer and to exploit a random sequence modulated to the carrier's phase to defeat malicious modifications. Our rigorous security analysis shows that BUPLE achieves desired security goals without affecting the cost of the reader and the passive tag.
2. BUPLE ensures that $\mathcal{A}$ receives a noisier signal than that of the valid reader, which presents a potential opportunity to further improve its eavesdropping resistance through the coding in the physical layer. Three Wiretap Channel Codes (WCCs) with practical parameters for passive tags and with trade-offs in the *information rate* (the proportion of the data-stream that is non-redundant), the *equivocation rate* (the degree to which the eavesdropper is confused) and the cost of implementation, are given – two of them are constructed from linear error correcting codes, and the other one is constructed, for the first time to the best of our knowledge, from resilient vector Boolean functions.
3. BUPLE and the proposed WCCs are implemented on the software defined radio platform (served as an RFID reader) and a programmable WISP tag. Results from our experimental data well support our theoretic hypothesis and security analysis. Additionally, performance comparison of the proposed WCC encoders with four lightweight ciphers from literature suggests that WCCs consume much less resource and have much higher throughput.

1.3   Related Work

There are a very few physical layer schemes targeting communication confidentiality and integrity in the context of RFID. To construct an unidirectional covert channel from the tag to the reader, cooperative-jamming methods are introduced in [16,5] for the key distribution. However, bitwise synchronization and required pre-shared secrets between the reader and the friendly jammer may be problematic in real-world applications. Moreover, Savry *et al.* in [25] designed a noisy reader by exploiting the fact that a passive tag modulates a noisy

---

[1] There exists another type of relay, for which a malicious passive tag wired with a malicious reader is placed in between the valid reader and the victim tag to relay the communication. Technically, this attack is one kind of tag impersonation, which violates our assumptions made to physical layer schemes thus is not considered here.

carrier generated by a reader during its reply. Nevertheless, the noisy carrier could cause severe disruption of all nearby RFID systems. To enable message integrity protection in general wireless communication, [7] presents variants of the Manchester code which make the communication immune to bit flipping and signal overshadowing attacks. By leveraging the physical characteristic that "nothing travels faster than light", the family of distance bounding protocols, e.g., [13,18,1,29], provides a potential way to solve the relay attack. However, besides the security vulnerabilities discovered in [18,1], this special-purpose protocol introduces additional communication overhead, and, the authenticity and integrity of the exchanged messages are ensured by symmetric cryptographic primitives.

1.4 Organization

In Section 2, we introduce basic concepts and definitions. In Section 3, we present BUPLE and its security analysis. In Section 4, we give our constructions of the wiretap channel codes for passive tags. A prototype implementation and experimental results are shown in Section 5, including a performance comparison with some lightweight ciphers. We conclude the paper in Section 6.

2 Preliminaries

In this section, we briefly introduce gradients for our scheme: the backscatter modulation, uncoordinated frequency hopping and Wyner's wiretap channel.

2.1 Backscattering for Passive RF Communication

Radar principles tell us that the amount of energy reflected by an object is proportional to the reflective area of the object. A passive RFID system is principally a radar system in which the reader provides an RF signal for communication in both directions, i.e., from the reader to the tag and the tag to the reader. To be specific, we consider a passive tag composed of an antenna with impedance Z_a and a load with impedance Z_l. The impedance is often a complex quantity, where the real part is the resistance (i.e., R_a, R_l), and the imaginary part is the reactance (i.e., X_a, X_l). According to the *maximum power theorem* in RLC circuit theory [15], if the antenna's impedance is matched to that of the load (i.e., $R_a = R_l$), no reflection occurs at the interface. On the contrary, if the load is shorted, total reflection occurs and the power is re-radiated by the antenna. Thus by switching between the two states, a backscattered signal is in fact modulated by the Amplitude Shift Keying (ASK).

2.2 Availability of Uncoordinated Frequency Hopping in Passive RFID Systems

Frequency Hopping (FH) communication [26], in which the carrier frequency of a transmitted signal constantly changes according to a pre-shared pseudorandom sequence, was developed to defeat unintended listeners. *Uncoordinated Frequency Hopping* (UFH) indicates that two entities establish FH communication without sharing any secret. Strasser *et. al.* in [23] considered applying UFH for fighting against a hostile jammer and proposed a hash-chain based pre-authentication scheme. However, implementing this probabilistic scheme is challenging, because: (1) the sender and receiver have less chance to "meet" in a particular channel at a certain time especially when the hopping set is large; (2) synchronization of the sender and the receiver is non-trivial when the hop rate is high, e.g., synchronization signals are vulnerable to jamming.

Nevertheless, we observed that UFH can be practically realized in passive RFID systems due to the following property: the reader changes the carrier frequency, while the tag only has to modulate responses on the carrier and reflect it without concerning which carrier frequency it uses. The reader is then able to center at the right frequency to capture the backscattered signal. Besides, the imperfect time synchronization, which is the main issue in a FH system, can be trivially solved, since the returned signal from the tag is strictly Δt second later than the emitted signal, where Δt is the sum of the tag's processing time and the signal's propagation delay in a small distance (< 20m). Finally, FH mechanism is standardized in EPCglobal UHF Class-1 Gen-2 [9] (EPC C1G2) as an optional strategy to eliminate interference in dense reader scenarios and implemented in commercial products. In the light of UFH, our scheme brings confidentiality, authenticity and integrity to the tag-to-reader communication for free. Note that although employing FH to avoid session hijacking was briefly mentioned in [34], the problem that FH signals are usually unable to power up passive tags is not considered, which is addressed in Section 3 of this paper.

2.3   Wiretap Channel

The wiretap channel model, as shown in Figure 1, is introduced by Wyner [33] and extended in [20,6]. In this model, when the main channel is better than the wiretap channel, i.e., $p_0 < p_w$, where p_0 and p_w are the error probabilities of the main channel and the wiretap channel respectively, it is possible through a particular coding to establish an (almost) perfectly secure source-destination link without relying on any pre-shared keys.

As shown in Figure 1, to send an m-bit message $\mathbf{s} = (s_1, ..., s_m) \in \mathbb{F}_2^m$, the sender first encodes it into an n-bit codeword $\mathbf{x}$, which is then propagated through the main channel and wiretap channel simultaneously. The legitimate receiver, e.g., RFID reader, received a corrupted version $\mathbf{y} \in \mathbb{F}_2^n$ of $\mathbf{x}$ while the eavesdropper receives an even more strongly corrupted binary stream $\mathbf{z} \in \mathbb{F}_2^n$. After decoding, all information of $\mathbf{s}$ is expected to be leant by the legitimate receiver at a code rate as high as possible, while no information about $\mathbf{s}$ is leaked to the eavesdropper. Stated in another way, a wiretap channel has an *achievable secrecy* (R, L), $0 \leq R, L \leq 1$, if there is an encoder-decoder pair such that for any $\eta > 0$ the following is true:

$$\frac{1}{m}\mathrm{Prob}[\mathbf{s} \neq \mathbf{s}''] \leq \eta, \quad \frac{m}{n} \geq R - \eta, \quad \Delta = \frac{H(\mathbf{s}|\mathbf{z})}{m} \geq L - \eta \tag{1}$$

where Δ is the equivocation rate and $H(\mathbf{s}|\mathbf{z})$ is the conditional entropy of $\mathbf{s}$ given $\mathbf{z}$. Wyner exhibited the set of achievable (R, L) pairs always forms a region $\{(R, L) : 0 \leq R, L \leq 1, R \times L \leq h(p_w) - h(p_o)\}$, where $h(p) = -p \log_2 p - (1 - p) \log_2(1 - p)$ is called the *binary entropy function* of p, and, $h(p_w) - h(p_o)$ is the *secrecy capacity* meaning the maximum rate of a code under which perfect secrecy can be achieved.

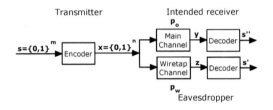

Fig. 1. Wiretap Channel Model [33,6]

Although this model offers a potential opportunity to achieve Shannon's perfect secrecy (i.e., $\Delta = 1$) without a pre-shared key, two strong assumptions make it less appealing to practitioners: (1) two channels are distinct and the main channel is apparently better. This is difficult to realize in reality; (2) given p_o and p_w, there must exist a code satisfying Eq. (1) (we call such a code *Wiretap Channel Code* or (n, m)-WCC hereafter). Note that general constructions of WCCs (especially those with satisfactory information rate, equivocation rate and finite codeword length) remain an open problem [28].

As shown in Section 3 and 4, our work firstly closes the gap between this theoretic model and practice as: (1) UFH is exploited to significantly degrade the tag-to-eavesdropper channel by increasing p_w; and (2) three WCCs with small codeword length, targeting practical security, are given which can be implemented in tags with modest computation/storage capability.

3   BUPLE and Its Security

For the rest of the paper, we keep the following notations.

- $\{f_1, ..., f_M\}$ represents a *hop set* with M possible frequencies and $W = \max(\{f_1, ..., f_M\}) - \min(\{f_1, ..., f_M\})$ is the *hopping band*.
- In one hop, t_h is the signal duration, called *hop duration*, (we ignore the transient *switching time* in this paper for simplicity) and W_h is the bandwidth for each frequency channel.
- v_T is the tag's data rate, while v, $v \gg v_T$, is the rate of a random binary sequence generated by the reader, and v_{cmd} is the data rate of reader's commands.
- τ_0 is the power-up time in second for a tag.

3.1 BUPLE Scheme

The BUPLE scheme works as follows:

1. During the time interval $[it_h, (i+1)t_h)$, $i = 1, ..., n$, the reader emits a carrier wave CW_i modulated by Minimum Shift Keying (MSK)[2], i.e., $CW_i = \sqrt{2E_b v_T} \cos\left(2\pi f_i t + b_{i,j} \frac{\pi v t}{2}\right)$, where $f_i \in \{f_1, ..., f_M\}$ is randomly selected by the reader, $\sqrt{2E_b v_T}$ is a positive constant indicating the carrier's amplitude, and $b_{i,j} \in \{+1, -1\}$, $j = 1, ..., \lfloor t_h v \rfloor$, is randomly selected by the reader at the rate v.
2. On this MSK-modulated carrier, the reader further ASK-modulates its commands at rate v_{cmd} if necessary, e.g., QUERY as specified in EPC C1G2.
3. Once the tag powers up, it starts to ASK-demodulate the double-modulated carrier to get the commands issued by the reader if there is any. The tag next computes a K-bit response $(r_1, ..., r_K)$ and backscatters "10" if $r_j = 1$ and "01" otherwise, at rate v_T, for $j = 1, .., K$.
4. The reader, with the receiver centered at f_i, receives the backscattered signal, which is denoted as $\widehat{CW}_i$. By amplitude-demodulation of $\widehat{CW}_i$ and further decoding "10" ("01" resp.) to "1" ("0" resp.), r_j is transmitted.
5. Above steps are repeated until the completion of the communication.

To exemplify our scheme, we present a toy instance in Figure 2 with $\tau_0 = 2/v$, $v = 3v_T$ and $v = 4v_{cmd}$, during the i-th time slot. As shown, a random sequence "10101111...1101" is MSK-modulated to the the carrier wave centered at f_i. Next, the reader's command "101" is ASK-modulated on the carrier wave (thus on the random sequence). After receiving the signal from the reader, the tag takes τ_0 second to power up and to process the reader's command. To respond with "10", the tag encodes "10" to "1001" and backscatters it. Note that the tag-to-reader message, i.e., "10", is now protected by BUPLE.

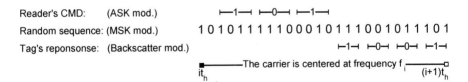

Fig. 2. An example of BUPLE with $\tau_0 = 2/v$, $v = 3v_T$ and $v = 4v_{cmd}$. The message sent from the tag is actually "10".

Choose of Parameters: Choosing appropriate parameters for our scheme is crucial to realize the expected security properties. One typical configuration of BUPLE satisfying Part 15 of Title 47 of the Federal Communications Commission (FCC) regarding the spread spectrum system is:

– Total bandwidth $W = 100$MHz.

---

[2] MSK is chosen because of its spectrum efficiency – power spectrum drops as the fourth power of frequency – and it provides constant energy to the tag.

- Size of hop set $M = 200$.
- Bandwidth for each frequency channel $W_h = 500\text{kHz}$.
- Hop duration $t_h = 20\mu s$.

BUPLE-S vs. BUPLE-W: As a result of spreading the power of the signal to hide the transmission, a technical challenge arises: FH signals are usually unable to power up a passive tag – providing the power of FH signals is strong enough to power up a tag, it is also detectable by $\mathcal{A}$'s envelope detector (even $\mathcal{A}$ is unaware of the carrier's frequency). To address this problem, BUPLE takes different values of E_b, which leads to the following *two sub-schemes.*

- BUPLE-S ("S" for strong): E_b is a great positive float to the extent that CW_i provides enough power for passive tags to operate, i.e., $\int_0^{T_0} \sqrt{2E_b v_T} dt > V_{in}$, where V_{in} is the tag's minimum operating voltage, e.g., $V_{in} = 1.8\text{v}$ for WISP v4.1 tags.
- BUPLE-W ("W" for weak): E_b has small numerical values such that CW_i is not detectable by the eavesdropper.

These two sub-schemes differ in several aspects as listed in Table 1: BUPLE-S provides more functionalities while BUPLE-W offers more security properties. For example, although BUPLE-W can neither power up tags nor issue commands, it has full resistance to eavesdropping in tag-to-reader communication when executed right after BUPLE-S. As confirmed by our experiments, few rounds of BUPLE-W could be executed immediately following one round execution of BUPLE-S. This is because the passive tag's capacitor stores constraint energy, which supplies the tag's circuit for a short while even without (enough) power supply from the reader. Depending on the design of upper protocols, BUPLE-S can be used independently, or with BUPLE-W alternatively.

Table 1. Functionalities V.S. security properties of BUPLE-S and BUPLE-W

	power-up tags	issue cmd	anti-modification	anti-eavesdropping	anti-relay
BUPLE-S	✓	✓	✓	limited	✓
BUPLE-W[a]	✗	✗	✓	✓	✓

[a] when BUPLE-W is executed right after BUPLE-S.

3.2   Security Analysis

Using the adversary model introduced in Section 1.1, we have the following analytical results.

Eavesdropping BUPLE-W: Generally speaking, the detection of FH signals is hard and all existed detectors exploit the known structure of signals [35], e.g., the hopping sequence is repeated after a short while. With the specified parameters, here we estimate the required *Signal-to-Noise Ratio* (SNR) to detect the presence of signals in BUPLE-W in terms of different types of FH detectors.

Following the calculations in [26], given the probability of detection $P_D = 0.7$ and the probability of false alarm $P_{FA} = 10^{-6}$, we have[3] (1) for a *wideband radiometer*, the required SNR at $\mathcal{A}$'s receiver is $SNR_{req} \approx 132$dB; (2) for a *partial-band filter bank combiner* (PB-FBC) with 50 branches, the required SNR for each channel $SNR_{req,I} \approx 128$dB; and (3) for an *optimum detector* with exact M branches, e.g., the legitimate reader, $SNR_{req} \approx 123$dB. This data suggests that $\mathcal{A}$'s wideband radiometer (PB-FBC resp.) has 9dB (4dB resp.) disadvantage relative to the optimum receiver owned by a legitimate reader. Thus, given the noise power spectrum in a specific environment, if E_b is carefully chosen, only the intended reader is able to receive messages backscattered by tags.

Eavesdropping BUPLE-S: Although BUPLE-S offers a poor eavesdropping resistance, it does differentiate the tag-to-reader channel and the tag-to-eavesdropper channel in the sense that the error probability of the latter is enlarged. Let a backscattered signal be $\widehat{CW}_i = \sqrt{2E_{b,k}V_t}\cos(2\pi f_i t)$, if $k = 0$ or 1 is sent by the tag (ignore the MSK-modulated sequence for the time being). According to the *minimum distance detection* [21], the bit error probability for the tag-to-reader channel is:

$$p_o = Q\left(\frac{\sqrt{E_{b,1}} - \sqrt{E_{b,0}}}{\sqrt{N_o}}\right). \tag{2}$$

where Q is the Gaussian cumulative distribution function.

Providing the eavesdropper listens at a wrong frequency, the received signal is passed through a band-pass filter, which leads a degradation, denoted as δ in dB, $\delta \leq 0$, to both $E_{b,0}$ and $E_{b,1}$, i.e., $E'_{b,0} = 10^{\delta/10}E_{b,0}$, $E'_{b,1} = 10^{\delta/10}E_{b,1}$. Thus the bit error probability for the tag-to-eavesdropper channel is:

$$p_w = Q\left(\frac{10^{\delta/20}(\sqrt{E_{b,1}} - \sqrt{E_{b,0}})}{\sqrt{N_o}}\right), \tag{3}$$

which is greater than p_o as Q is a decreasing function. Given an numerical example, let $E_{b,0} = 4$, $E_{b,1} = 25$, $\delta = -20$ and $N_o = 1$, we have $p_o = 0.0013$ for the intended receiver while $p_w = 0.3821$ for the eavesdropper.

Message Modification: First of all, the *signal overshadowing* is prevented: to inject a high amplitude signal to the channel, $\mathcal{A}$ has to know at which frequency the reader's receiver is working at; otherwise, the inserted signal will be filtered. In BUPLE, the attacker has $\frac{1}{M}$ chance to hit the right frequency. Transmitting the same message N times in different hops further decreases this probability

---

[3] To enable a tractable analysis, we assume: (1) the tag-to-eavesdropper channel is *Additive White Gaussian Noise* (AWGN); (2) $\{f_1, f_2, ..., f_M\}$, W, t_{msg}, M, t_h and W_h are public; and (3) $\mathcal{A}$ has exact knowledge of both the time at which a transmission originates and stops; otherwise, $\mathcal{A}$ has 1dB extra disadvantage [26].

to $\frac{1}{M^N}$, which is negligible when N is large[4]. Secondly, the *bit flipping* could be eliminated: in order to change "$r_j = 1$" to "$r_j = 0$", $\mathcal{A}$ needs to modify "10" to "01" in the channel (note that "00" or "11" are illegal codewords that help the reader to detect modification). To change the first bit in "10", $\mathcal{A}$ has to predict the shape of its carrier and sends the inverted signal to cancel it out. However, this is impossible since, besides the carrier frequency is unknown, the phase of the backscattered carrier is randomized by the MSK-modulated sequence and the channel condition is unpredictable as analyzed in [7].

Relay: In this case, $\mathcal{A}$ produces a well-formatted signal centered at f_i' carrying the relayed information to respond to the reader. The reader ignores this signal generated by the relayer with probability $1 - \frac{1}{M}$ since the reader's receiver always listens at f_i and filters out signals happening in other bands, where the probability, for $\mathcal{A}$, to have $f_i' = f_i$ is $\frac{1}{M}$. Multiple rounds of executions, say N, further decrease this probability to be negligible, i.e., $\frac{1}{M^N}$.

4   Enhanced BUPLE through Wiretap Channel Codes

As indicated by Eq. (2) and (3), if $\mathcal{A}$'s receiver tunes to a wrong frequency, a portion of energy of the backscattered signal is filtered and the demodulated and decoded bit streams are apparently noisier than those received by the intended receiver. Therefore, the wiretap channel model is realized by BUPLE. In this section, we further enhance BUPLE by considering *how could BUPLE-S achieve immunity to eavesdropping to the practical maximum extent possible?*

Our solution relies on the wiretap channel code. As shown in Figure 3, the tag's message is WCC-encoded before transmission and WCC-decoded by the reader launching BUPLE. Considering the moderate processing/storage capability of passive tags, we require a candidate WCC to have a equivocation rate close to 1 (rather than perfect secrecy), a relatively high information rate and a small codeword length n. In what follows, we assume both channels are *Binary Symmetric Channel* (BSC) with $p_o = 0$ and $p_w > 0$ for simplicity, otherwise a suitable error correction code can be employed to make $p_o = 0$ while keeping $p_w > 0$ (remember $p_w > p_o$). All "$\oplus$"s are addition operations in $\mathbb{F}_2$ unless otherwise stated and superscript T is the transpose of a vector.

4.1   Parameterized WCCs from Linear Error Correcting Codes

The *coset coding* based on linear error correcting codes with infinite codeword length was first used in Wyner's proof [33] of the existence of a secrecy-capacity-achieving WCC (see Appendix A). Along this line, our first two constructions concentrate more on: (1) carefully selecting the underlying linear code to maximize the desired security with small n; and (2) designing of a storage efficient

---

[4] There is a confliction that repeated transmissions impair the eavesdropping resistance. In reality, which security property is more important depends on upper layer protocols, e.g., modification resistance is more imperative to protocols in HB$^+$ family [19,14].

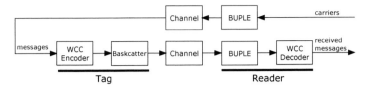

Fig. 3. Enhanced BUPLE Through Wiretap Channel Codes

encoding algorithm, i.e., reducing the storage complex from $O(2^{2m})$ to $O(2^m)$. We thus have the following constructions.

Construction I: (8, 1)-WCC The encoder works as follows: to transmit $s \in \{0, 1\}$, the encoder outputs a random vector $\mathbf{x} = (x_1, ..., x_8) \in \mathbb{F}_2^8$ satisfying $x_1 \oplus x_2 \oplus ... \oplus x_8 = s$. The decoder at the receiver's side evaluates $x_1 \oplus x_2 \oplus ... \oplus x_8$ (or $z_1 \oplus z_2 \oplus ... \oplus z_8$ for $\mathcal{A}$) to obtain s (or $s \oplus \Sigma_{i=1}^8 e_i$ resp.), where, as received by $\mathcal{A}$, $z_i = x_i \oplus e_i$ and e_i is an error bit introduced by the channel, i.e., $\text{Prob}\{e_i = 1\} = p_w$. We calculate its rate, equivocation rate and $R \times L$ for different p_w, which are listed in Table 2. Similarly, we could construct a (16, 1)-WCC.

Construction II: (8, 4)-WCC Let $g(.) : \{0, 1\}^4 \mapsto i, 0 \le i \le 15$ be a public injective function and H be the parity check matrix of a (8, 4)-extended hamming code $\mathcal{C}$, i.e.,

$$H = \begin{pmatrix} 1 & 1 & 1 & 1 & 1 & 1 & 1 & 1 \\ 0 & 0 & 0 & 1 & 1 & 1 & 1 & 0 \\ 0 & 1 & 1 & 0 & 0 & 1 & 1 & 0 \\ 1 & 0 & 1 & 0 & 1 & 0 & 1 & 0 \end{pmatrix}.$$

Moreover, the *cosets* of $\mathcal{C}$ is denoted as C_i, $0 \le i \le 15$.

To transmit a 4-bit message s, the encoder randomly selects a code $\mathbf{c} \in \mathcal{C}$ and XOR it with the coset leader $\mathbf{a}$ of $C_{g(s)}$ to produce $\mathbf{x}$. The decoder at the receiver's side evaluates $H\mathbf{x}^T$ (or $H\mathbf{z}^T = H(\mathbf{x} \oplus \mathbf{e})^T$ for $\mathcal{A}$) to obtain $H\mathbf{a}^T = s$ (or $H(\mathbf{a} \oplus \mathbf{e})^T$ resp.). Here $H\mathbf{a}^T$ is called the *syndrome* of $\mathcal{C}$. In terms of implementation, this tag needs to store: (1) g of 64-bit; (2) $\mathcal{C}$ of (8×16)-bit; (3) coset leaders of (8×16)-bit; and (4) the syndromes of (16×4)-bit in the tag's memory. That is 384 bits in all. We calculate its rate, equivocation rate and $R \times L$ for different p_w, which are listed in Table 2.

Security Analysis: It is intuitive that after decoding the noise-corrupted codeword $\mathbf{z} = (z_1, ..., z_n)$, where each z_i can be seen as a random binary variable, $\mathcal{A}$ is ignorant of $s = (s_1, ..., s_m)$ if and only if the output of the decoder appears (almost) equally likely ranging from "$\underbrace{0...0}_{m}$" to "$\underbrace{1...1}_{m}$". This is achieved by the above WCCs because of the following theorem, the proof of which is deferred to the full version of this paper.

Theorem 1. *Let $s = (s_1, ..., s_m) \in \mathbb{F}_2^m$ be the message to be sent and let codewords in the dual of a linear code $\mathcal{C}$ have minimum distance d and let $wt(H_i)$ be the hamming weight of the i-th row of the parity check matrix H of $\mathcal{C}$ (thus $wt(H_i) \ge d$). Above WCCs achieve:*

$$\text{Prob}\{s_1 = 0|\mathbf{z}\} = \Sigma^{wt(H_1)}_{j \ even}\binom{wt(H_1)}{j}p^j_w(1-p_w)^{wt(H_1)-j} = \frac{1}{2}+\frac{1}{2}(1-2p_w)^{wt(H_1)}$$

$$\text{Prob}\{s_1 = 1|\mathbf{z}\} = \Sigma^{wt(H_1)}_{j \ odd}\binom{wt(H_1)}{j}p^j_w(1-p_w)^{wt(H_1)-j} = \frac{1}{2}-\frac{1}{2}(1-2p_w)^{wt(H_1)}$$

$$\text{Prob}\{s_i = 0|s_1,...,s_{i-1},\mathbf{z}\} = \frac{1}{2}\pm\frac{1}{2}(1-2p_w)^{wt(H_1\oplus...\oplus H_{i-1})} = \frac{1}{2}\pm\frac{1}{2}(1-2p_w)^d, i>1$$

$$\text{Prob}\{s_i = 1|s_1,...,s_{i-1},\mathbf{z}\} = \frac{1}{2}\mp\frac{1}{2}(1-2p_w)^{wt(H_1\oplus...\oplus H_{i-1})} = \frac{1}{2}\mp\frac{1}{2}(1-2p_w)^d, i>1$$

$$(\frac{1}{2}-\frac{1}{2}(1-2p_w)^d)^m \le \text{Prob}\{\mathbf{s}|\mathbf{z}\} = \text{Prob}\{s_1|\mathbf{z}\}\times\prod^{m}_{i=2}\text{Prob}\{s_i|s_1,...,s_{i-1},\mathbf{z}\}$$

$$\le (\frac{1}{2}+\frac{1}{2}(1-2p_w)^d)^m.$$

Therefore, above WCCs have an achievable secrecy (R,L), as defined by Eq. (1), such that

$$R = \frac{m}{n}, \quad -\log_2(\frac{1}{2}+\frac{1}{2}(1-2p_w)^d) \le L \le 1.$$

4.2 WCCs Constructed from Resilient Boolean Functions

As we observed, the decoding process (e.g., $H(\mathbf{x}\oplus\mathbf{e})^T : \{0,1\}^n \mapsto \{0,1\}^m$ in Construction II) can be generalized as passing the noise-corrupted codeword through a well-designed S-box as shown below: when $(\mathbf{x}\oplus\mathbf{e})^T$ is not random as $p_w < 0.5$, the output of the S-box can be sufficiently random such that each output bit appears to be "0" and "1" (almost) equally likely. The tool of design for such an S-box is the *Boolean theory*, particularly, *vector resilient Boolean functions*. We refer the reader to [3] for unexplained definitions.

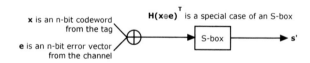

Fig. 4. The WCC decoder can be generalized as an S-box

We propose the following theorem without proof here, which provides a striking connection between (n,m)-WCC and (n,m,t)-resilient vector Boolean functions for the first time to our best knowledge.

Theorem 2. *An (n,m,t)-resilient Boolean function $f(.)$ can be used to construct an (n,m)-WCCs by letting the encoder be $f^{-1}(.)$ and the decoder be $f(.)$. All results in Theorem 1 is still valid by replacing d with $t+1$.*

Theorem 2 generalizes the two aforementioned WCCs as there exists a linear (n, m, t)-resilient vector Boolean function if and only if there exists a $[n, m, d = t + 1]$-linear code [3]. More importantly, we are interested in nonlinear WCCs with better overall performance, which is rooted in the fact that a nonlinear code with good parameters may exist while a linear function with the same parameters does not exist [24]. In light of the Kerdock code as studied in [24], we have the following novel construction of a WCC using the nonlinear code.

Construction III: (16, 8)-WCC Let $\mathbf{x} = (x_1, ..., x_{16}) \in \mathbb{F}_2^{16}$, where $f(\mathbf{x}) = (f_1(\mathbf{x}), ..., f_8(\mathbf{x})) =$

$$(x_9 \oplus (x_1 \oplus x_2 \oplus x_4 \oplus x_7 \oplus x_8 \oplus (x_1 \oplus x_5)(x_2 \oplus x_3 \oplus x_4 \oplus x_6) \oplus (x_2 \oplus x_3)(x_4 \oplus x_6)),$$
$$x_{10} \oplus (x_2 \oplus x_3 \oplus x_5 \oplus x_1 \oplus x_8 \oplus (x_2 \oplus x_6)(x_3 \oplus x_4 \oplus x_5 \oplus x_7) \oplus (x_3 \oplus x_4)(x_5 \oplus x_7)),$$
$$x_{11} \oplus (x_3 \oplus x_4 \oplus x_6 \oplus x_2 \oplus x_8 \oplus (x_3 \oplus x_7)(x_4 \oplus x_5 \oplus x_6 \oplus x_1) \oplus (x_4 \oplus x_5)(x_6 \oplus x_1)),$$
$$x_{12} \oplus (x_4 \oplus x_5 \oplus x_7 \oplus x_3 \oplus x_8 \oplus (x_4 \oplus x_1)(x_5 \oplus x_6 \oplus x_7 \oplus x_2) \oplus (x_5 \oplus x_6)(x_7 \oplus x_2)),$$
$$x_{13} \oplus (x_5 \oplus x_6 \oplus x_1 \oplus x_4 \oplus x_8 \oplus (x_5 \oplus x_2)(x_6 \oplus x_7 \oplus x_1 \oplus x_3) \oplus (x_6 \oplus x_7)(x_1 \oplus x_3)),$$
$$x_{14} \oplus (x_6 \oplus x_7 \oplus x_2 \oplus x_5 \oplus x_8 \oplus (x_6 \oplus x_3)(x_7 \oplus x_1 \oplus x_2 \oplus x_4) \oplus (x_7 \oplus x_1)(x_2 \oplus x_4)),$$
$$x_{15} \oplus (x_7 \oplus x_1 \oplus x_3 \oplus x_6 \oplus x_8 \oplus (x_7 \oplus x_4)(x_1 \oplus x_2 \oplus x_3 \oplus x_5) \oplus (x_1 \oplus x_2)(x_3 \oplus x_5)),$$
$$\Sigma_{i=1}^{16} x_i). \tag{4}$$

Let the encoder be $f^{-1}(\mathbf{x})$ and the decoder be $f(\mathbf{x})$. To transmit an 8-bit message $\mathbf{s}$, the encoder outputs a 16-bit random binary vector $\mathbf{x}$ such that $f(\mathbf{x}) = \mathbf{s}$. The decoder at the receiver's side simply evaluates $f(\mathbf{x})$ (or $f(\mathbf{x} \oplus \mathbf{e})$ for $\mathcal{A}$) given $\mathbf{x}$ (or $\mathbf{x} \oplus \mathbf{e}$ resp.) is received. This construction is optimum as its $R \times L$ is closest to the secrecy capacity as shown in Table 2.

Table 2. Comparison of performances of proposed WCCs

(n, m)	underlying code	rate	equivocation rate	$R \times L$
$p_w = 0.20$, secrecy capacity $= h(p_w) = 0.721928094887$				
(8, 1)	parity check	0.1250	0.99979649036	0.12497456129
(8, 4)	ext. hamming	0.5000	0.96977096204	0.48488548102
(16, 8)	Kerdock	0.5000	0.98711512719	0.49355756360
$p_w = 0.10$, secrecy capacity $= h(p_w) = 0.468995593589$				
(8, 1)	parity check	0.1250	0.97959953172	0.12244994146
(8, 4)	ext. hamming	0.5000	0.78495689709	0.39247844855
(16, 8)	Kerdock	0.5000	0.82311413681	0.41155706840
$p_w = 0.05$, secrecy capacity $= h(p_w) = 0.286396957116$				
(8, 1)	parity check	0.1250	0.86186434726	0.10773304341
(8, 4)	ext. hamming	0.5000	0.53233802320	0.26616901160
(16, 8)	Kerdock	0.5000	0.55356866398	0.27678433199

4.3   Visualize the Security of Proposed WCCs

We calculate the information rate, the exact equivocation rate and $R \times L$ of each WCC with different p_w, which are listed in Table 2. As seen, there is no one-size-fits-all WCC: Construction I is an extreme case when confidentiality is to be taken care of, with an imperative shortcoming in its lowest transmission

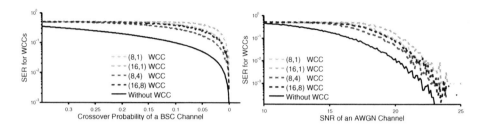

Fig. 5. Simunlink Simulation for RFID systems

rate; Construction II and Construction III are rate-efficient codes at the cost of lower equivocation rates.

To observe the real-world effects of the proposed WCCs, with Simulink, we built a digital communication system composing of a random message generator, a WCC encoder/decoder, an ASK modulator with 915MHz carrier, a BSC or AWGN channel and an envelope detector. The Symbol Error Rate (SER) is simulated and calculated to validate that WCCs further improves the eavesdropping resistance. As shown in Figure 5, the SER in BSC increases with p_w if no coding is involved (the given plots use a logarithmic scale for the y-axis). An interesting result is that the distance or resiliency of each WCC can be visualized as its maximum geometric distance away from the solid line. Besides, the plot of SER in AWGN on the right shows that the intended receiver has approximately 5dB advantage of SNR (relative to the eavesdropper) to achieve the same SER.

5   Proof-of-Concept Implementation and Testing

In the following, we present our proof-of-concept implementation and testing of BUPLE and proposed WCCs.

5.1   Experiment Setup

We built a physical-layer programmable reader using the Universal Software Radio Peripherals (USRP v1.0) [10] together with two RFX900 daughter boards (with the filters bypassed to get a 500mW peak output power): we use one RFX900 with a VERT900 antenna [30] to serve as the frontend of the transmitter (call them RFX900-Tx hereafter) and another RFX900 with a circular polarity panel antenna [4] to be the frontend of a narrowband receiver (call them RFX900-Rx hereafter). In the receiving path, RFX900-Rx samples raw UHF signals by an ADC and then converts them to baseband signals by a digital downconverter (DDC). The baseband digital signals out of USRP are sent via USB 2.0 interface to the Thinkpad T410 laptop running GNU Radio [12], a free software toolkit for signal processing from the physical layer, under the 32-bit Ubuntu 10.04. The transmission path is similar, but consists of digital upconverters (DUC) and a DAC. Parallel to this, a DPO7104 digital phosphor oscilloscope is used for measurements.

To observe behaviors of a passive tag, the WISP v4.1 tag [32], is employed. The reasons for the selection are: (1) it is programmable due to its 16-bit general purpose MSP430F2132 microcontroller. Programs for MSP430F2132 are written in embedded C and compiled, debugged and profiled with IAR Embedded Workbench 5.10.4, in conjunction with TI FET430UIF debugger; (2) it simulates every aspect of a passive tag in terms of limited and ephemeral energy storage and backscatter communication; (3) it implements a significant portion of EPC C1G2 commands, e.g., QUERY and QUERYREP.

Table 3. Actual measures of the output voltages at port TX/RX of RFX900 with respect to the scale factor

scale factor	output voltage	scale factor	output voltage
10	0.00mv	5000	2.124v
500	144mv	10000	2.880v
1000	396mv	25000	3.208v
2000	864mv	32767	3.312v

In what follows, we use an integer called *scale factor* in $[-2^{16}+1, 2^{16}-1]$ to represent the amplitude of a signal without unit. The actual measures of the output voltages at port TX/RX of RFX900 (without antenna) with respect to this scale factor is provided shown in Table 3.

5.2 Our Implementation

In our implementation, BUPLE-W and BUPLE-S are executed alternatively. We first developed a signal processing block for GNU Radio, in conjunction with our customized FPGA firmware, to generate a two leveled carrier signal with period 0.5s, where the high level of the amplitude 25000 represents BUPLE-S while the low level of the amplitude 3000 represents BUPLE-W (this amount, as we tested in an independent session, cannot drive the tag). In addition, our block randomly tunes the frequency of both RFX900-Tx and RFX900-Rx every 0.5s. Finally, we wrote a Python script to create and control *signal flow graphs*, in which, the gain of the receiver's antenna is set to 20dB, and the received signal is decimated by USRP with a factor of 32; right before demodulation, the decimated signals are again filtered by an 8-th order low-pass filter with gain 2, cutoff frequency of 400KHz. Therefore a narrowband receiver is realized. Note that here the specified hop rate cannot be implemented as there are many delays along the digitization path of USRP such as RF frontend settling time, FPGA FIFO filling time, USB transferring time, etc..

For the tag side, we slightly modified the firmware of the WISP tag to let it intermittently answers "1010101010101010"[5] at $v_T = 250$KHz followed each time by a sleep, when it has enough power, rather than implementing the command-based reader-tag interaction. This is because our physical layer scheme is essentially independent from upper layer protocols. Figure 7 exhibits how our scheme

---

[5] This actually transmits a "1": the tag encodes "1" as "11111111" with the $(8, 1)$-WCC, and each "1" in "11111111" is mapped to "10" as specified by BUPLE.

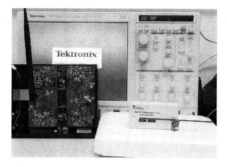

Fig. 6. Devices employed in our implementation and testing: one DP07104 oscilloscope, one USRP (v1.0), two RFX900 daughterboards, one VERT900 antenna, one circular polarity panel antenna, one WISP tag (v4.1) and one TI FET430UIF debugger

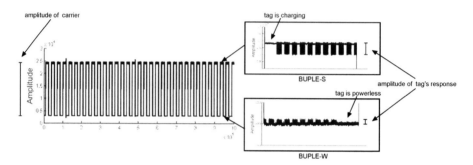

Fig. 7. Time domain measurements when BUPLE works with a WISP tag

works in a standard office setting with the tag placed in between the transceiver and receiver – it is 9.8cm away from RFX900-Tx's antenna and 131cm away from RFX900-Rx's antenna. As we can see, the backscatter communication carries out normally in BUPLE-S while it can only last for a while in BUPLE-W before the tag uses up its power. As long as the execution time of BUPLE-W is reduced, it is possible to keep the tag always alive.

Eavesdropping BUPLE Enhanced Communication: To further investigate the eavesdropper's performance while BUPLE is running, we conducted the following tests in the same physical environment: centering RFX900-Tx at 915MHz while centering RFX900-Rx at frequencies ranging from 915MHz to 918MHz, we measured the amplitudes of the backscattered signals on BUPLE-S and BUPLE-W respectively, which are expected to exhibit the loss of communication reliability if the eavesdropper works at a wrong frequency.

We tabulated the results in Table 4. In both BUPLE-S and BUPLE-W, the carrier's amplitudes as well as those of the tag's responses drop quickly if the eavesdropper's receiver is not centered at the right frequency. By "N/A", we mean the signal is submerged in noise and cannot be observed. The experimental evidences support the theoretic hypothesis that to detect the presence of frequency hopped signals in BUPLE-W is non-trivial, let alone demodulate and decode them. We conducted this experiment for reader/tag/eavesdropper with varying distances/angles and get the similar results.

Table 4. Amplitudes of signals captured by the eavesdropper working at 915MHz to 918MHz

Rx's Freq.	BUPLE-S		BUPLE-W	
	amp. of carrier	amp. of tag's response	amp. of carrier	amp. of tag's response
915MHz	24700	564	2980	91
916MHz	6000	389	600	N/A
917MHz	4300	210	270	N/A
918MHz	300	N/A	200	N/A

Implementing On-tag WCC Encoders: To evaluate the cost of WCC encoders, we implemented them on the MSP430F2132 of a WISP tag (without WISP's firmware since the firmware itself consumes a considerable portion of SRAM [27]) and tested memory consumption and throughput. We employ a 23-stage LFSR with each stage in $\mathbb{F}_2^8$ as the random source for each WCC. To be mentioned, the encoding processes of $(8, 1)$-WCC and $(8, 4)$-WCC are implemented using pre-computed lookup tables while that of $(16, 8)$-WCCs is computed on-the-fly by the underlying Boolean calculations. This is because when $n = 16$, the desired lookup table (of size 128KB) is far greater than the memory provided. To generate the code with maximal speed, we set the optimization level to be "high-speed" for the compiler. We then record the cycle counts through the FET debugger by letting the encoders execute at 8MHz on MSP430F2132 for 1000 times with random messages as inputs.

Table 5. Performance comparison of the proposed WCC encoders and four lightweight ciphers from literature. Note that PRESENT is implemented on a different-but-similar microcontroller platform – Atmel AVR ATmega163.

	SRAM [byte]	Flash [byte]	Initialization [cycle]	Throughput [bits/sec]
$(8, 1)$-WCC	690	0	0	740,936
$(8, 4)$-WCC	732	0	0	621,346
$(16, 8)$-WCC	1,348	0	0	86,776
Hummingbird[8]	1,064	0	9,667	53,024
AES[17]	13,448	92	1,745	199,377
KASUMI[17]	9,541	64	1,381	90,395
PRESENT[22]	2,398	528	–	53,361

Table 5 summarizes the performance of WCC encoders, together with that of four lightweight ciphers implemented on the same or similar microcontroller platforms. Thanks to the simple operations, WCCs consume less resource and have higher throughput. The $(16, 8)$-WCC encoder is resource-hungry because the pure embedded C code, as we used, is inefficient to process Boolean functions such as Eq. (4). Appropriate mixing of inline assembly code will allow the consumed resource be further decreased; this is part of our future work. Another noteworthy merit is that WCCs are more survivable in a frequent-loss-of-power environment since (1) they have the zero initialization time; and (2) they have a very small computation granularity, e.g., the only operation needed is a simple mapping from $\{0,1\}^m$ to $\{0,1\}^n$. On the contrary, an on-tag cipher, composing of many operations in series, is more likely to be interrupted. In all, together with Table 2, we found that $(8,4)$-WCC makes the information rate, the security and the implementation cost well-balanced, which is a favorable choice for practitioners.

6   Conclusion

Given the likely importance of RFID technology in practice, security and privacy problems should be solved before worldwide deployment. In this paper, we propose to enhance the physical layer of the passive RFID communication. The security and usability are further confirmed by our implementations and testing results. Through the BUPLE scheme and proposed WCCs, a confidentiality-, authenticity- and integrity-preserving channel is created for tag-to-reader communication. It is also worth emphasizing that our solutions are designed for, but not limited to passive RFID systems, e.g, it is applicable to the backscatter wireless sensor network, e.g., [31], for establishing secret communication.

References

1. Avoine, G., Floerkemeier, C., Martin, B.: RFID Distance Bounding Multistate Enhancement. In: Roy, B., Sendrier, N. (eds.) INDOCRYPT 2009. LNCS, vol. 5922, pp. 290–307. Springer, Heidelberg (2009)
2. Bogdanov, A., Knudsen, L., Leander, G., Paar, C., Poschmann, A., Robshaw, M., Seurin, Y., Vikkelsoe, C.: PRESENT: An Ultra-Lightweight Block Cipher. In: Paillier, P., Verbauwhede, I. (eds.) CHES 2007. LNCS, vol. 4727, pp. 450–466. Springer, Heidelberg (2007)
3. Carlet, C.: Vectorial Boolean Functions For Cryptography. Cambridge University Press (2010)
4. Circular Polarity Pane Antenna,
   http://www.arcadianinc.com/datasheets/4123.pdf
5. Castelluccia, C., Avoine, G.: Noisy Tags: A Pretty Good Key Exchange Protocol for RFID Tags. In: Domingo-Ferrer, J., Posegga, J., Schreckling, D. (eds.) CARDIS 2006. LNCS, vol. 3928, pp. 289–299. Springer, Heidelberg (2006)
6. Csiszar, I., Korner, J.: Broadcast channels with confidential messages. IEEE Transactions on Information Theory 24(3), 339–348 (2002)
7. Cagalj, M., Capkun, S., Rengaswamy, R., Tsigkogiannis, I., Srivastava, M., Hubaux, J.P.: Integrity (I) codes: message integrity protection and authentication over insecure channels. In: 29th IEEE Symposium on Security and Privacy, S&P 2008, pp. 279–294 (2006)
8. Engels, D., Fan, X., Gong, G., Hu, H., Smith, E.M.: Hummingbird: Ultralightweight cryptography for resource-constrained devices. In: Sion, R., Curtmola, R., Dietrich, S., Kiayias, A., Miret, J.M., Sako, K., Sebé, F. (eds.) RLCPS, WECSR, and WLC 2010. LNCS, vol. 6054, pp. 3–18. Springer, Heidelberg (2010)

9. EPC Global, Class 1 Generation 2 UHF air interface protocol standard v1.2 (2008), http://www.epcglobalinc.org
10. Ettus Research LLC, The USRP and RFX900 daughter boards, http://www.ettus.com/products
11. Francis, L., Hancke, G., Mayes, K., Markantonakis, K.: Practical NFC Peer-to-Peer Relay Attack Using Mobile Phones. In: Ors Yalcin, S.B. (ed.) RFIDSec 2010. LNCS, vol. 6370, pp. 35–49. Springer, Heidelberg (2010)
12. GNU Radio, http://www.gnu.org/software/gnuradio
13. Hancke, G., Kuhn, M.: An RFID distance bounding protocol. In: Conference on Security and Privacy for Emerging Areas in Communication Networks, SecureComm 2006 (2005)
14. Gilbert, H., Robshaw, M.J.B., Seurin, Y.: HB#: Increasing the Security and Efficiency of HB$^+$. In: Smart, N.P. (ed.) EUROCRYPT 2008. LNCS, vol. 4965, pp. 361–378. Springer, Heidelberg (2008)
15. Dobkin, D.M.: The RF in RFID: passive UHF RFID in practice, Newnes (2007)
16. Juels, A., Rivest, R.L., Szydlo, M.: The blocker tag: selective blocking of RFID tags for consumer privacy. In: 10th ACM Conference on Computer and Communications Security, CCS 2003, pp. 103–111 (2003)
17. Law, Y.W., Doumen, J., Hartel, P.: Survey and benchmark of block ciphers for wireless sensor networks. ACM Transactions on Sensor Networks 2(1), 65–93 (2006)
18. Munilla, J., Peinado, A.: Distance bounding protocols for RFID enhanced by using void-challenges and analysis in noisy channels. Wireless Communications and Mobile Computing 8(9), 1227–1232 (2008)
19. Ouafi, K., Overbeck, R., Vaudenay, S.: On the Security of HB# Against a Man-in-the-Middle Attack. In: Pieprzyk, J. (ed.) ASIACRYPT 2008. LNCS, vol. 5350, pp. 108–124. Springer, Heidelberg (2008)
20. Ozarow, L.H., Wyner, A.D.: Wire-tap Channel II. In: Beth, T., Cot, N., Ingemarsson, I. (eds.) EUROCRYPT 1984. LNCS, vol. 209, pp. 33–50. Springer, Heidelberg (1985)
21. Pursley, M.B.: Introduction to Digital Communications. Pearson Prentice Hall (2005)
22. Poschmann, A.: Lightweight cryptography - cryptographic engineering for a pervasive world, Ph.D. Thesis, Ruhr-Universitaet Bochum, Germany (2009)
23. Strasser, M., Capkun, S., Popper, C., Cagalj, M.: Jamming-resistant key establishment using uncoordinated frequency hopping. In: 29th IEEE Symposium on Security and Privacy, S&P 2008, pp. 64–78 (2008)
24. Stinson, D.R., Massey, J.L.: An infinite class of counterexamples to a conjecture concerning nonlinear resilient functions. Journal of Cryptology 8(3), 167–173 (1995)
25. Savry, O., Pebay-Peyroula, F., Dehmas, F., Robert, G., Reverdy, J.: RFID noisy reader how to prevent from eavesdropping on the communication? In: Paillier, P., Verbauwhede, I. (eds.) CHES 2007. LNCS, vol. 4727, pp. 334–345. Springer, Heidelberg (2007)
26. Simon, M.K., Omura, J.K., Scholtz, R.A., Levitt, B.K.: Spread Spectrum Communications Handbook. McGraw-Hill Professional Publishing (2001)
27. Saxena, N., Voris, J.: We can remember it for you wholesale: implications of data remanence on the use of RAM for true random number generation on RFID tags. In: Workshop on RFID Security, RFIDSec 2009 (2009)
28. Thangaraj, A., Dihidar, S., Calderbank, A.R., McLaughlin, S.W., Merolla, J.M.: Applications of LDPC codes to the wiretap channel. IEEE Transactions on Information Theory 53(8), 2933–2945 (2007)

29. Trujillo-Rasua, R., Martin, B., Avoine, G.: The Poulidor Distance-Bounding Protocol. In: Ors Yalcin, S.B. (ed.) RFIDSec 2010. LNCS, vol. 6370, pp. 239–257. Springer, Heidelberg (2010)
30. VERT900 Antenna, http://www.ettus.com/downloads/VERT900.pdf
31. Vannucci, G., Bletsas, A., Leigh, D.: A software-defined radio system for backscatter sensor networks. IEEE Transactions on Wireless Communications 7(6), 2170–2179 (2008)
32. Wireless Identification and Sensing Platform (WISP),
http://wisp.wikispaces.com
33. Wyner, A.D.: The wire-tap channel. Bell Systems Technical Journal 54, 1355–1387 (1975)
34. Weis, S.A., Sarma, S.E., Rivest, R.L., Engels, D.W.: Security and Privacy Aspects of Low-Cost Radio Frequency Identification Systems. In: Hutter, D., Müller, G., Stephan, W., Ullmann, M. (eds.) Security in Pervasive Computing. LNCS, vol. 2802, pp. 201–212. Springer, Heidelberg (2004)
35. Haykin, S.: Cognitive radio: brain-empowered wireless communications. IEEE Journal on Selected Areas in Communications 23(2), 201–220 (2005)

A   Wyner's Coset Coding

Let C be an $[n, n-m]$ binary linear code with the parity check matrix H. We can partition the n-bit vector space $\mathbb{F}_2^n$ into 2^{n-m} subsets in the following fashion. For any fixed vector $\mathbf{a} \in \mathbb{F}_2^n$, the set,

$$C_i = \mathbf{a} \oplus C = \{\mathbf{a} \oplus \mathbf{c} | \mathbf{c} \in C\},$$

is called a *coset* of C. Two cosets are either disjoint or coincide (partial overlap is impossible). The minimum weight vector in a coset is called the *coset leader*. It may have more than one coset leaders, then just randomly chooses one. In addition, let $g_1(.) : \{0,1\}^m \mapsto i$, $0 \le i \le 2^m - 1$, $g_2(.) : \{0,1\}^m \mapsto \{0,1\}^m$ be two public injective functions.

To transmit an m-bit secret message $\mathbf{s}$, the sender propagates over the channel an n-bit vector $\mathbf{x}$, which is selected randomly among all vectors in $C_{g_1(\mathbf{s})}$. Let $\mathbf{a}$ be the coset leader of $C_{g_1(\mathbf{s})}$. The intended receiver decodes by computing:

$$H\mathbf{x}^T = H(\mathbf{c}^T \oplus \mathbf{a}^T) = H\mathbf{a}^T, \quad \mathbf{s} = g_2(H\mathbf{a}^T),$$

where the second last identity comes from $H\mathbf{c}^T = \mathbf{0}$, which is the property of the linear code C. On the other hand, after receiving $\mathbf{z} = \mathbf{x} + \mathbf{e}$ where $\mathbf{e} \in \mathbb{F}_2^n$ is a binary error vector introduced by the noisy channel, the eavesdropper does the following:

$$H(\mathbf{x} \oplus \mathbf{e})^T = H(\mathbf{c}^T \oplus \mathbf{a}^T \oplus \mathbf{e}^T) = H(\mathbf{a}^T \oplus \mathbf{e}^T), \quad \mathbf{s}' = g_2(H(\mathbf{a}^T \oplus \mathbf{e}^T)),$$

which implies that the transmitted message is masked by a true random sequence $\mathbf{e}$. In our implementations, $g_2(.)$ is saved by arranging the syndrome in a proper order.

A Scalable RFID Authentication Protocol Supporting Ownership Transfer and Controlled Delegation

Albert Fernàndez-Mir, Rolando Trujillo-Rasua,
Jordi Castellà-Roca, and Josep Domingo-Ferrer

Universitat Rovira i Virgili
UNESCO Chair in Data Privacy
Departament d'Enginyeria Informàtica i Matemàtiques
Av. Països Catalans 26,
E-43007 Tarragona, Catalonia
{albert.fernandez,rolando.trujillo,
jordi.castella,josep.domingo}@urv.cat

Abstract. RFID systems allow fast and automatic identification of RFID tags through a wireless channel. Information on product items like name, model, purpose, expiration date, etc., can be easily stored and retrieved from RFID tags attached to items. That is why, in the near future, RFID tags can be an active part of our everyday life when interacting with items around us. Frequently, such items may change hands during their life-cycle. Therefore, beyond RFID identification protocols, there is a need for secure and private ownership transfer protocols in RFID systems. To ensure privacy to tag owners, the keys of tags are usually updated during the ownership transfer process. However, none of the previous proposals takes advantage of this property to improve the system scalability. To the best of our knowledge, we propose the first RFID identification protocol supporting ownership transfer that is secure, private and scalable. Furthermore, our proposal achieves other valuable properties related to ownership transfer, such as controlled delegation and decentralization.

Keywords: RFID, Identification, Security, Privacy, Scalability, Ownership transfer, Controlled delegation.

1 Introduction

A basic RFID scheme consists of a reader that uses radio waves in order to identify several small devices named *RFID tags*. This technology is gaining more and more momentum for identification, because it does not need physical or visual contact to identify tags. A few years ago, Gillette announced their plans of purchasing 500 million RFID tags for inventory control in their supply chain. RFID systems are not only useful to identify single items, but also to identify items in batches that logically should be placed together, *e.g.* a razor and a razor blade into a box.

A. Juels and C. Paar (Eds.): RFIDSec 2011, LNCS 7055, pp. 147–162, 2012.

A good use of the RFID technology by a company may enable a positive return of the investments in a short time [7]. However, although the price of a tag can be small, the fact that companies should often buy millions of these devices ties down their price to be not higher than 5 dollar cents [13]. That is why low-cost tags are, in general, more suitable for large-scale systems.

Even though this technology offers important advantages to the users, it also poses serious privacy and security risks to them. Considering that RFID tags respond to any reader query without the tag holder being aware of it, an adversary may be able to create a profile of a user by just reading the data of the tags in the user's possession. On the other hand, security measures must be carefully adopted because simply eavesdropping the communication channel between tags and readers could be enough to spoof a tag's identity. For example, if a tag attached to a Cohiba cigar box sends its identifier in plaintext, this identifier can be easily cloned in order to fake this expensive product in an inventory. Thus, it is necessary to develop secure schemes that prevent attackers from misusing the information managed in RFID systems. Notice that this point is earnestly suggested by the European Union in [15]. However, low-cost tags are very constrained devices that can only perform basic and simple cryptographic operations. Asymmetric-key cryptography is considered too expensive for low-cost tags; symmetric-key cryptography is more suitable for resource-constrained devices. Although several identification protocols using symmetric-key cryptography have been proposed for RFID systems, combining privacy and scalability through resource-constrained devices is still an issue [1].

In addition to the security and privacy problems, key management becomes an issue when the owner of a tagged item changes. Let us consider a manufacturer distributing RFID-tagged products to the point of sale. Later, these products are sold to buyers who can resell them to other buyers. In order to track RFID-tagged products across buyers, each reader could connect to the central server that manages all the tags' keys. However, this solution does not only cause bottlenecks and overloads on the server side, but also causes privacy issues when the product changes hands. The opposite solution is to share the keys of the tags among the different owners. But, with this scheme, privacy issues arise because previous and future owners of a tag are able to identify it even when it is not in their possession. Indeed, the tag key and secret information must be transferred from previous owners to new owners ensuring the security and privacy of past and future tag identifications *ownership transfer* [12]).

In some special cases, such as for after-sale service of an RFID-tagged object, the previous owner of a tag might need to temporarily recover the means of interacting with it. For instance, this happens when the buyer goes back to the seller to have a guaranteed appliance repaired. In this case, the current owner of a tag should be able to transfer its identification rights over a tag to another reader and to recover the exclusive right of identifying this tag at any moment. If the reader to whom the identification rights over a tag were transferred is a previous owner of this tag, the process is called *authorization recovery* [6]), otherwise the process is called *controlled delegation* [17].

1.1   Contribution and Plan of This Article

Preserving privacy among owners is a challenging task when the ownership of tagged products is transferred between them. Ownership transfer, authorization recovery and controlled delegation schemes should be designed to be secure and private not only against external adversaries, but also against previous owners. In this paper, to the best of our knowledge, we propose the first RFID identification protocol that is secure, private, scalable and able to perform ownership transfer, authorization recovery and controlled delegation.

The rest of this article is organized as follows. In Section 2 we summarize the current literature in the field of ownership transfer and put our contribution in context. In Section 3 we describe our proposal and in Section 4 we analyze its security. Section 5 contains conclusions and suggestions for future work.

2   Related Work

A great number of authentication/identification protocols for RFID systems have been proposed in the literature [9]. However, just a few of them have been extended to support ownership transfer, authorization recovery or controlled delegation. When the RFID system supports ownership transfer, the tags can be used by different owners, so they have a longer life cycle. Authorization recovery and controlled delegation are properties especially designed for after-sale and maintenance service.

In identification/authentication protocols, RFID systems typically use a shared key between the tag and the owner's reader. Since the shared key is only known by the owner's reader, this reader alone can complete the tag identification successfully. In ownership transfer protocols there are two players, the current owner and the future owner. Before the protocol, only the current owner can identify the tag; after the protocol is completed, only the new owner can identify the tag successfully. This process is repeated every time the owner of the tag changes. So far, two assumptions have been extensively used in order to achieve the property mentioned above:

- **Centralized scheme:** There exists a Trusted Third Party (TTP) which every entity (owner) trusts. It is assumed that entities can establish a secure communication.
- **Isolated environment:** There exists a secure environment, so that each entity can execute the protocol with the tag without being eavesdropped by an adversary.

Both assumptions make sense depending on the application. A centralized scheme might be used in inventory control or supply-chain management applications, where all tags are identified by readers belonging to the same company. However, when a user buys a product, she does not necessarily trust anyone. Hence, a centralized scheme is not suitable. In this case, it is assumed that the user can go to an isolated environment (*e.g.* the user's home), where he can change the tag key without being eavesdropped by an adversary.

2.1 Ownership Transfer Model

An ownership transfer protocol allows transfering the rights over a tag T from the current owner to the new owner in a secure and private way. According to [14, 17], there are three different roles (entities) in an ownership transfer protocol:

- *The previous owner.* In the past, this entity had the ability to identify or track T as much as he wanted, but now she cannot do these operations any more.
- *The current owner.* At present, only this entity can identify and track T.
- *The new owner.* She cannot identify or track T at the beginning of the protocol . When the protocol finishes, T can only be identified or tracked by this entity.

When it is required to transfer the ownership of T, the current owner and the new owner run an ownership transfer protocol on T. The secrets and data stored in T are transferred from the current owner to the new owner. Thus, roles change. The current owner of T becomes the previous owner of T, while the new owner of T becomes the current owner of T.

The ownership transfer process motivates the requirements of authorization recovery and controlled delegation mentioned in the introduction.

Figure 1 shows the players that can be involved in an ownership transfer protocol.

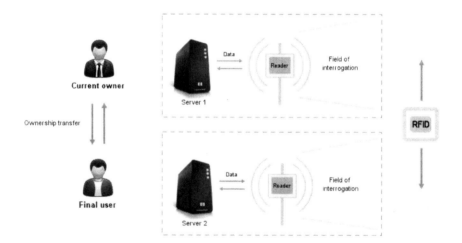

Fig. 1. A generic scenario for ownership transfer

2.2 Previous Proposals

The first solution to the ownership transfer problem based on a centralized scheme was proposed by Saito *et al.* in [12]. In this protocol, tags receive encrypted messages using the TTP key (K_{TTP}). Since all tags know K_{TTP}, they are able to correctly decrypt the messages coming from the trusted third party. However, tags are not tamper-resistant and, hence, tampering just one tag is enough to break the security of the whole system by finding K_{TTP}. Saito *et al.* [12] also consider the case where a centralized scheme cannot be used. In this case, they assume that the backward channel (from tag to reader) is unreadable by adversaries. Therefore, a secure communication between tags and readers is achieved by the reader encrypting messages using a nonce sent by the reader to the tag that is refreshed at each session. However, although the range of the backward channel is shorter than the range of the forward channel from reader to tag, in general the backward channel cannot be considered as unreadable by adversaries.

Another centralized scheme for ownership transfer and controlled delegation is proposed by Molnar *et al.* in [10]. They use a centralized trusted center named TC to manage tag keys in a tree structure. The delegation property is achieved when the trusted center gives a subtree of pseudonyms to a reader. Using this subtree of pseudonyms, a reader is able to identify a tag q times where q is the number of leaves of this subtree. The keys shared by several tags are a protocol weakness that reduces security. Therefore, the privacy of the whole system decreases quickly when more tags are compromised [2].

Unlike Molnar *et al.*'s protocol [10], other proposals use a counter into the non-volatile memory of tags in order to control how many identifications can be done after the execution of a controlled delegation protocol. The basic idea is that tags give different responses depending on whether the counter c is less than some threshold c_{max} or equals c_{max}. As shown by Fouladgar and Afifi [6], while $c < c_{max}$ the tag responds using a key known just by the trusted center and by the readers (the trusted center gave rights to the readers previously). Once the counter reaches its maximum value, the tag encrypts its responses using a key known just by the trusted center and hence, the tag identification is only possible through the trusted server. However, using a counter on the tag side raises two main issues: i) the counter must be in the non-volatile memory of the tag; ii) giving rights to more than one reader causes that tag keys to be shared by several readers. Notice that a reader that knows the identification key of some tag is able to know where and when this tag is being identified by any other reader.

Schemes based on a centralized and trusted third party require that readers be online at each execution of the ownership transfer protocol. Further, some of the parties involved in the ownership transfer process may not actually trust the TTP. There exist some proposals without a TTP. To the best of our knowledge, the first decentralized protocol relying on the assumption that owners are able to change the tag key in an isolated environment was proposed by Yoon and Yoo [16]. However, this protocol has security vulnerabilities well described in [8]. Under the same assumption, Chen *et al.* [3] proposed an improvement of Osaka *et al.*'s scheme [11] through authentication of the reader by the tag before changing the tag key. Although this protocol guarantees a successful ownership transfer process, a previous owner can neither check whether a tag was in its possession nor can temporarily recover the means of interacting with a tag.

The property of authorization recovery [14] allows a previous owner of a tag to identify it again. This property is considered a particular case of delegation and could be achieved simply restoring the key of the previous owner into the tag. For instance, Dimitriou [4] proposes a simple *tag release* command that restores the manufacture key of the tag. However, this solution gives authorization recovery rights just to the tag manufacturer. Song *et al.* [14] solve this drawback in their proposal. Each tag owner remembers the key of the previous tag owner. Hence, updating the tag key to the key used by the previous owner is enough for authorization recovery. Although both protocols [4, 14] do not support controlled delegation, they have the advantage of not needing a trusted third party. The recent work in ownership transfer [17] shows that ownership transfer and controlled delegation are possible in a decentralized scheme. The authors propose a scheme that achieves all the desired properties defined so far in ownership transfer. However, their scheme can be used only in those identification/authentication protocols where: i) keys are not updated; or ii) keys are updated using Song *et al.*'s protocol [14]. Such a constraint has severe effects on the scalability of the identification process. Note that, although most identification protocols with key updating are not private against active adversaries, they can scale better than protocols without key updating.

In this paper, a new decentralized identification protocol with ownership transfer and controlled delegation is proposed. On the reader's side, tag identification is scalable in the number of tags. Once the tag has been identified, its identification key is updated. This property is used in the ownership transfer process in order to update the owner's key. Similarly to the proposals [10] and [14], the protocol has the advantage of supporting controlled delegation without needing a counter on the tag's side. Also, although it is based on synchronization unlike previous proposals [4, 14, 17], our protocol is still secure and private against active adversaries.

3   Our Protocol

As discussed in Section 2, there exist several secure and private RFID identification protocols with ownership transfer [3, 4, 6, 10–12, 14, 16, 17]. However, just a few of them can deal with controlled delegation [4, 6, 14, 17]. Besides, none of these protocols leverages the updating phase performed during the ownership transfer process in order to efficiently identify the tags.

We propose an RFID identification protocol that is efficient both at the tag and at the server sides. Our protocol is based on the synchronization between the server and the tag, but even when these are desynchronized, it still can be scalable and resistant against denial-of-service attacks. The protocol has been designed to guarantee that an attacker cannot distinguish whether a tag is synchronized or not. This fact adds one more degree of difficulty for an attacker who wants to trace a tag or mount a denial-of-service attack. Together with the above mentioned features, our proposal supports ownership transfer and controlled delegation in a decentralized scheme. The result is a secure, private and scalable RFID identification protocol that supports ownership transfer and controlled delegation.

Our proposal is partially based on the Fernández-Mir *et al.* protocol [5] and consists of five phases: initialization, synchronized identification, desynchronized identification, update and ownership transfer. The update phase is executed after each successful identification. If the tag cannot be updated and the system is desynchronized, it can still be identified by a desynchronized identification phase that preserves all the security and privacy properties. Table 1 summarizes the notation used to describe the new proposal.

Table 1. Notation used in the protocol

R	Reader
T	Tag
id	Tag identifier
ik	Identification key
uk	Update key
r_i	Random number
$h()$	One-way hash function
$h_k()$	Keyed hash function (HMAC)
$PRNG$	Pseudo-random number generator
$SYNC$	Synchronization state
C_i	Pseudo-random bit sequence
S	Pseudo-random bit sequence
m_i	Update message
k_δ	Hash chain
$\|$	Concatenation operator
$\oplus$	XOR operator

3.1 System Environment

The proposed protocol requires a server that hosts its own database and readers that transmit information from tags to the server. For each tag, the server stores a record containing the following data (see Table 2):

- id: The tag identity.
- $Info_{id}$: The tag information.
- uk: An update key uk that only changes after the execution of a successful ownership transfer protocol. This key is only known by the current tag owner.
- ik *and* $h_{id}(ik)$: A tag identification key ik and its associated hash value $h_{id}(ik)$ using the tag identifier as key. As described, the hash value is used to identify a tag in a lookup table.
- ik_{old} *and* $h_{id}(ik_{old})$: A previous tag identification key ik_{old} and its associated hash value $h_{id}(ik_{old})$ are kept in order to prevent denial-of-service attacks.

- *Table k*: A table used to identify a tag in case of desynchronization between the tag and the server. Row 1 and row 2 in the table store hash chains of size MAX starting from ik_{old} and ik, respectively.

Table 2. DB values for each tag

Tag data		Table k	
id		k_i^{old}	k_i
$Info_{id}$	0	$h_{id}(ik_{old})$	$h_{id}(ik)$
uk	1	$h_{uk}(k_0^{old}\|\|id)$	$h_{uk}(k_0\|\|id)$
ik	2	$h_{uk}(k_1^{old}\|\|id)$	$h_{uk}(k_1\|\|id)$
$h_{id}(ik)$	⋮	⋮	⋮
ik_{old}			
$h_{id}(ik_{old})$	MAX	$h_{uk}(k_{MAX-1}^{old}\|\|id)$	$h_{uk}(k_{MAX-1}\|\|id)$

3.2   Protocol Phases

In this section we describe the five different phases of our protocol. Table 4 in Appendix A depicts the four phases after initialization.

Initialization. Two unique keys, ik and uk, are generated for each tag. Then, ik, uk and id are written on the non-volatile memory of the tag via a secure channel. This information will be used later by the tag to perform identification and ownership transfer. After tag initialization, the server stores the tag data in its database (see Table 2).

Synchronized Identification Phase. When the tags are synchronized, they execute this phase in order to be identified by a legitimate reader.

1. First, the reader broadcasts a nonce r_0.
2. Then, the synchronized tag answers with the following information: $h_{id}(ik)$, $C_0 = PRNG(ik\|\|r_0\|\|r_1)$[1] and r_1. After sending all data, the tag switches to a desynchronized state $(SYNC = 0)$ until the update phase ends.
3. Upon reception of these data, the reader forwards them to the server.
4. Then, the server searches inside a lookup table the value $h_{id}(ik)$ and obtains the tag's data ik and id. Using the identification key ik and the nonces r_0 and r_1, the server checks C_0 and decides whether to send id to the reader. Note that by checking C_0 the server avoids phishing or replay attacks. Finally, the server saves r_0 and r_1. These values are used in the update phase.

Update Phase. All the features of our protocol are mainly based on this phase.

1. The server composes m by concatenating a new identification key $m_L = ik_{new}$ and its hash value $m_R = h_{id}(ik_{new})$. Finally, the server computes $C_1 = m \oplus S$ where $S = PRNG(h_{uk}(ik)\|\|id\|\|r_0\|\|r_1)$ is an unpredictable pseudorandom sequence. The server sends C_1 to the reader.

---

[1] The pseudo-random number generator PRNG is supposed to be secure and unpredictable.

2. The reader forwards C_1 to the tag.
3. Upon reception of C_1, the tag generates its own pseudorandom sequence $S' = PRNG(h_{uk}(ik)||id||r_0||r_1)$, and computes $m' = C_1 \oplus S'$. By splitting m', the tag obtains m'_R and m'_L and checks whether $m'_R = h_{uk}(m'_L)$. If so, the tag can be sure that m' is, indeed, m; otherwise the tag rejects the reader's response. After the reader authentication, the tag splits m and updates its data: $ik = m'_L$ and $SYNC = 1$.

Desynchronized Identification Phase. This phase is executed when reader and tag are desynchronized, *e.g.* the message C_1 corresponding to the update phase was incorrect or it had not been received. The steps are as follows:

1. The reader sends r_0 to the tag, like in the synchronized identification phase.
2. The tag generates a new nonce r_1 and computes:
   $C_0 = PRNG(h_{uk}(k_{delta})||id||r_0||r_1)$, $\delta = \delta + 1$, and $k_\delta = h_{ik}(k_{\delta-1})$ where $k_0 = h_{id}(ik)$. Finally, the tag sends k_δ and C_0 to the reader.
3. Upon reception of the tag's response, the reader forwards the data to the server, who will search the value k_δ in the database using a lookup table generated with all the $Table\,k$ in the database (see Table 2). If the k_δ value is not found, the identification process fails. Otherwise, if k_δ is found in one or more records of the database, the server obtains the correct identifier through search of the id matching the C_0 value.
4. After a correct identification of the tag, the reader starts the Update phase.

It should be remarked that, the desynchronized identification phase can be executed consecutively just MAX times. If the number of consecutive identifications by a desynchronized identification phase is greater than MAX, the server will not be able to identify the tag any more (denial of service). The value of the parameter MAX is extensively discussed in [5].

Controlled Delegation Phase. This phase is run when the current owner needs to delegate identification rights to a new reader.

1. First, the current owner runs a successful synchronized identification phase but skips the update phase. At this stage, the tag is desynchronized and therefore responds with k_δ values when queried.
2. Then, the current owner just needs to give to the new reader the following infomation: id and n pairs $(k_\delta, h_{uk||ik}(k_\delta))$.
3. Later, the current owner is able to recover full control over the tag using one of the two following strategies: i) run a successful synchronized identification phase together with an update phase or ii) query the tag n times where n is the number of values given to the new reader.

When the new reader identifies a tag n times by controlled delegation, loose the right to identify this tag and only the current owner is able to identify the tag again. If the new reader needs to identify this tag again, it must request authorization to the current owner one more time
   This procedure is also described in Table 3 in Appendix 5.

Owner Transfer Phase. This phase is used to transfer ownership of the tag from the current owner to the new owner. The basic idea is to use a temporary key, as shown in Figure 2.

1. First, the current owner updates the key uk with uk_{tmp}. This prevents the new owner from backward tracking the tag.
2. Next, the current owner gives to the new owner the key uk_{tmp}.
3. Finally, the new owner updates uk_{tmp} with uk_{new} to prevent the old owner from forward tracking the tag.

After the previous protocol, the current owner plays the role of the previous owner while the new owner becomes the current owner. It should be remarked that a tag can know that uk is being updated by computing the left part of C_2. On the other hand, the new owner should update uk in an isolated environment in order to prevent the current owner from eavesdropping the messages and computing uk_{new}.

$$uk \longrightarrow uk_{tmp} \longrightarrow uk_{new}$$

Fig. 2. Life-cycle of the update key during the ownership transfer process

Authorization Recovery. In our scheme, an authorization recovery process can be performed as a controlled delegation process. However, we must assume that the current owner is unwilling to give the tag's identifier to another reader. The previous owner must search in its data base an identifier that matches C_0 using one of the provided pairs $(k_\delta, h_{uk||ik}(k_\delta))$. Note that this checking process can be only performed by a previous owner of a tag and, hence, the tag can be identified only by a legitimate previous owner.

3.3   Protocol States

In this protocol, a tag can be in one of the following states: initialized, synchronized, desynchronized and owner transfer. The tag changes its state by means of the following operations:

- (a) Initializing a tag. Once a tag has been initialized, it goes to the synchronized state.
- (b) Identifying a tag when it is synchronized. Once the tag is synchronized, if an identification is requested then its state changes to desynchronized.
- (c) Updating a tag. After a tag has been identified, the reader sends an update message. If the message is verified properly by the tag, the tag goes to the synchronized state.
- (d) Identifying a tag when it is desynchronized does not change the tag's state. Thus, the tag will remain desynchronized.
- (e) Running an owner transfer protocol. When the current owner runs the owner transfer phase, the tag changes its state to owner transfer. When the operation is verified successfully, the tags state is set to synchronized.

- (f) Disabling a tag. If the desynchronized identification phase is run more than MAX consecutive times, the tag is disabled (denial of service).

Figure 3 shows the different states and operations that are possible in the protocol.

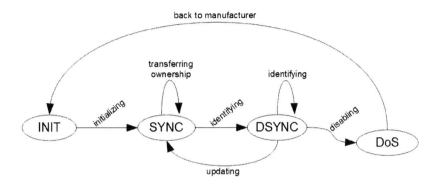

Fig. 3. The state diagram contains the states and transitions of an RFID tag in our scheme. The states are the following: i) tag initialized (INIT), ii) tag synchronized (SYNC), iii) tag desynchronized (DSYNC), and iv) tag disabled (DoS).

4   Analysis

The protocol has the following security and privacy properties.

4.1   Privacy

We consider the following privacy property:

Monitoring and Location. Location privacy is guaranteed because, in each identification, the data sent are always different, thanks to the use of nonces r_0 and r_1. Indeed, values ik, $h_{id}(ik)$, C_0 and r_1 are updated in each identification. If the reader and the tag are not synchronized, then the updated elements are: k_δ, C_0 and r_1. If both devices are synchronized, $h_{id}(ik)$ can appear twice with a probability of $1/2^\ell$ where ℓ is the size of the hash function.

The probability for k_δ is the same as $h_{id}(ik)$ in consecutive secondary identifications.

4.2   Security

Below are the most common attacks which can be launched on RFID schemes:

Denial of Service. An attacker can query the tag or interrupt the update phase $MAX + 1$ times, so that after that, a legitimate reader will not find k_δ in the database and will not be able to identify the tag. Since MAX is a security parameter of our system, we can set this value in order to increase the resistance of the proposed protocol against this attack. If the table is large enough, the time needed to consume all the values will be high enough. For instance, for $MAX = 100,000$ the required time to obtain all values of $Table\ k$ by an attacker, taking into account that each identification needs an interval of 200 ms, is 5.5 hours. By contrast, the disk space needed in a system with only 100,000 tags is 24 Tb.

To prevent massive attacks, the system can identify the tags regurarly. In this case, if an attacker is trying to knock out a tag, once the system updates that tag, the attacker must restart the DoS attack from zero. Furthermore, the value of MAX can be parameterized to resist DoS attacks. The fact that a high value of MAX behave a high space in disk is assumed due to the low cost of storage units today, yet this is one aspect to improve in a future versions of this protocol.

Impersonation of Devices

- *Impersonating a certain tag.* An attacker does not know values ik, uk and id. These elements are sent in the initialization phase using a secure communication channel. An attacker trying to impersonate a certain tag without the knowledge of these values will be detected by the reader. If an attacker is able to obtain the tag values, this information does not compromise other tags. Hence, impersonating a tag requires physically tampering with it and, in that case, it allows impersonating only that tag.
- *Impersonating the server.* This case is similar to the previous property. The server can only be impersonated by an attacker who knows the entire database. We assume that the database is hosted in a secure environment.
- *Replay attacks.* This type of attack is not possible in this protocol because, in each identification, each of the sides (tag and server) provides a new value which is computed at random. In this way, a replay attack at the server side will be successful only if the message which has been captured previously contains the expected r_0 value. The same happens at the tag side but with the value r_1. Random nonces r_0 and r_1 are generated in each device and they are unlikely to be repeated over a short period of time. In this way, value $h_{id}(ik)$ is different in each synchronized identification phase. In the desynchronized identification phase case, k_δ is always different.

4.3   Ownership Transfer

Our proposal satisfies the following properties.

New Owner Privacy. Our protocol is designed to guarantee that the transactions between the current owner and the tag cannot be traced by the previous owner. When the ownership of the tag is transferred, uk and ik are randomly updated, thereby ensuring that previous owners cannot identify the tag anymore unless the current owner allows controlled delegation.

Previous Owner Privacy. Since the update key is changed twice ($uk \rightarrow uk_{tmp} \rightarrow ik$), the previous owner's privacy is also guaranteed. As a result, the current owner cannot trace previous transactions between the previous owner and the tag.

Authorization Recovery. The protocol satisfies this property because the current owner can delegate the reading of the tag in a controlled fashion.

5   Conclusions

The novelty of our proposal consists of leveraging the update phase, that is used in the RFID identification protocol, in order to implement the ownership transfer protocol. Moreover, the protocol allows controlled delegation without the need of a counter in the non-volatile memory of tags. This feature is especially important considering that: i) tags are resource-constrained devices; ii) readers should not share the identification key of a tag. Finally, the protocol does not need a TTP, so that the users can perform ownership transfers any time and anywhere.

Disclaimer and Acknowledgments. The authors are solely responsible for the views expressed in this paper, which do not necessarily reflect the position of UNESCO nor commit that organization. This work was partly supported by the Spanish Ministry of Education through projects IPT-430000-2010-0031 AUDIT TRANSPARENCY, TSI2007-65406-C03-01 "E-AEGIS" and CONSOLIDER CSD2007-00004 "ARES", by the Spanish Ministry of Industry, Commerce and Tourism through project "SECloud" TSI-020302-2010-153 and by the Government of Catalonia under grant 2009 SGR 1135. The last author is partly supported as an ICREA Acadmia Researcher by the Government of Catalonia.

References

1. Alomair, B., Poovendran, R.: Privacy versus scalability in radio frequency identification systems. Computer Communications 33(18), 2155–2163 (2010)
2. Avoine, G., Dysli, E., Oechslin, P.: Reducing Time Complexity in RFID Systems. In: Preneel, B., Tavares, S. (eds.) SAC 2005. LNCS, vol. 3897, pp. 291–306. Springer, Heidelberg (2006)
3. Chen, H.B., Lee, W.B., Zhao, Y.H., Chen, Y.L.: Enhancement of the RFID security method with ownership transfer. In: Proceedings of the 3rd International Conference on Ubiquitous Information Management and Communication, pp. 251–254. ACM (2009)
4. Dimitriou, T.: rfidDOT: RFID delegation and ownership transfer made simple. In: Proceedings of the 4th International Conference on Security and Privacy in Communication Netowrks, pp. 1–8. ACM (2008)
5. Fernàndez-Mir, A., Castellà-Roca, J., Viejo, A.: Secure and Scalable RFID Authentication Protocol. In: Garcia-Alfaro, J., Navarro-Arribas, G., Cavalli, A., Leneutre, J. (eds.) DPM 2010 and SETOP 2010. LNCS, vol. 6514, pp. 231–243. Springer, Heidelberg (2011)
6. Fouladgar, S., Afifi, H.: An efficient delegation and transfer of ownership protocol for RFID tags. In: First International EURASIP Workshop on RFID Technology, Vienna, Austria (2007)

7. Goebel, C., Tribowski, C., Gunther, O., Troeger, R., Nickerl, R.: RFID in the Supply Chain: How to Obtain a Positive ROI-The Case of Gerry Weber. In: 11th International Conference on Enterprise Information Systems (ICEIS 2009), Milan, Italy, vol. 10, pp. 95–102 (May 6, 2009)

8. Kapoor, G., Piramuthu, S.: Vulnerabilities in some recently proposed RFID ownership transfer protocols. In: 2009 First International Conference on Networks & Communications, pp. 354–357. IEEE (2009)

9. Langheinrich, M.: A survey of RFID privacy approaches. Personal and Ubiquitous Computing 13(6), 413–421 (2009)

10. Molnar, D., Soppera, A., Wagner, D.: A Scalable, Delegatable Pseudonym Protocol Enabling Ownership Transfer of RFID Tags. In: Preneel, B., Tavares, S. (eds.) SAC 2005. LNCS, vol. 3897, pp. 276–290. Springer, Heidelberg (2006)

11. Osaka, K., Takagi, T., Yamazaki, K., Takahashi, O.: An Efficient and Secure RFID Security Method with Ownership Transfer. In: 2006 International Conference on Computational Intelligence and Security, vol. 2, pp. 1090–1095. IEEE (2007)

12. Saito, J., Imamoto, K., Sakurai, K.: Reassignment Scheme of an RFID Tag's Key for Owner Transfer. In: Enokido, T., Yan, L., Xiao, B., Kim, D.Y., Dai, Y.-S., Yang, L.T. (eds.) EUC-WS 2005. LNCS, vol. 3823, pp. 1303–1312. Springer, Heidelberg (2005)

13. Sarma, S.E.: Towards the five-cent tag. Technical report (2001)

14. Song, B., Mitchell, C.J.: Scalable RFID security protocols supporting tag ownership transfer. In: Computer Communications (2010)

15. European Union. Commission recommendation of 12 may 2009 on the implementation of privacy and data protection principles in applications supported by radiofrequency identification. Technical Report Official Journal of the European Union (May 2009)

16. Yoon, E.J., Yoo, K.Y.: Two security problems of RFID security method with ownership transfer. In: IFIP International Conference on Network and Parallel Computing, NPC 2008, pp. 68–73. IEEE (2008)

17. Yu Ng, C., Susilo, W., Mu, Y., Safavi-Naini, R.: Practical RFID Ownership Transfer Scheme. Journal of Computer Security - Special Issue on RFID System Security (2010)

A   Tables

Table 3. Controlled delegation and owner transfer phases

Current User	Tag	Final User

Controlled delegation phase

Synchronized identification phase

$\longrightarrow$

$SYNC = 0$

id and n pairs $(k_\delta, h_{uk||ik}(k_\delta))$ (with secure channel)

$\longrightarrow$

Desynchronized identification phase

$\longleftarrow$

$SYNC = 0$

Owner transfer phase

$m_L = uk_{new}, \; m_R = h_{uk}(uk_{new})$
$m = m_L||m_R$
$S = PRNG(h_{uk}(id)||r_0||r_1)$
$C_2 = m \oplus S$

C_2

$\longrightarrow$

$S^{'} = PRNG(h_{uk}(id)||r_0||r_1)$
$m^{'} = C_2 \oplus S^{'}$
$m^{'}_R \overset{?}{=} h_{uk}(m^{'}_L)$
$uk = m^{'}_L$

all data of the tag (with secure channel)

$\longrightarrow$

Owner transfer phase

$\longleftarrow$

Table 4. Our protocol

Server	Reader	Tag
Initialization phase (with secure channel)		
	ik, uk, id $\longrightarrow$	
Synchronized identification phase		
	$r_0 \in R\{0,1\}^*$ $\xrightarrow{r_0}$	
		$r_1 \in R\{0,1\}^*$ $C_0 = PRNG(ik\|r_0\|r_1)$ $\delta = 0$ Computes $h_{id}(ik)$ $SYNC = 0$
$\xleftarrow{h_{id}(ik), C_0, r_1, r_0}$	$\xleftarrow{h_{id}(ik), C_0, r_1}$	
Searches $h_{id}(ik)$ Checks C_0		
Update phase		
$m_L = ik_{new}, \ m_R = h_{uk}(ik_{new})$ $m = m_L\|m_R$ $S = PRNG(h_{uk}(id)\|r_0\|r_1)$ $C_1 = m \oplus S$		
$\xrightarrow{C_1}$	$\xrightarrow{C_1}$	
		$S' = PRNG(h_{uk}(id)\|r_0\|r_1)$ $m' = C_1 \oplus S'$ $m'_R \stackrel{?}{=} h_{uk}(m'_L)$ $ik = m'_L$ $SYNC = 1$
Desynchronized identification phase		
	$r_0 \in R\{0,1\}^*$ $\xrightarrow{r_0}$	
		$r_1 \in R\{0,1\}^*$ $k_0 = h_{id}(ik)$ $\delta = \delta + 1$ $k_\delta = h_{ik}(k_{\delta-1}\|id)$ $C_0 = PRNG(h_{uk}(k_{delta})\|id\|r_0\|r_1)$
$\xleftarrow{k_\delta, C_0, r_1}$	$\xleftarrow{k_\delta, C_0, r_1}$	
Searches k_δ on $Table\,k$. Checks C_0 Start update phase		

ROTIV: RFID Ownership Transfer with Issuer Verification

Kaoutar Elkhiyaoui, Erik-Oliver Blass, and Refik Molva

Eurecom, Sophia-Antipolis, France
{kaoutar.elkhiyaoui,erik-oliver.blass,refik.molva}@eurecom.fr

Abstract. RFID tags travel between partner sites in a supply chain. For privacy reasons, each partner *owns* the tags present at his site, i.e., the owner is the only entity able to authenticate his tags. When passing tags on to the next partner in the supply chain, ownership of the old partner is *transferred* to the new partner. In this paper, we propose ROTIV, a protocol that allows secure ownership transfer against malicious owners. ROTIV offers as well issuer verification to prevent malicious partners from injecting fake tags not originally issued by some trusted party. As part of ownership transfer, ROTIV provides a constant-time, privacy-preserving authentication. ROTIV's main idea is to combine an HMAC-based authentication with public key encryption to achieve constant time authentication and issuer verification. To assure privacy, ROTIV implements key update techniques and tag state re-encryption techniques, performed on the reader. ROTIV is especially designed for lightweight tags which are only required to evaluate a hash function.

1 Introduction

Supply chain management is one of the main applications of RFID tags today. Each RFID tag is physically attached to a product to allow product tracking and inventorying. As products travel in a supply chain, their ownership is transferred from one supply chain partner to another, and so is the ownership of their corresponding RFID tags. Tag ownership in this setting is the capability that allows an owner of tag T to authenticate, access, and transfer the ownership of T. Generally, the supply chain partners are reluctant into sharing their private information. Therefore, each partner requires to be the only authorized entity that can interact with tags in his site. To that effect, tags and partners in the supply chain must implement a secure ownership transfer protocol.

A secure ownership transfer protocol should fulfill two main *security* requirements: **1)** mutual authentication between the owner of a tag T (partner in the supply chain) and tag T to tell apart legitimate tags from counterfeits. **2)** exclusive ownership: non-authorized parties must not be able to transfer the ownership of tag T without the consent of T's owner. Furthermore, ownership transfer must be privacy preserving. It must ensure **1)** tag backward unlinkability: ownership transfer has to prevent the previous owner of a tag from tracing a tag once he releases its ownership, see Lim and Kwon [13]. **2)** tag forward unlinkability:

A. Juels and C. Paar (Eds.): RFIDSec 2011, LNCS 7055, pp. 163–182, 2012.

ownership transfer must prevent the new owner of a tag from tracing the tag's past interactions.

In addition to the basic features of tag ownership transfer as previously addressed in [14, 13, 7, 18], this paper proposes an *efficient* ownership transfer protocol that also allows a party possessing the right references to *verify the issuer* of a tag. A possible scenario for issuer verification is a supply chain where partners want to check that a product originates from a trusted partner.

An efficient ownership transfer protocol calls for an efficient authentication protocol. Current RFID authentication schemes based on symmetric cryptographic primitives require at least a logarithmic cost in the number of tags, see Burmester et al. [4]. Previously proposed tag/reader authentication protocols that achieve constant time authentication rely on public key cryptography performed on the tag as in [12]. However, RFID tags are constrained devices that cannot implement asymmetric cryptography.

The above schemes are designed to be privacy preserving against a *strong* adversary as defined by Juels and Weis [9], who can *continuously* eavesdrop on tags' communications. We claim that such an adversary is unrealistic in distributed supply chains which is the targeted setting by ROTIV. In ROTIV, we relax some privacy requirements to achieve mutual authentication in constant time while the tag performs only *symmetric* cryptographic operations (hash functions).

In ROTIV, a tag T stores in addition to its *symmetric* key, a public key encryption of its identification information computed by T's owner. The public key encryption helps the owner to identify the tag T first, then the symmetric key is used to authenticate both T and its current owner. In order to ensure tag privacy, we update T's state after each successful authentication. Moreover, each tag T in ROTIV is associated with a set of ownership references. T's ownership references allow T's owner to authenticate T and to transfer T's ownership. Finally, to allow tag issuer verification by third parties, a tag T stores an encryption of the issuer's signature. Provided with some trapdoor information from T's owner(the randomness used to encrypt $\mathcal{I}$'s signature), a third party verifier can verify whether the signature stored on T corresponds to a legitimate issuer or not.

In summary, ROTIV's contributions are:

- ownership transfer that ensures both tag forward unlinkability against the tag's new owner and tag backward unlinkability against the tag's previous owner.
- a *privacy-preserving*, and *constant time* authentication while tags are only required to compute a hash function.
- contrary to related work [17, 14, 7, 11], ROTIV does not require a trusted third party to perform tag ownership transfer.
- issuer verification protocol that allows prospective owners of a tag T to check the identity of the party issuing T.
- formal definitions of privacy and security requirements of tag ownership transfer.
- formal proofs of ROTIV security and privacy.

2   RFID Ownership Transfer with Issuer Verification

An ownership transfer protocol with issuer verification involves the following entities.

2.1   Entities

- **Tags** T_i: Each tag is attached to a single item. A tag T_i has a re-writable memory representing T_i's current state $s_{(i,j)}$ at time j. Tags can compute hash function G. $\mathcal{T}$ denotes the set of legitimate tags T_i.
- **Issuer** $\mathcal{I}$: The issuer $\mathcal{I}$ initializes tags and attaches each tag T_i to a product. For each tag T_i, $\mathcal{I}$ creates a set *ownership references* $\text{ref}^O_{T_i}$ that he gives to T_i's owner. $\mathcal{I}$ writes an initial state $s_{(i,0)}$ into T_i.
- **Owner** $O_{(T_i,k)}$: Is the owner of a tag T_i at time k. $O_{(T_i,k)}$ stores a set of ownership references $\text{ref}^O_{T_i}$ that allows him to authenticate tags T_i and to transfer T_i's ownership to a new owner. $\mathbb{O}$ denotes the set of all owners $O_{(T_i,k)}$. An owner $O_{(T_i,k)}$ comprises a database $\mathcal{D}_k$ and an RFID reader R_k.
- **Verifier** $\mathcal{V}$: Before accepting the ownership of some tag T_i, any prospective owner $O_{(T_i,k+1)}$ wants to verify the identity of tag T_i's issuer, therewith becoming a verifier $\mathcal{V}$. Owner $O_{(T_i,k)}$ of T_i provides $\mathcal{V}$ with *verification references* $\text{ref}^V_{T_i}$ allowing $\mathcal{V}$ to verify the identity of the issuer of T_i.

2.2   RFID Ownership Transfer with Issuer Verification

Secure ownership transfer raises four major requirements as follows:

1.) During daily operations, current owner $O_{(T_i,k)}$ of tag T_i in the supply chain has to be able to perform a number of *mutual authentications* with T_i.

2.) Eventually, $O_{(T_i,k)}$ has to pass T_i to the next owner $O_{(T_i,k+1)}$ in the supply chain. Therefore, $O_{(T_i,k)}$ and $O_{(T_i,k+1)}$ must *exchange* the *ownership references*.

3.) Once previous owner $O_{(T_i,k)}$ releases ownership of a tag T_i, new owner $O_{(T_i,k+1)}$ must securely *update* any *secrets* stored on T_i, such that only $O_{(T_i,k+1)}$ is able to authenticate T_i and eventually pass T_i to the next owner $O_{(T_i,k+2)}$.

4.) Before accepting tag ownership, a prospective owner $O_{(T_i,k+1)}$, has to perform *issuer verification*. That is, upon receipt of T_i verification references $\text{ref}^V_{T_i}$ from T_i's current owner, $O_{(T_i,k+1)}$ is able to verify whether T_i has been originally issued by $\mathcal{I}$.

3   Problem Statement

Recently proposed protocols on RFID tag ownership transfer [13, 7, 18] rely on symmetric primitives to perform privacy preserving mutual authentication and secure ownership transfer. As depicted in Figure 1, a tag T_i in these protocols

- stores a state $s_{(i,j)} = k_{(i,j)}$. This state corresponds to a secret key which is shared between T_i and T_i's owner $O_{(T_i,k)}$.

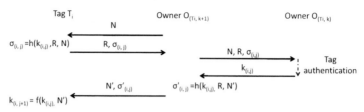

Fig. 1. Ownership transfer protocol

- computes a secure symmetric primitive h that is used to authenticate mutually T_i and $O_{(T_i,k)}$ using the secret key $k_{(i,j)}$.
- computes a function f that is used to update the secret key of T_i after a successful mutual authentication.

However, such protocols suffer from inherent limitations:

1) Linear complexity: As previously proposed protocols in [13, 18, 11] use symmetric primitives to authenticate a tag T_i, an owner has to try all the tags' keys in his database to authenticate T_i. Thus, in these schemes the authentication takes a linear time in the number of tags.

2) Denial of service: To ensure forward unlinkability, tag T_i updates its key $k_{(i,j)}$ using a secure hash function g even if the authentication with its owner $O_{(T_i,k)}$ is not successful as shown by Ohkubo et al. [15]. Also, $O_{(T_i,k)}$ keeps a limited set of η keys $(k_{(i,j+1)}, k_{(i,j+2)}, ..., k_{(i,j+\eta)}) = (g(k_{(i,j)}), g^2(k_{(i,j)}), ..., g^\eta(k_{(i,j)}))$ in his database $\mathcal{D}_k$ after each successful authentication with T_i. Thus, $O_{(T_i,k)}$ will still be able to authenticate T_i even if the authentication fails up to $\eta - 1$ times. However, an adversary can query T_i up to $p > \eta$ times, and therefore desynchronize T_i and $O_{(T_i,k)}$.

3) No tag issuer verification: Without tag issuer verification, owners and therewith partners in the supply chain will be able to inject tags that were not issued by trusted parties. We claim that in the real world, the prospective owner of tag T_i will require verifying the origin of T_i before accepting it.

To cope with these limitations we propose ROTIV. To achieve constant time authentication, a tag T_i in ROTIV stores in addition to its symmetric key $k_{(i,j)}$, an Elgamal ciphertext $c_{(i,j)}$ of T_i's identification information. When T_i is queried, it replies with $c_{(i,j)}$ and an HMAC computed using $k_{(i,j)}$. The owner decrypts $c_{(i,j)}$ and identifies T_i. Once T_i is identified, the owner authenticates T_i through HMAC. Furthermore, to prevent denial of service, a tag in ROTIV does not update its symmetric key unless the authentication is successful. Finally, to provide tag issuer verification, the ciphertext $c_{(i,j)}$ encrypts the signature of T_i's identifier by the issuer.

Note that protocols presented above [13, 7, 18] are designed to be forward privacy preserving against a *strong adversary* that continuously monitors tags [9, 19, 16]. However, in order to achieve both constant time authentication and denial of service resistance while the tag only computes hash functions, ROTIV must consider a more *realistic* adversary model. The adversary cannot continuously monitor a tag, i.e., there is at least *one* communication between the tag and its owner that is *unobserved* by the adversary.

Hence, ROTIV defines new privacy and security requirements that will be further discussed in Section 5. These requirements are along the same lines as recent research on RFID security such as [9, 19, 16].

Now, we present ROTIV in §4, followed by our privacy and security models in §5.

4   ROTIV

ROTIV takes place in subgroups of elliptic curves that support bilinear pairings.

4.1   Preliminaries

Bilinear pairing. Let $\mathbb{G}_1$, $\mathbb{G}_2$ and $\mathbb{G}_T$ be groups, such that $\mathbb{G}_1$ and $\mathbb{G}_T$ have the same prime order q. Pairing e: $\mathbb{G}_1 \times \mathbb{G}_2 \to \mathbb{G}_T$ is a bilinear pairing if:

1. e is *bilinear*: $\forall\, x, y \in \mathbb{Z}_q$, $g_1 \in \mathbb{G}_1$ and $g_2 \in \mathbb{G}_2$, $e(g_1^x, g_2^y) = e(g_1, g_2)^{xy}$;
2. e is *computable*: there is an efficient algorithm to compute $e(g_1, g_2)$ for any $(g_1, g_2) \in \mathbb{G}_1 \times \mathbb{G}_2$;
3. e is *non-degenerate*: if g_1 is a generator of $\mathbb{G}_1$ and g_2 is a generator of $\mathbb{G}_2$, then $e(g_1, g_2)$ is a generator of $\mathbb{G}_T$.

ROTIV's security and privacy rely on two assumptions.

Definition 1 (BCDH Assumption). *Let g_1 be a generator of $\mathbb{G}_1$ and g_2 be a generator of $\mathbb{G}_2$. We say that the BCDH assumption holds if, given $g_1, g_1^x, g_1^y, g_1^z \in \mathbb{G}_1$ and $g_2, g_2^x, g_2^y \in \mathbb{G}_2$ for random $x, y, z \in \mathbb{F}_q$, the probability to compute $e(g_1, g_2)^{xyz}$ is negligible.*

Definition 2 (SXDH Assumption). *The SXDH assumption holds if $\mathbb{G}_1$ and $\mathbb{G}_2$ are two groups with the following properties:*

1. *There exists a bilinear pairing $e : \mathbb{G}_1 \times \mathbb{G}_2 \to \mathbb{G}_T$.*
2. *The decisional Diffie-Hellman problem (DDH) is hard in both $\mathbb{G}_1$ and $\mathbb{G}_2$.*

Thus, ROTIV uses bilinear groups where DDH is hard, see Ballard et al. [3], Ateniese et al. [1, 2]. Such groups can be chosen as specific subgroups of MNT curves. Also, results by Galbraith et al. [8] indicate the high efficiency of such pairings.

4.2   ROTIV Description

1. Overview In ROTIV, a tag T_i stores a state $s_{(i,j)} = (k_{(i,j)}, c_{(i,j)})$, where $k_{(i,j)}$ is a key shared with the owner of T_i, and $c_{(i,j)}$ is an Elgamal encryption of T_i's identification information.

When an owner $O_{(T_i,k)}$ starts a mutual authentication with T_i, T_i replies with $c_{(i,j)}$ along with an HMAC computed using T_i's secret key $k_{(i,j)}$. Upon receipt of $c_{(i,j)}$, $O_{(T_i,k)}$ uses his Elgamal secret key to decrypt $c_{(i,j)}$. After decryption, $O_{(T_i,k)}$ checks if the resulting plaintext is in his database $\mathcal{D}_k$. If so, $O_{(T_i,k)}$ looks up the symmetric key $k_{(i,j)}$ of tag T_i in his database and verifies the HMAC sent by T_i. Therefore, ROTIV allows for mutual authentication with tag T_i in constant time, while the tag is only required to compute a symmetric primitive, i.e., HMAC.

To perform ownership transfer of tag T_i, the current owner $O_{(T_i,k)}$ of T_i gives $O_{(T_i,k+1)}$ T_i's ownership references $\text{ref}_{T_i}^O$ that will be used by $O_{(T_i,k+1)}$ to authenticate himself to T_i and to update T_i's state.

In order to ensure T_i's forward and backward privacy, the owner $O_{(T_i,k)}$ of T_i updates the ciphertext stored on T_i in every authentication he runs with T_i, using Elgamal re-encryption mechanisms. Moreoever, T_i updates its key $k_{(i,j)}$ after each successful authentication.

Finally, to achieve tag issuer verification, the ciphertext $c_{(i,j)}$ stored on T_i encrypts a signature of $\mathcal{I}$ on T_i's identifier. To perform issuer verification for tag T_i, a verifier $\mathcal{V}$ is provided with the ciphertext $c_{(i,j)}$ stored in T_i along with some trapdoor information called verification references $\text{ref}_{T_i}^V$. Then, given $c_{(i,j)}$ and $\text{ref}_{T_i}^V$, $\mathcal{V}$ is able to verify if $c_{(i,j)}$ is an encrypted signature by $\mathcal{I}$ of T_i's identifier.

2. Description A ROTIV system comprises l owners $O_{(T_i,k)}$ and n tags T_i. Each tag T_i can evaluate a cryptographic hash function G to compute an HMAC. The HMAC is used to authenticate T_i and T_i's owner, and to update the symmetric key after each successful authentication.

In the rest of this section we use the notation $\text{HMAC}_k(m, m') = \text{HMAC}_k(\text{m}||\text{m}')$, where $||$ denotes concatenation.

Setup. The issuer $\mathcal{I}$ outputs $(q, \mathbb{G}_1, \mathbb{G}_2, \mathbb{G}_T, g_1, g_2, e)$, where $\mathbb{G}_1$, $\mathbb{G}_T$ are subgroups of prime order q, g_1 and g_2 are random generators of $\mathbb{G}_1$ and $\mathbb{G}_2$ respectively, and $e : \mathbb{G}_1 \times \mathbb{G}_2 \to \mathbb{G}_T$ is a bilinear pairing. The issuer chooses $x \in \mathbb{Z}_q^*$ and computes g_2^x. $\mathcal{I}$'s secret key is $sk = x$ and his public key is $pk = g_2^x$.

For each owner $O_{(T_i,k)}$ $\mathcal{I}$ randomly selects $\alpha_k \in \mathbb{Z}_q^*$ and computes the pair $(g_1^{\alpha_k^2}, g_2^{\alpha_k})$. The system supplies each owner $O_{(T_i,k)}$ with his secret key $sk = \alpha_k$ and his public key $pk = (g_1^{\alpha_k^2}, g_2^{\alpha_k})$. All owners know each other's public key.

Tag Initialization. The issuer $\mathcal{I}$ initializes a tag T_i owned by $O_{(T_i,k)}$. $\mathcal{I}$ picks a random number $t_i \in \mathbb{F}_q$. Using a cryptographic hash function $H : \mathbb{F}_q \to \mathbb{G}_1$, $\mathcal{I}$ computes $h_i = H(t_i) \in \mathbb{G}_1$. Then, $\mathcal{I}$ computes $u_{(i,0)} = 1$ and $v_{(i,0)} = h_i^x$. Finally, $\mathcal{I}$ chooses randomly a key $k_{(i,0)} \in \mathbb{F}_q$. Tag T_i stores: $s_{(i,0)} = (k_{(i,0)}, c_{(i,0)})$, where $c_{(i,0)} = (u_{(i,0)}, v_{(i,0)})$. $\mathcal{I}$ gives $O_{(T_i,k)}$ the tag T_i and the corresponding ownership references $\text{ref}_{T_i}^O = (k_i^{\text{old}}, k_i^{\text{new}}, x_i, y_i) = (k_{(i,0)}, k_{(i,0)}, t_i, h_i^x)$.

Before accepting the tag, $O_{(T_i,k)}$ reads T_i and checks if the ownership references verify the equation: $e(H(x_i), g_2^x) = e(y_i, g_2)$. If so, this implies that T_i is actually issued by $\mathcal{I}$, that is $y_i = H(x_i)^x$.

The owner $O_{(T_i,k)}$ adds an entry E_{T_i} for tag T_i in his database $\mathcal{D}_k$: $E_{T_i} = (y_i, \text{ref}_{T_i}^O)$. y_i acts as the index of T_i in $O_{(T_i,k)}$'s database $\mathcal{D}_k$. Once the owner

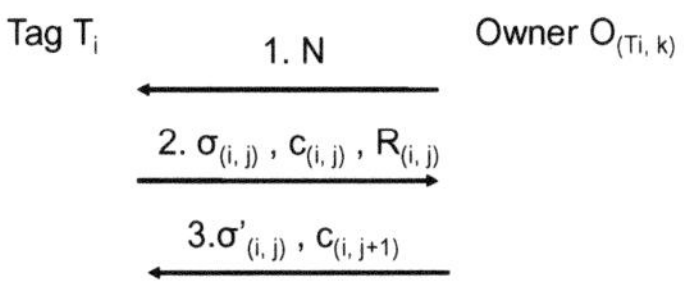

Fig. 2. Authentication in ROTIV

$O_{(T_i,k)}$ accepts the tag, he overwrites its content. He chooses randomly $r_{(i,1)} \in \mathbb{F}_q$ and computes an Elgamal encryption of y_i using his public key $g_1^{\alpha_k^2}$: $c_{(i,1)} = (u_{(i,1)}, v_{(i,1)}) = (g_1^{r_{(i,1)}}, y_i g_1^{\alpha_k^2 r_{(i,1)}})$. Therefore, $s_{(i,1)} = (k_{(i,1)} = k_{(i,0)}, c_{(i,1)})$.

Authentication protocol. To authenticate a tag T_i, the owner $O_{(T_i,k)}$ decrypts the ciphertext $c_{(i,j)} = (u_{(i,j)}, v_{(i,j)})$ sent by T_i and gets y_i. Using y_i, $O_{(T_i,k)}$ identifies T_i and starts a hash-based mutual authentication. If the mutual authentication succeeds, both the owner $O_{(T_i,k)}$ and the tag T_i update their keys.

1. To start an authentication with tag T_i, the owner $O_{(T_i,k)}$ sends a random nonce N to T_i as depicted in Figure 2.
   Once T_i receives N, it generates a random number $R_{(i,j)} \in \mathbb{F}_q$. Using its secret key $k_{(i,j)}$, T_i computes: $\sigma_{(i,j)} = \mathrm{HMAC}_{k_{(i,j)}}(N, R_{(i,j)}, c_{(i,j)})$. This HMAC serves two purposes, it authenticates T_i and ensures the integrity of the message sent by T_i.
2. T_i replies with $(R_{(i,j)}, c_{(i,j)} = (u_{(i,j)}, v_{(i,j)}), \sigma_{(i,j)})$.
   Upon receiving T_i's reply, the owner $O_{(T_i,k)}$ decrypts $c_{(i,j)}$ using his secret key α_k and gets $y_i = \frac{v_{(i,j)}}{(u_{(i,j)})^{\alpha_k^2}}$. $O_{(T_i,k)}$ checks if $y_i \in \mathcal{D}_k$. If not, $O_{(T_i,k)}$ aborts authentication. Otherwise, $O_{(T_i,k)}$ looks up T_i's ownership references $\mathrm{ref}_{T_i}^O = (k_i^{\mathrm{old}}, k_i^{\mathrm{new}}, t_i, h_i^x)$ in $\mathcal{D}_k$ and checks if: $\sigma_{(i,j)} = \mathrm{HMAC}_{k_i^{\mathrm{new}}}(N, R_{(i,j)}, c_{(i,j)})$ or $\sigma_{(i,j)} = \mathrm{HMAC}_{k_i^{\mathrm{old}}}(N, R_{(i,j)}, c_{(i,j)})$. If not, $O_{(T_i,k)}$ aborts authentication. If $\mathrm{HMAC}_{k_i^{\mathrm{old}}}(N, R_{(i,j)}, c_{(i,j)}) = \sigma_{(i,j)}$ then $k_{(i,j)} = k_i^{\mathrm{old}}$, otherwise $k_{(i,j)} = k_i^{\mathrm{new}}$. $O_{(T_i,k)}$ chooses a new random number $r_{(i,j+1)} \in \mathbb{F}_q^*$ and computes:

$$c_{(i,j+1)} = (u_{(i,j+1)}, v_{(i,j+1)}) = (g_1^{r_{(i,j+1)}}, y_i g_1^{\alpha_k^2 r_{(i,j+1)}})$$
$$\sigma'_{(i,j)} = \mathrm{HMAC}_{k_{(i,j)}}(R_{(i,j)}, c_{(i,j+1)})$$

   Finally, $O_{(T_i,k)}$ updates the symmetric keys k_i^{old} and k_i^{new} in his database $\mathcal{D}_k$: $(k_i^{\mathrm{old}}, k_i^{\mathrm{new}}) = (k_{(i,j)}, G(k_{(i,j)}, N))$.
3. $O_{(T_i,k)}$ sends $c_{(i,j+1)}$ and $\sigma'_{(i,j)}$ to T_i.
   Once T_i receives $\sigma'_{(i,j)}$ and $c_{(i,j+1)}$, it checks if $\sigma'_{(i,j)} = \mathrm{HMAC}_{k_{(i,j)}}(R_{(i,j)}, c_{(i,j+1)})$. If not T_i aborts authentication. Otherwise, T_i updates its key such that $k_{(i,j+1)} = G(k_{(i,j)}, N)$ and rewrites its state $s_{(i,j+1)} = (k_{(i,j+1)}, c_{(i,j+1)})$.

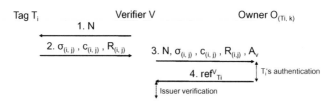

Fig. 3. Issuer verification in ROTIV

Desynchronization. If the last message of the authentication protocol is lost, tag T_i will not update its state and therewith, T_i will not update its symmetric key $k_{(i,j)}$. However, as the owner $O_{(T_i,k)}$ keeps both keys $k_i^{\text{old}} = k_{(i,j)}$ and $k_i^{\text{new}} = G(k_{(i,j)}, N)$, $O_{(T_i,k)}$ can always re-synchronize with T_i using k_i^{old}.

In the rest of this section, we assume that the channels between the owners are secure.

Issuer verification protocol. In order to verify whether a tag T_i owned by $O_{(T_i,k)}$ is actually issued by $\mathcal{I}$, a verifier $\mathcal{V}$ proceeds as follows:

1. $\mathcal{V}$ sends a nonce N to T_i, as depicted in Figure 3.

   Upon receiving N, T_i replies with $c_{(i,j)} = (u_{(i,j)}, v_{(i,j)}) = (g_1^{r_{(i,j)}}, h_i^x g_1^{\alpha_k^2 r_{(i,j)}})$, a random number $R_{(i,j)}$, and $\sigma_{(i,j)} = \text{HMAC}_{k_{(i,j)}}(N, R_{(i,j)}, c_{(i,j)})$.

2. Once $\mathcal{V}$ receives T_i's reply, he chooses a random number $r_v \in \mathbb{F}_q^*$ and computes $A_v = (u_{(i,j)})^{r_v} = g_1^{r_{(i,j)} r_v}$.

3. Then, $\mathcal{V}$ sends $N, R_{(i,j)}, c_{(i,j)}, \sigma_{(i,j)}$ along with A_v to $O_{(T_i,k)}$. Note that r_v and therewith A_v is used to prevent replay attacks by $O_{(T_i,k)}$.

   When receiving the tuple $(N, R_{(i,j)}, c_{(i,j)}, \sigma_{(i,j)}, A_v)$, $O_{(T_i,k)}$ identifies and authenticates T_i. If $O_{(T_i,k)}$ is not willing to run the verification protocol for T_i he aborts the verification. Otherwise, $O_{(T_i,k)}$ computes: $\text{ref}_{T_i}^V = (A_{(i,j)}, B_{(i,j)}, C_{(i,j)}) = (t_i, H(t_i)^x, A_v^{\alpha_k})$.

4. $O_{(T_i,k)}$ sends $\text{ref}_{T_i}^V = (A_{(i,j)}, B_{(i,j)}, C_{(i,j)})$ to $\mathcal{V}$.

Given the verification references $\text{ref}_{T_i}^V$, $\mathcal{V}$ checks whether the following equations hold:

$$e(H(A_{(i,j)}), g_2^x) = e(B_{(i,j)}, g_2) \tag{1}$$

$$e(C_{(i,j)}, g_2) = e(A_v, g_2^{\alpha_k}) \tag{2}$$

Equation (1) verifies whether $B_{(i,j)} = H(A_{(i,j)})^x$, i.e., whether $B_{(i,j)}$ is the signature of $A_{(i,j)}$ by issuer $\mathcal{I}$. Equation (2) checks whether $C_{(i,j)} = A_v^{\alpha_k}$.

Finally, $\mathcal{V}$ verifies whether $c_{(i,j)}$ is the encryption of $B_{(i,j)}$ with the public key $g_1^{\alpha_k^2}$ by checking if the following equation holds:

$$e(v_{(i,j)}, g_2)^{r_v} = e(B_{(i,j)}, g_2)^{r_v} e(C_{(i,j)}, g_2^{\alpha_k})$$

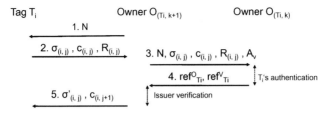

Fig. 4. Ownership transfer in ROTIV

Note that if $c_{(i,j)}$ is the encryption of $B_{(i,j)}$ with the public key $g_1^{\alpha_k^2}$, we have:
$c_{(i,j)} = (u_{(i,j)}, v_{(i,j)}) = (g_1^{r_{(i,j)}}, B_{(i,j)}g_1^{\alpha_k^2 r_{(i,j)}})$. Therefore,

$$e(v_{(i,j)}, g_2)^{r_v} = e(B_{(i,j)}, g_2)^{r_v} e(g_1^{\alpha_k^2 r_{(i,j)}}, g_2)^{r_v} = e(B_{(i,j)}, g_2)^{r_v} e(g_1^{r_v r_{(i,j)}}, g_2^{\alpha_k^2})$$

$$= e(B_{(i,j)}, g_2)^{r_v} e(A_v, g_2^{\alpha_k^2}) = e(B_{(i,j)}, g_2)^{r_v} e(A_v^{\alpha_k}, g_2^{\alpha_k})$$

$$= e(B_{(i,j)}, g_2)^{r_v} e(C_{(i,j)}, g_2^{\alpha_k})$$

If all the equations hold, $\mathcal{V}$ outputs $b = 1$ meaning that $\mathcal{I}$ is T_i's issuer. Otherwise, $\mathcal{V}$ outputs $b = 0$ meaning that $\mathcal{I}$ is not the issuer of T_i.

Ownership transfer protocol. The setup of the ownership transfer in ROTIV consists of a current owner $O_{(T_i,k)}$, a prospective owner $O_{(T_i,k+1)}$ and a tag T_i as shown in Figure 4. The ownership transfer consists of: **a)** a mutual authentication between T_i and $O_{(T_i,k+1)}$, **b)** an exchange of verification references $\mathrm{ref}_{T_i}^V$ between $O_{(T_i,k)}$ and $O_{(T_i,k+1)}$ to perform issuer verification, and **c)** an exchange of ownership references $\mathrm{ref}_{T_i}^O$ between $O_{(T_i,k)}$ and $O_{(T_i,k+1)}$ to allow $O_{(T_i,k+1)}$ authentication.

The ownership transfer protocol between $O_{(T_i,k)}$ and $O_{(T_i,k+1)}$ for tag T_i is as follows:

1. The owner $O_{(T_i,k+1)}$ sends a nonce N to tag T_i.
2. T_i replies with $c_{(i,j)} = (u_{(i,j)}, v_{(i,j)})$, a random number $R_{(i,j)}$ and HMAC $\sigma_{(i,j)}$.
3. $O_{(T_i,k+1)}$ selects a random number r_v and computes $A_v = u_{(i,j)}^{r_v}$. $O_{(T_i,k+1)}$ sends N, $R_{(i,j)}$, $c_{(i,j)}$, $\sigma_{(i,j)}$ and A_v to T_i's owner $O_{(T_i,k)}$.
   Given N, $R_{(i,j)}$, $c_{(i,j)}$ and $\sigma_{(i,j)}$, $O_{(T_i,k)}$ authenticates T_i. If the authentication fails, $O_{(T_i,k)}$ informs $O_{(T_i,k+1)}$, who re-sends his first message to T_i. Otherwise, $O_{(T_i,k)}$ supplies $O_{(T_i,k+1)}$ with: $\mathrm{ref}_{T_i}^O = (k_i^{old}, k_i^{new}, x_i, y_i) = (k_{(i,j)}, k_{(i,j)}, t_i, h_i^x = H(t_i)^x)$ and $\mathrm{ref}_{T_i}^V = (A_{(i,j)}, B_{(i,j)}, C_{(i,j)}) = (t_i, h_i^x, A_v^{\alpha_k})$.
4. Provided with $\mathrm{ref}_{T_i}^O$, $O_{(T_i,k+1)}$ checks if the equation $\sigma_{(i,j)} = \mathrm{HMAC}_{k_{(i,j)}}(N, R_{(i,j)}, c_{(i,j)})$ holds. If it does, this implies that the key $k_{(i,j)}$ provided by $O_{(T_i,k)}$ corresponds to tag T_i.
   Given $\mathrm{ref}_{T_i}^V$, $O_{(T_i,k+1)}$ verifies whether the issuer of T_i is $\mathcal{I}$. If the verification fails, $O_{(T_i,k+1)}$ aborts the ownership transfer. If not, $O_{(T_i,k+1)}$ adds the entry $(y_i, \mathrm{ref}_{T_i}^O)$ into his database $\mathcal{D}_{k+1}$, and finishes the authentication with T_i. $O_{(T_i,k+1)}$ chooses a new random number $r_{(i,j+1)} \in \mathbb{F}_q^*$ and computes:

$$c_{(i,j+1)} = (u_{(i,j+1)}, v_{(i,j+1)}) = (g_1^{r(i,j+1)}, y_i g_1^{\alpha_{k+1}^2 r(i,j+1)})$$
$$\sigma'_{(i,j)} = \text{HMAC}_{k_{(i,j)}}(R_{(i,j)}, c_{(i,j+1)})$$

So, $c_{(i,j+1)}$ is the encryption of y_i with $O_{(T_i,k+1)}$'s public key $g_1^{\alpha_{k+1}^2}$.

5. $O_{(T_i,k+1)}$ sends $c_{(i,j+1)}$ and $\sigma'_{(i,j)}$ to T_i, and updates its database $\mathcal{D}_{k+1}$ as in the authentication protocol presented above.

Upon receiving $c_{(i,j+1)}$ and $\sigma'_{(i,j)}$, T_i authenticates $O_{(T_i,k+1)}$. If the authentication succeeds T_i updates its state accordingly.

Note. To prevent the old owner $O_{(T_i,k)}$ from tracing the tag later in the future, the new owner $O_{(T_i,k+1)}$ has to run a mutual authentication with T_i *outside* the range of $O_{(T_i,k)}$ after the ownership transfer. In this manner, T_i and $O_{(T_i,k+1)}$ will share a symmetric key that $O_{(T_i,k)}$ cannot retrieve without physical access to tag T_i.

5   Privacy and Security Models

We assume that the communication channel between owners during an ownership transfer and an owner and a verifier during an issuer verification protocol are secure. That is, an adversary $\mathcal{A}$ has only access to the interactions between tags and owners and the wireless interactions between tags and verifiers.

5.1   Privacy

Inspired by previous work on ownership transfer[13, 5], we formally define using experiments the two major privacy requirements for ownership transfer which are *tag forward unlinkability* and *tag backward unlinkability*. In the setting of *tag ownership transfer*, forward unlinkability ensures that when a *new* owner $O_{(T,k+1)}$ acquires T's secrets after a successful ownership transfer at time $k + 1$, he still cannot tell whether T has participated in protocol runs at time $t < k+1$. On the other hand, backward unlinkability, ensures that when a *previous* owner $O_{(T,k)}$ releases tag's ownership at time $k + 1$, he still cannot tell whether T is involved in interactions that occured at time $t > k + 1$.

In the remainder of this section, we assume that the adversary $\mathcal{A}$ has access to oracles:

- $\mathcal{O}_{\mathcal{T}}$ is an oracle that, when queried, randomly returns a tag T from the set of tags $\mathcal{T}$.

- $\mathcal{O}_{\text{flip}}$ is an oracle that, when queried with two tags T_0 and T_1, randomly chooses $b \in \{0, 1\}$ and returns T_b.

- $\mathcal{O}_{\mathbb{O}}$ is an oracle that, when queried, returns a randomly selected owner O from the set of legitimate owners $\mathbb{O}$.

Forward unlinkability. The forward unlinkability experiment captures the capabilities of adversary $\mathcal{A}$ who is allowed to own a tag T at the *end* of his attack, and who has to decide if T was already involved in *previous* interactions.

Note that in scenarios where mutual authentication is required, the notion of *forward* unlinkability has been proven to be unachievable without tag performing public key cryptography operations, see Paise and Vaudenay [16].

Thus, as discussed in Section 3, in order to achieve constant time authentication and denial of service resistance, we assume that there is at least one communication between T and its owner that is un-observed by $\mathcal{A}$.

Our forward unlinkability experiment is indistinguishability based as proposed by Juels and Weis [9]. Adversary $\mathcal{A}(r, s, t, \epsilon)$ has access to tags in two phases. In the learning phase, as depicted in Algorithm 1, oracle $\mathcal{O}_T$ gives $\mathcal{A}$ two tags T_0 and T_1 that he can eavesdrop on by calling OBSERVEINTERACTION(T_i) for a maximum of t times. Note that OBSERVEINTERACTION(T_i) eavesdrops on tag T_i during mutual authentications, ownership transfer or issuer verification.

In addition to T_0 and T_1, $\mathcal{O}_T$ gives $\mathcal{A}$ a set of r tags T_i'. The ownership of T_i' is then transferred to $\mathcal{A}$ through TRANSFEROWNERSHIP$(T_i', O_{(T_i',k)}, \mathcal{A})$. $\mathcal{A}$ is now allowed to run up to s mutual authentication with T_i'.

In the challenge phase as depicted in Algorithm 2, T_0 and T_1 run once a mutual authentication with their respective owners (cf., RUNAUTH) *outside* the range of the adversary $\mathcal{A}$. Then, the oracle $\mathcal{O}_{\mathrm{flip}}$ queried with the tags T_0 and T_1, selects randomly $b \in \{0, 1\}$ and returns the tag T_b to $\mathcal{A}$. Then, the ownership of tag T_b will be transferred to $\mathcal{A}$. Then, $\mathcal{A}$ can run up to t mutual authentication with tag T_b.

$\mathcal{A}$ calls as well oracle $\mathcal{O}_T$ that supplies him with r tags T_i''. Then, the ownership of T_i'' is transferred to $\mathcal{A}$, who now can run up to s mutual authentication with T_i''. Finally, $\mathcal{A}$ outputs his guess of the value of b.

$\mathcal{A}$ is *successful*, if his guess of b is correct.

```
T_0 ← O_T;
T_1 ← O_T;
for j := 1 to t do
  | OBSERVEINTERACTION(T_0);
  |  OBSERVEINTERACTION(T_1);
end
for i := 1 to r do
  | T_i' ← O_T;
  | TRANSFEROWNERSHIP(T_i', O_(T_i',k), A);
  |
  | for j := 1 to s do
  |   | RUNAUTH(T_i', A)
  | end
end
```

Algorithm 1. $\mathcal{A}$'s forward unlinkability learning phase

```
RUNAUTH(T_0, O_(T_0,k));
// Unobserved by A.
RUNAUTH(T_1, O_(T_1,k));
// Unobserved by A.
T_b ← O_flip{T_0, T_1};
TRANSFEROWNERSHIP(T_b, O_(T_b,k), A);

for j := 1 to t do
  | RUNAUTH(T_b, A);
end
for i := 1 to r do
  | T_i'' ← O_T;
  | TRANSFEROWNERSHIP(T_i'', O_(T_i'',k), A);
  |
  | for j := 1 to s do
  |   | RUNAUTH(T_i'', A)
  | end
end
OUTPUT b;
```

Algorithm 2. $\mathcal{A}$'s forward unlinkability challenge phase

Definition 3 (Forward Unlinkability). *ROTIV provides forward unlinkability* $\Leftrightarrow$ *For any adversary* $\mathcal{A}$, *inequality* $Pr(\mathcal{A}$ *is successful*$) \leq \frac{1}{2} + \epsilon$ *holds, where* ϵ *is negligible.*

Backward unlinkability. It has been shown in [19] that is impossible to achieve backward unlinkability without public key cryptography on tags. In order to achieve at least a slightly weaker notion of backward unlinkability, we add the assumption that a previous owner $O_{(T,k)}$ of tag T *cannot continuously* monitor T after releasing T's ownership. This has been previously suggested by, e.g., Lim and Kwon [13], Dimitrou [5].

The backward unlinkability experiment captures the capabilities of an adversary $\mathcal{A}$ who *releases* the ownership of tag T *during* his attack and has to tell whether T is involved in future protocol transactions.

In the learning phase, cf., Algorithm 3, oracle $\mathcal{O}_T$ selects randomly two tags T_0 and T_1. Then, the ownership of these two tags is transferred to $\mathcal{A}$. $\mathcal{A}$ is allowed to run up to t mutual authentications with tags T_0 and T_1.

$\mathcal{O}_T$ gives $\mathcal{A}$ also a set of r tags T_i'. Then, the ownership of tags T_i' is transferred to $\mathcal{A}$, who can then perform up to s mutual authentications with tags T_i'.

At the end of the learning phase, the oracle $\mathcal{O}_{\mathbb{O}}$ supplies $\mathcal{A}$ with two randomly selected owners. $\mathcal{A}$ then, releases the ownership of tags T_0 and T_1.

$T_0 \leftarrow \mathcal{O}_T$;
$T_1 \leftarrow \mathcal{O}_T$;
TRANSFEROWNERSHIP$(T_0, O_{(T_0,k)}, \mathcal{A})$;

TRANSFEROWNERSHIP$(T_1, O_{(T_1,k)}, \mathcal{A})$;

for $j := 1$ **to** t **do**
   | RUNAUTH$(T_0, \mathcal{A})$;
   | RUNAUTH$(T_1, \mathcal{A})$;
end
for $i := 1$ **to** r **do**
   | $T_i' \leftarrow \mathcal{O}_T$;
   | TRANSFEROWNERSHIP$(T_i', O_{(T_i',k)}, \mathcal{A})$;

   | **for** $j := 1$ **to** s **do**
      | RUNAUTH$(T_i', \mathcal{A})$
   | **end**
end
$O_{(T_0,k+1)} \leftarrow \mathcal{O}_{\mathbb{O}}$;
TRANSFEROWNERSHIP$(T_0, \mathcal{A}, O_{(T_0,k+1)})$;

$O_{(T_1,k+1)} \leftarrow \mathcal{O}_{\mathbb{O}}$;
TRANSFEROWNERSHIP$(T_1, \mathcal{A}, O_{(T_1,k+1)})$;

Algorithm 3. $\mathcal{A}$'s backward unlinkability learning phase

RUNAUTH$(T_0, O_{(T_0,k+1)})$;
// **Unobserved by** $\mathcal{A}$.
RUNAUTH$(T_1, O_{(T_1,k+1)})$;
// **Unobserved by** $\mathcal{A}$.
$T_b \leftarrow \mathcal{O}_{\text{flip}}\{T_0, T_1\}$;
for $j := 1$ **to** t **do**
   | OBSERVEINTERACTION(T_b);
end
for $i := 1$ **to** r **do**
   | $T_i'' \leftarrow \mathcal{O}_T$;
   | TRANSFEROWNERSHIP$(T_i'', O_{(T_i'',k)}, \mathcal{A})$;

   | **for** $j := 1$ **to** s **do**
      | RUNAUTH$(T_i'', \mathcal{A})$
   | **end**
end
OUTPUT b;

Algorithm 4. $\mathcal{A}$'s backward unlinkability challenge phase

In the challenge phase as depicted in Algorithm 4, T_0 and T_1 run a mutual authentication with their respective owners *outside* the range of the adversary

$\mathcal{A}$. The oracle $\mathcal{O}_{\text{flip}}$ queried with tags T_0 and T_1, chooses randomly $b \in \{0,1\}$ and returns the tag T_b to $\mathcal{A}$. $\mathcal{A}$ is allowed to eavesdrop on T_b for a maximum of t times.

$\mathcal{A}$ queries also the oracle $\mathcal{O}_\mathcal{T}$ that supplies $\mathcal{A}$ with r tags T_i''. The ownership of T_i'' is transferred to $\mathcal{A}$, who is allowed to run up to s mutual authentication with T_i''. Finally, $\mathcal{A}$ outputs his guess of the value of b. $\mathcal{A}$ is *successful*, if his guess of b is correct.

Definition 4 (Backward Unlinkability). *ROTIV provides backward unlinkability* $\Leftrightarrow$ *For any adversary* $\mathcal{A}$, *inequality* $Pr(\mathcal{A}$ *is successful*$) \leq \frac{1}{2} + \epsilon$ *holds, where* ϵ *is negligible.*

5.2 Security

As ROTIV consists of two main protocols, an ownership transfer protocol and an issuer verification protocol, we introduce the security requirements for each protocol separately. The adversary $\mathcal{A}$ in this section is a direct adaptation of the non-narrow destructive adversary by Vaudenay [19] and Paise and Vaudenay [16] to tag ownership transfer in supply chains.

Ownership transfer. A secure ownership transfer must assure the following properties:

a) Mutual authentication. A secure ownership transfer protocol must ensure that, when a tag T runs a successful mutual authentication with owner O, this implies that O is T's current owner with high probability. Also, when an owner O runs a successful mutual authentication with a tag T, it yields that T is a legitimate tag with high probability.

We define an authentication game in accordance with Lim and Kwon [13], Vaudenay [19] and Paise and Vaudenay [16]. This game proceeds in two phases. During the learning phase as depicted in Algorithm 5, an adversary $\mathcal{A}(r,s,t,\epsilon)$ is supplied with a challenge tag T_c from oracle $\mathcal{O}_\mathcal{T}$. $\mathcal{A}$ is not allowed to read the internal state of T_c. $\mathcal{A}$ is allowed to eavesdrop on r mutual authentications between T_c and its owner $O_{(T_c,k)}$, cf., RUNAUTH$(T_c, O_{(T_c,k)})$. He can also alter authentications by modifying the messages exchanged between T_c and its owner $O_{(T_c,k)}$, cf., ALTERAUTH$(T_c, O_{(T_c,k)})$. $\mathcal{A}$ is allowed as well to start s authentications with T_c while impersonating $O_{(T_c,k)}$, (cf., RUNAUTH$(T_c, \mathcal{A})$). Also he can start t authentications with $O_{(T_c,k)}$ while impersonating T_c, cf., RUNAUTH$(\mathcal{A}, O_{(T_c,k)})$.

$\mathcal{A}$'s goal in the challenge phase is **either** to run a successful mutual authentication with T_c, i.e., $\mathcal{A}$ succeeds in impersonating $O_{(T_c,k)}$, **or** to run a successful mutual authentication with $O_{(T_c,k)}$, i.e., $\mathcal{A}$ succeeds in impersonating T_c.

In the challenge phase as depicted in Algorithm 6, $\mathcal{A}(r,s,t,\epsilon)$ interacts with T_c and initiates an authentication protocol run to impersonate $O_{(T_c,k)}$, cf., RUNAUTH$(T_c, \mathcal{A})$. At the end of the authentication, T_c outputs a bit b_{T_c}, $b_{T_c} = 1$ if the authentication with $\mathcal{A}$ was successful, and $b_{T_c} = 0$ otherwise.

$T_c \leftarrow \mathcal{O}_T$;
for $i = 1$ **to** r **do**
  $\mid$ RUNAUTH($T_c, O_{(T_c,k)}$);
  $\mid$ ALTERAUTH($T_c, O_{(T_c,k)}$);
end
for $i = 1$ **to** s **do**
  $\mid$ RUNAUTH($T_c, \mathcal{A}$);
end
for $i = 1$ **to** t **do**
  $\mid$ RUNAUTH($\mathcal{A}, O_{(T_c,k)}$);
end

Algorithm 5. $\mathcal{A}$'s authentication learning phase

RUNAUTH($T_c, \mathcal{A}$);
T_c OUTPUTS b_{T_c};
RUNAUTH($\mathcal{A}, O_{(T_c,k)}$);
$O_{(T_c,k)}$ OUTPUTS $b_{O_{(T_c,k)}}$;

Algorithm 6. $\mathcal{A}$'s authentication challenge phase

$\mathcal{A}$ can interact as well with $O_{(T_c,k)}$ and initiates an authentication protocol run to impersonate T_c, cf., RUNAUTH($\mathcal{A}, O_{(T_c,k)}$). At the end of this authentication, $O_{(T_c,k)}$ outputs a bit $b_{O_{(T_c,k)}} = 1$, if the authentication was successful, $b_{O_{(T_c,k)}} = 0$ otherwise.

$\mathcal{A}$ is *successful* if, $b_{T_c} = 1$ or $b_{O_{(T_c,k)}} = 1$.

Definition 5 (Authentication). *ROTIV is secure with regard to authentication* $\Leftrightarrow$ *For any adversary* $\mathcal{A}$, *inequality* $Pr(\mathcal{A}$ *is successful*$) \le \epsilon$ *holds, where* ϵ *is negligible.*

b) Exclusive ownership It ensures that an adversary $\mathcal{A}$ who does not have T's ownership references noted ref_T^O, cannot transfer the ownership of T, unless he rewrites the content of T.

In the learning phase as shown in Algorithm 7, the oracle $\mathcal{O}_T$ supplies $\mathcal{A}(r, s, t, \epsilon)$ with r tags T_i, then, the ownership of tag T_i is transferred to $\mathcal{A}$. $\mathcal{A}$ can run up to s successful mutual authentications with T_i, cf., RUNAUTH($T_i, \mathcal{A}$). He can as well at the end of the learning phase, transfer the ownership of tag T_i to an owner O_i selected randomly from the set of owners $\mathbb{O}$.

for $i := 1$ **to** r **do**
  $T_i \leftarrow \mathcal{O}_T$;
  TRANSFEROWNERSHIP($T_i, O_{(T_i,k)}, \mathcal{A}$);
  for $j := 1$ **to** s **do**
    $\mid$ RUNAUTH($T_i, \mathcal{A}$);
  end
  $O_i \leftarrow \mathcal{O}_{\mathbb{O}}$;
  TRANSFEROWNERSHIP($T_i, \mathcal{A}, O_i$);
end

Algorithm 7. $\mathcal{A}$'s exclusive ownership learning phase

$T_c \leftarrow \mathcal{O}_T$;
for $j := 1$ **to** t **do**
  $\mid$ $s_{(T_c,j)} :=$ READSTATE(T_c);
  $\mid$ OBSERVEINTERACTION(T_c);
end
$O_c \leftarrow \mathcal{O}_{\mathbb{O}}$;
TRANSFEROWNERSHIP($T_c, \mathcal{A}, O_c$);
O_c OUTPUTS b;

Algorithm 8. $\mathcal{A}$'s exclusive ownership challenge phase

In the challenge phase, cf., Algorithm 8, the oracle $\mathcal{O}_T$ gives $\mathcal{A}(r, s, t, \epsilon)$ a challenge tag T_c.

$\mathcal{A}$ can read T_c's internal state, cf., READSTATE(T_c), and eavesdrop on T_c's up to t times. However, $\mathcal{A}$ is not allowed to alter T_c's internal state. At the end of the challenge phase, $\mathcal{A}$ queries the oracle $\mathcal{O}_{\mathbb{O}}$. $\mathcal{O}_{\mathbb{O}}$ returns a challenge owner O_c.

$\mathcal{A}$ runs an ownership transfer protocol for T_c with O_c. O_c outputs a bit $b = 1$, if the ownership transfer was successful, and $b = 0$ otherwise. $\mathcal{A}$ is *successful*, if $b = 1$.

Definition 6 (Exclusive ownership). *ROTIV provides exclusive ownership* $\Leftrightarrow$ *For any adversary $\mathcal{A}$, inequality $Pr(\mathcal{A}$ is successful$) \leq \epsilon$ holds, where ϵ is negligible.*

Issuer verification The security of issuer verification ensures that when a verifier $\mathcal{V}$ outputs that the issuer of tag T is $\mathcal{I}$, it implies that $\mathcal{I}$ is the issuer of T with high probability.

An adversary $\mathcal{A}$'s goal is to run an issuer verification protocol with $\mathcal{V}$ for tag T that was not issued by $\mathcal{I}$, and still $\mathcal{V}$ outputs that $\mathcal{I}$ is the issuer of T.

In the learning phase, $\mathcal{A}$ queries the oracle $\mathcal{O}_T$ that gives $\mathcal{A}$ a total of r random tags T_i. The ownership of T_i is then transferred to $\mathcal{A}$, cf. TRANSFEROWNER-SHIP$(O_{(T_i,k)}, \mathcal{A}, T_i)$. $\mathcal{A}$ can run up to s mutual authentications with tag T_i, cf., RUNAUTH$(T_c, \mathcal{A})$. The adversary can also run s issuer verification protocol for tag T_i with the verifier $\mathcal{V}$, cf., VERIFY$(T_i, \mathcal{A}, \mathcal{V})$ and to transfer T_i's ownership to an owner O_i randomly selected from the set of owners $\mathbb{O}$.

for $i := 1$ **to** r **do**
   $T_i \leftarrow \mathcal{O}_T$;
   TRANSFEROWNERSHIP$(O_{(T_i,k)}, \mathcal{A}, T_i)$;

   for $j := 1$ **to** s **do**
      RUNAUTH$(T_i, \mathcal{A})$;
      VERIFY$(T_i, \mathcal{A}, \mathcal{V})$;
   end
   $O_i \leftarrow \mathcal{O}_\mathbb{O}$;
   TRANSFEROWNERSHIP$(T_i, \mathcal{A}, O_i)$;
end

Algorithm 9. $\mathcal{A}$'s issuer verification security learning phase

CREATETAG T_c;
MODIFYSTATE(T_c, s'_{T_c});
VERIFY $(T_c, \mathcal{A}, \mathcal{V})$;
$\mathcal{V}$ OUTPUTS b;

Algorithm 10. $\mathcal{A}$'s issuer verification security challenge phase

In the challenge phase, $\mathcal{A}$ creates a tag $T_c \notin \mathcal{T}$ and write some state s'_{T_c} in it. Then, $\mathcal{A}$ starts a verification protocol for tag T_c with the verifier $\mathcal{V}$, cf. VERIFY $(T_c, \mathcal{A}, \mathcal{V})$. Finally, $\mathcal{V}$ outputs a bit $b = 1$, if the issuer verification protocol outputs $\mathcal{I}$, and $b = 0$ otherwise. $\mathcal{A}$ is *successful*, if $b = 1$ and s'_{T_c} does not correspond to a state of tag T_i that was given to $\mathcal{A}$ in the learning phase.

Definition 7 (Issuer verification security). *ROTIV is secure with regard to issuer verification* $\Leftrightarrow$ *For any adversary $\mathcal{A}$, inequality $Pr(\mathcal{A}$ is successful$) \leq \epsilon$ holds, where ϵ is negligible.*

6 Privacy and Security Analysis

In this section, we state the main proofs of ROTIV's privacy and security.

Due to space limitations, we give only proof sketches. The detailed proofs could be found in the extended version of this paper [6].

6.1   Privacy

We prove that ROTIV provides forward unlinkability and backward unlinkability under the SXDH assumption (DDH is hard in both $\mathbb{G}_1$ and $\mathbb{G}_2$).

Theorem 1 (Forward unlinkability). *ROTIV provides forward unlinkability under the SXDH assumption.*

Proof (sketch). Assume there is an adversary $\mathcal{A}$ who breaks the forward unlinkability ROTIV with a non negligible advantage ϵ. We show that there is an adversary $\mathcal{A}'$ that uses $\mathcal{A}$ to break the DDH assumption, that is, given $(g_1, g_1^\alpha, g_1^\beta, g_1^\gamma)$, it is hard to decide whether $\gamma = \alpha\beta$.

To break DDH, $\mathcal{A}'$ creates a ROTIV system with **1.)** issuer $\mathcal{I}$ whose public key is g_2^x where x is selected randomly from $\mathbb{F}_q$. **2.)** Owner O whose public key is g_1^α.

To issue the challenge tags $T_i, i \in \{0, 1\}$, $\mathcal{A}'$ randomly selects t_i, $k_{(i,0)}$ and $r_{(i,0)} \in \mathbb{F}_q$, then computes $h_i = H(t_i)$, and $c_{(i,0)} = (u_{(i,0)}, v_{(i,0)}) = (g_1^{\beta r_{(i,0)}}, h_i^x g_1^{\gamma r_{(i,0)}})$. Finally, $\mathcal{A}'$ stores $s_{(i,0)} = (k_{(i,0)}, c_{(i,0)})$ in tag T_i.

In the challenge phase, $\mathcal{A}'$ starts authentications outside the range of $\mathcal{A}$ with T_0 by sending a nonce N_0 and with T_1 by sending a nonce N_1. We assume T_0 stores $s_{(0,j)} = (k_{(0,j)}, c_{(0,j)})$ and T_1 stores $s_{(1,j)} = (k_{(1,j)}, c_{(1,j)})$.

At the end of an authentication, $\mathcal{A}'$ updates the state of T_0 and T_1 as follows: $s_{(i,j+1)} = (k_{(i,j+1)}, c_{(i,j+1)})$, $i \in \{0, 1\}$, where $k_{(i,j+1)} = G(N_i, k_{(i,j)})$ and $c_{(i,j+1)} = (g_1^{r_{(i,j+1)}}, h_i^x g_1^{\alpha r_{(i,j+1)}})$.

Given that $\mathcal{A}$ does not have access to $N_i, i \in \{0, 1\}$, $k_{(i,j+1)} = G(k_{(i,j)}, N_i)$ cannot give $\mathcal{A}$ any information about T_b's past interactions. So, the privacy of ROTIV is reduced to the security of ciphertexts stored in T_0 and T_1.

In the challenge phase, $\mathcal{A}'$ selects randomly a coin $b \in \{0, 1\}$ and transfers the ownership of T_b to $\mathcal{A}$. T_b now stores a state $s_{(b,j+1)} = (k_{(b,j+1)}, c_{(b,j+1)})$ where $c_{(b,j+1)} = (g_1^{r_{(b,j+1)}}, h_b^x g_1^{\alpha r_{(b,j+1)}})$.

At the end of the challenge phase, $\mathcal{A}$ outputs his guess of b.

If $\gamma = \alpha\beta$, then $c_{(b,j+1)}$ is re-encryption of $c_{(b,j)}$. $\mathcal{A}$ then can output a correct guess for the tag corresponding to T_b with a non-negligible advantage ϵ. Thus, $\mathcal{A}'$ can tell that $\gamma = \alpha\beta$ with a non negligible advantage ϵ.

If $\gamma \neq \alpha\beta$, the probability that $\mathcal{A}'$ can break the DDH is a random guess, i.e., $\frac{1}{2}$.

Let E_1 be the event that $\mathcal{A}'$ can break DDH, and E_2 is the event that $\gamma = \alpha\beta$ holds. The probability of event E_2 is $\frac{1}{2}$.

$$Pr(E_1) = Pr(E_2) \cdot Pr(E_1|E_2) + Pr(\overline{E_2}) \cdot Pr(E_1|\overline{E_2})$$
$$= \frac{1}{2}Pr(E_1|E_2) + \frac{1}{2}Pr(E_1|\overline{E_2}) \geq \frac{1}{2}(\frac{1}{2} + \epsilon) + \frac{1}{2} \cdot \frac{1}{2} = \frac{1}{2} + \frac{\epsilon}{2}$$

Therefore, with $\mathcal{A}$'s non negligible advantage in breaking forward unlinkability of ROTIV, $\mathcal{A}'$'s advantage in breaking DDH in $\mathbb{G}_1$ is also non negligible.

Theorem 2 (Backward unlinkability). *ROTIV provides backward unlinkability under the SXDH assumption.*

The same reasoning of the above proof sketch applies for ROTIV's backward unlinkability.

6.2 Security

We prove that ROTIV is secure with regards to the security properties introduced in Section 5.2.

Theorem 3 (Secure authentication). *The ownership transfer protocol in ROTIV provides secure authentication under the security of HMAC.*

Proof (sketch). Assume there is an adversary $\mathcal{A}$ who breaks the mutual authentication of ROTIV with a non-negligible advantage. We show that there is an adversary $\mathcal{A}'$ who breaks the security of HMAC with a non-negligible advantage.

Note that if $\mathcal{A}$ breaks the mutual authentication of ROTIV, then this means that $\mathcal{A}$ is able to either impersonate the challenge tag T_c or to impersonate the owner of T_c.

Let k denotes the secret key shared between T_c and T_c's owner in the challenge phase of the mutual authentication experiment.

1) If $\mathcal{A}$ impersonates T_c: this implies that $\mathcal{A}$ receives a nonce N from T_c's owner and then replies with a ciphertext c , a random number R and $\sigma = \mathrm{HMAC}_k(N, R, c)$.

An adversary $\mathcal{A}'$ who wants to break the security of HMAC outputs the message $m = (N, R, c)$ and $\sigma = \mathrm{HMAC}_k(m)$. This leads to a contradiction under the security of HMAC.

2) If $\mathcal{A}$ impersonates T_c's owner: this yields that $\mathcal{A}$ sends a nonce N to T_c. Then, $\mathcal{A}$ receives a ciphertext c, a random number R and $\sigma = \mathrm{HMAC}_k(N, R, c)$ from tag T_c. Finally, $\mathcal{A}$ replies with a ciphertext c' and $\sigma' = \mathrm{HMAC}_k(R, c')$.

An adversary $\mathcal{A}'$ who wants to break the security of HMAC outputs the message $m' = R \parallel c'$ and $\sigma' = \mathrm{HMAC}_k(m')$. This leads to a contradiction under the security of HMAC.

Theorem 4 (Exclusive ownership). *The ownership transfer protocol in ROTIV provides exclusive ownership under the security of hash function H.*

Proof (sketch). Assume there is an adversary $\mathcal{A}$ who breaks the exclusive ownership of ROTIV with a non negligible advantage. We construct an adversary $\mathcal{A}'$ who breaks the one wayness of the hash function H with a non negligible advantage.

Let $\mathcal{A}'$ denotes an adversary against the one wayness of H. That is, given $h = H(t)$, $\mathcal{A}'$ outputs t.

To break the one wayness of H, $\mathcal{A}'$ writes a valid state $s_{(T_c, j)} = (k_{(T_c, j)}, c_{(T_c, j)})$ into the challenge tag T_c, such that $c_{(T_c, j)}$ is an encryption of $h^x = H(t)^x$. At the end of the challenge phase of the exclusive ownership experiment, $\mathcal{A}$ is required to transfer the ownership of tag T_c to a challenge owner O_c.

If $\mathcal{A}$'s advantage in the exclusive ownership experiment is non-negligible, then this means that $\mathcal{A}$ is able to supply O_c with valid ownership references of tag T_c: $\mathrm{ref}_{T_c}^O = (t, h^x, k_{\mathrm{old}}, k_{\mathrm{new}})$ with non negligible advantage.

To break the one wayness of H, $\mathcal{A}'$ outputs t as provided by $\mathcal{A}$. This leads to a contradiction under the one wayness of H.

Theorem 5 (Issuer verification security). *The issuer verification protocol in ROTIV is secure under the BCDH assumption.*

Proof (sketch). Assume there is an adversary $\mathcal{A}$ who can break the security of the issuer verification protocol with a non-negligible advantage. We build an adversary $\mathcal{A}'$ who breaks the BCDH assumption, that is, given $g_1, g_1^x, g_1^y, g_1^z \in \mathbb{G}_1$ and $g_2, g_2^x, g_2^y \in \mathbb{G}_2$ for random $x, y, z \in \mathbb{F}_q$, the probability to compute $e(g_1, g_2)^{xyz}$ is negligible.

To break BCDH assumption, $\mathcal{A}'$ simulates an issuer of ROTIV whose secret key is $sk = x$ and public key $pk = g_2^x$. $\mathcal{A}'$ also simulates the output of the hash function H during the issuer verification experiment. In the challenge phase, when $\mathcal{A}$ creates a tag T_c, he selects a random identifier t_c. Then, $\mathcal{A}$ queries H with t_c. To compute $H(t_c)$, $\mathcal{A}'$ selects randomly $r_c \in \mathbb{F}_q$ and returns $h_c = H(t_c) = g_1^{zr_c}$.

If $\mathcal{A}$ has a non-negligible advantage in breaking the issuer verification security, then this yields that $\mathcal{A}$ is able to output valid verification references for T_c, $\mathrm{ref}_{T_c}^V = (A_c, B_c, C_c) = (t_c, h_c^x, C_c) = (t_c, g_1^{xzr_c}, C_c)$.

Therefore, to break BCDH $\mathcal{A}'$ outputs $e(g_1, g_2)^{xyz} = e(g_1^{xzr_c}, g_2^y)^{r_c^{-1}}$.

7   Related Work

Molnar et al. [14] address the problem of ownership transfer in RFID systems by using tag pseudonyms and relying on a trusted third party. Here, the TTP is the only entity than can identify tags. To transfer ownership of tag T, the current owner of T $O_{(T,k)}$, and the prospective owner of T $O_{(T,k+1)}$, contact the TTP, who then provides $O_{(T,k+1)}$ with T's identity. Once the ownership transfer of T takes place, the TTP refuses identity requests from T's previous owner $O_{(T,k)}$. However, relying on a TTP is a drawback: in many scenarios, the availability of a trusted third party during tag ownership transfer is probably unrealistic.

Other solutions based on symmetric primitives have been proposed by Lim and Kwon [13], Fouladgar and Afifi [7], Song [18], and Kulseng et al. [11]. These schemes however suffer as discussed in section 2.2 from three major drawbacks: **1.)** tag identification and authentication is linear in the number of tags, **2.)** desynchronization and **3.)** no tag issuer verification.

Kapoor and Piramuthu [10] suggests a two party ownership transfer protocol based on keyed hash functions. In order to provide forward unlinkability, the new owner of tag T, $O_{(T,k+1)}$ does not have access to the key of the previous owner $O_{(T,k+1)}$. Also, to cope with desynchronization, T's owner does not update the shared key unless he receives an acknowledgment from T. However, as the scheme relies on symmetric primitives it still suffers from linear time authentication and lack of issuer verification.

Dimitrou [5] proposes a solution to ownership transfer that relies on symmetric cryptography while relaxing the privacy requirements for both backward and forward unlinkability. Unlike previous schemes on ownership transfer, this solution allows an owner of a tag to revert the tag to its original state. This is useful for after sales services where a retailer can recognize a sold tag T. Note that ROTIV offers the same feature: a tag T's unique identifier will allow any owner to verify whether he owned T before or not.

8   Conclusion

In this paper, we presented ROTIV to address security and privacy issues related to RFID ownership transfer in supply chains. Moreover, ROTIV enables ownership transfer together with issuer verification. Such verification will prevent partners in a supply chain from injecting fake products. ROTIV's main idea is to store a signature of the issuer in tags that can be verified by every partner in the supply chain. Also, to allow for efficient ownership transfer, ROTIV comprises an efficient, constant time authentication protocol. To guarantee tag privacy, we use re-encryption and key update techniques. Despite the high security and privacy properties, ROTIV is lightweight and requires a tag to only evaluate a hash function.

References

[1] Ateniese, G., Camenisch, J., de Medeiros, B.: Untraceable rfid tags via insubvertible encryption. In: CCS 2005: Proceedings of the 12th ACM Conference on Computer and Communications Security, pp. 92–101. ACM, New York (2005) ISBN 1-59593-226-7

[2] Ateniese, G., Kirsch, J., Blanton, M.: Secret handshakes with dynamic and fuzzy matching. In: Proceedings of the Network and Distributed System Security Symposium, NDSS. The Internet Society (2007)

[3] Ballard, L., Green, M., de Medeiros, B., Monrose, F.: Correlation-resistant storage via keyword-searchable encryption. In: Cryptology ePrint Archive, Report 2005/417 (2005), http://eprint.iacr.org/

[4] Burmester, M., de Medeiros, B., Motta, R.: Robust, anonymous RFID authentication with constant key-lookup. In: Proceedings of the 2008 ACM Symposium on Information, Computer and Communications Security, ASIACCS 2008, pp. 283–291. ACM, New York (2008) ISBN 978-1-59593-979-1

[5] Dimitrou, T.: rfidDOT: RFID delegation and ownership transfer made simple. In: Proceedings of International Conference on Security and Privacy in Communication Networks, Istanbul, Turkey (2008) ISBN 978-1-60558-241-2

[6] Elkhiyaoui, K., Blass, E.-O., Molva, R.: ROTIV: RFID Ownership Transfer with Issuer Verification. In: Cryptology ePrint Archive, Report 2010/634 (2010), http://eprint.iacr.org/

[7] Fouladgar, S., Afifi, H.: An Efficient Delegation and Transfer of Ownership Protocol for RFID Tags. In: First International EURASIP Workshop on RFID Technology, Vienna, Austria (September 2007)

[8] Galbraith, S.D., Paterson, K.G., Smart, N.P.: Pairings for cryptographers. Discrete Appl. Math. 156, 3113–3121 (2008) ISSN 0166-218X

[9] Juels, A., Weis, S.A.: Defining Strong Privacy for RFID. In: PerCom Workshops, White Plains, USA, pp. 342–347 (2007) ISBN 978-0-7695-2788-8

[10] Kapoor, G., Piramuthu, S.: Single RFID Tag Ownership Transfer Protocols. IEEE Transactions on Systems, Man, and Cybernetics 99, 1–10 (2011) ISSN 1094-6977

[11] Kulseng, L., Yu, Z., Wei, Y., Guan, Y.: Lightweight mutual authentication and ownership transfer for rfid systems. In: INFOCOM, pp. 251–255 (2010)

[12] Lee, Y.K., Batina, L., Singelée, D., Verbauwhede, I.: Low-Cost Untraceable Authentication Protocols for RFID. In: Wetzel, S., Nita-Rotaru, C., Stajano, F.:Proceedings of the 3rd ACM Conference on Wireless Network Security – WiSec 2010, Hoboken, New Jersey, USA, pp. 55–64. ACM, ACM Press (March 2010)

[13] Lim, C.H., Kwon, T.: Strong and Robust RFID Authentication Enabling Perfect Ownership Transfer. In: Ning, P., Qing, S., Li, N. (eds.) ICICS 2006. LNCS, vol. 4307, pp. 1–20. Springer, Heidelberg (2006)

[14] Molnar, D., Soppera, A., Wagner, D.: A Scalable, Delegatable Pseudonym Protocol Enabling Ownership Transfer of RFID Tags. In: Preneel, B., Tavares, S. (eds.) SAC 2005. LNCS, vol. 3897, pp. 276–290. Springer, Heidelberg (2006)

[15] Ohkubo, M., Suzuki, K., Kinoshita, S.: Cryptographic Approach to "Privacy-Friendly" Tags. In: RFID Privacy Workshop. MIT, Massachusetts (2003)

[16] Paise, R., Vaudenay, S.: Mutual authentication in RFID: security and privacy. In: Proceedings of the 2008 ACM Symposium on Information, Computer and Communications Security, ASIACCS 2008, pp. 292–299. ACM, New York (2008) ISBN 978-1-59593-979-1

[17] Saito, J., Imamoto, K., Sakurai, K.: Reassignment Scheme of an RFID Tag's Key for Owner Transfer. In: Enokido, T., Yan, L., Xiao, B., Kim, D.Y., Dai, Y.-S., Yang, L.T. (eds.) EUC-WS 2005. LNCS, vol. 3823, pp. 1303–1312. Springer, Heidelberg (2005)

[18] Song, B.: RFID Tag Ownership Transfer. In: Workshop on RFID Security – RFID-Sec 2008, Budapest, Hungary (July 2008)

[19] Vaudenay, S.: On Privacy Models for RFID. In: Kurosawa, K. (ed.) ASIACRYPT 2007. LNCS, vol. 4833, pp. 68–87. Springer, Heidelberg (2007) ISBN 3-540-76899-8, 978-3-540-76899-9

Hierarchical ECC-Based RFID Authentication Protocol

Lejla Batina[1,2], Stefaan Seys[1], Dave Singelée[1], and Ingrid Verbauwhede[1]

[1] K.U.Leuven ESAT/SCD-COSIC and IBBT
Kasteelpark Arenberg 10, B-3001 Leuven-Heverlee, Belgium
`firstname.lastname@esat.kuleuven.be`
[2] Radboud University Nijmegen, CS Dept./Digital Security group
Heyendaalseweg 135, 6525 AJ Nijmegen, The Netherlands
`lejla@cs.ru.nl`

Abstract. RFID (Radio Frequency Identification) technology enables readers to scan remote RFID tags, and label the objects and people to which they are attached. Current cryptographic authentication protocols deployed in heterogeneous environments are often not compatible, or reveal too much information to the RFID readers. To tackle this problem, we introduce the concept of RFID groups and propose a hierarchical RFID authentication protocol. By using this protocol, an RFID tag can tune its identification process to the type of reader it is communicating with. Only a subset of readers can learn the identity of a particular tag, while others can only acquire information on the group to which the tag belongs. Our protocol offers impersonation resistance and is narrow-strong privacy-preserving. Furthermore, we extend the concept to multiple level of subgroups, and demonstrate the feasibility of our proposed protocols for RFID tags.

Keywords: RFID, Authentication, ECC, Hierarchical Groups, Privacy.

1 Introduction

Radio Frequency Identification is a technology designed to automatically identify objects and people. RFID systems are rapidly expanding their applications to many areas: inventory systems, supply chains, access control, vehicle tracking, toll payments, e-ticketing, pharmaceutics, *etc.* However, due to the wide spread of tags, there are potentially various security and privacy risks. Nowadays, the vast majority of the tags being used only provide an identity number (or Electronic Product Code), and neither authentication nor any kind of privacy is achieved. To tackle the identified threats, there is a clear demand for secure and privacy-preserving RFID protocols.

A large part of the RFID security research is currently focused on RFID identification protocols. The protocols differ in the cryptographic building blocks they use, their efficiency, message flows, and security and privacy properties they offer. But all of them are carried out between a tag and a reader, in which the latter learns the identity of the tag at the end of a successful protocol run.

A. Juels and C. Paar (Eds.): RFIDSec 2011, LNCS 7055, pp. 183–201, 2012.
© Springer-Verlag Berlin Heidelberg 2012

In many real life situations a tag will not reside in one place, but will be located in different environments during its lifetime. For example, an RFID tag attached to an object will move from the manufacturer to the costumer. Throughout the supply chain, the tag will travel across several companies, and communicate to readers which are not operated by the same organization. At the various stages during the lifetime of a tag, there will be different requirements regarding the identification of the product to which the tag is attached. While it is important for the manufacturer to identify the tag (*i.e.*, to learn its exact identity), it could be sufficient for intermediate parties or the customer to only know the manufacturer of the product, or the type of product. This translates to a need for a more granular approach, in which the tag only reveals the necessary information to which that specific reader is entitled.

1.1   RFID Groups

To realize this notion, we introduce the concept of an "RFID group". Each tag belongs to one of these groups, and can be identified both by its unique identity and by the group to which it belongs. During the authentication process, the level of detail of the information revealed by the tag (*i.e.*, its identity or its RFID group) is determined by the reader to which it is communicating. Some readers are authorized to learn the tag's identity, while other readers can only obtain the tag's RFID group (or no information at all). One might notice that this concept is quite similar to the notion of anonymous credentials [3,7,8]. There is one important difference. When using credential systems, the prover constructs a message (*i.e.*, the credential) depending on the properties it wants to prove. In our setting, the information that is revealed depends on the reader that is participating in the protocol, and is not chosen by the tag.

Introducing the concept of RFID groups significantly improves scalability and compatibility of large RFID systems. Without using groups, all readers need a list of all tags' keys to successfully carry out an authentication protocol. Without these keys, a reader cannot verify the authenticity of a tag. However, distributing these keys among all readers is quite cumbersome and potentially even undesirable, since the readers can be controlled by different parties. By using the notion of RFID groups, readers are destined to belong to an authentication group. Depending on the group they belong to, they will obtain a set of verification keys. Readers belonging to other groups do not have to know these keys.

We demonstrate the use of RFID groups with two practical examples. The first example is related to the supply chain we mentioned above. Suppose that in the near future many consumer goods will come with an RFID as a bar-code replacement. By employing no security or conventional authentication mechanisms, the tag will reveal its unique identity to the reader. The privacy problems resulting from employing no security has been extensively criticized (see [14] for an overview). Privacy-preserving authentication methods such as [6,20] protect the privacy of the user from eavesdroppers, but still reveal the unique identifier to an authorized reader. Using the concept of RFID groups presented in this paper, we can create tags that are capable of proving group membership to any reader with the correct group verification key. In this way we could, for example, manufacture tags for medicine packages that contain a unique identifier (that uniquely identifies this particular package and all its details), but also an identifier of a group that only specifies the type of drug and a third identifier that specifies the fact that this is an FDA approved drug. RFID readers in the supply chain will have access to the unique ID and thus access to all the details, the same holds for hospitals, emergency response units and any other entity that need this detailed information. Everybody else will be able to obtain a reader that only has access to the group that specifies that this drug has been FDA approved. This enables people to perform an independent check of the drug's validity, but does not allow them to obtain any other information; thus preventing malicious individuals from obtaining details of medicines carried around by other people.

A second example is access control. Assume a large corporate building is protected with an access control system based on RFID. Further suppose that each employee is part of one "access group" that allows them access to a set of hallways or rooms within the building. Using RFID groups, their RFID card could contain the identities of the group they belong to and their unique employee number. Instead of always providing this unique employee number to any reader in the building (as is the case now), readers will only obtain information on the access group of the user. Once inside the building, the user can use the same RFID tag to log in to his terminal using the unique employee number of the card. This allows fine grained access control (using multiple groups), but still protects the privacy of the employee (as readers will only obtain the access group and not the unique ID of the employee).

1.2 Contributions and Outline

In this paper, we propose a hierarchical, secure, privacy-preserving RFID authentication protocol, which incorporates the concept of RFID groups. Depending on the keys used during the verification process, the reader will learn the necessary information to which it is entitled to. This can be the identity of the tag or the group to which the the tag belongs. We prove that the protocol is narrow-strong privacy-preserving and is resistant to impersonation attacks. It is exclusively based on ECC (Elliptic Curve Cryptography) [19,23] and can be easily extended to the case with n levels in the group hierarchy. Moreover, we present the performance results of our protocol on an ECC coprocessor, to show that the protocols are feasible for RFID tags.

The remainder of the paper is organized as follows. In Sect. 2, RFID authentication protocols are reviewed. In Sect. 3 we describe the setting of hierarchical RFID groups. Next, we present our basic hierarchical RFID authentication protocol in Sect. 4, and show that it can be easily extended to the setting where there are multiple levels of RFID subgroups. The security and privacy properties of the protocol are discussed in Sect. 5. The performance results of our protocol are outlined in Sect. 6. We conclude our work in Sect. 7.

2   Related Work

To solve the security and privacy issues posed by RFID technology, various RFID authentication protocols have been proposed in the literature. So far, most schemes rely exclusively on symmetric-key cryptography. One of the first was the work of Feldhofer *et al.* [12] that proposed a challenge-response protocol based on the AES block-cipher. The implementation consumes a chip area of 3,595 gates and has a current consumption of 8.15 μA at a frequency of 100 kHz. Juels and Weis proposed the HB+ protocol [18], which was designed as an efficient solution, as it even can be implemented on tags of 5-10 cents, and offers protection against active adversaries. Later other variants of HB followed. However, it is shown that these are vulnerable to various security flaws. For example, Gilbert *et al.* [15] presented a man-in-the-middle attack that uses failed authentications to extract the HB+ key. As a fix, a new protocol called HB++ from Bringer *et al.* [5] was proposed. HB++ is claimed to be secure against man-in-the-middle attacks but it requires additional secret key material and a universal hash function to detect the attacks. In the follow-up work Bringer and Chabanne [4] proposed a new HB+ variant (so-called Trusted-HB) using special linear feedback shift register (LFSR) constructions. However Frumkin and Shamir [13] discovered several weaknesses of Trusted-HB. Various other symmetric-key based authentication protocols have been proposed for RFID, each having specific security and privacy properties. However, since these protocols are not the main focus of the paper, we will not discuss them further.

The main reason why most work focused on symmetric-key solutions lies in the common perception of public-key cryptography being too slow, complex and power-hungry for RFID. However, recent publications on compact and efficient Elliptic Curve Cryptography (ECC) implementations challenge this assumption [16,20,22]. Using public-key protocols solves the scalability issues that often burden symmetric-key based solutions and can offer strong privacy protection [26]. One of the first ECC based authentication protocols is the EC-RAC (Elliptic Curve Based Randomized Access Control) protocol that has been proposed to address tracking attacks. However, in [6,9,10,11], it is shown that EC-RAC is vulnerable to various man-in-the-middle and replay attacks. As a result, the EC-RAC protocol has been gradually revised in [20,21] to tackle the known attacks and offer narrow-strong privacy. Furthermore, Bringer, Chabanne and Icart proposed the randomized Schnorr protocol [6] (an extension of the basic Schnorr protocol [25]) as an efficient alternative that is also narrow-strong privacy-preserving. The hierarchical RFID authentication protocol we propose in this paper is inspired by this protocol.

3   Setting

3.1   Notation

Let us first introduce the notation used in this work. We denote P as the base point on an Elliptic Curve. As will be discussed later, a reader has multiple

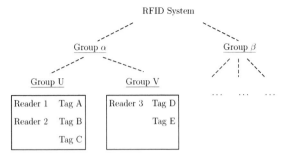

Fig. 1. Example RFID system divided into groups α and β, in which group α is subdivided into subgroups U and V

key pairs. We denote these reader's private and public-key pairs as y_i and $Y_i (= y_i P)$, where $y_i P$ denotes the point derived by the point multiplication operation on the Elliptic Curve group. Also an RFID tag will have multiple key pairs, corresponding to its identity and the (sub)groups where it belongs to. These private and public-key pairs are respectively denoted by x_i and X_i.

3.2   Group Structure

In our setting there are two types of entities involved: tags and readers. Each tag has a unique identity and communicates to a (potentially untrusted) reader during the execution of the hierarchical authentication protocol. A reader that is part of the RFID system is denoted as an authorized reader, all other readers are unauthorized readers. Only authorized readers are allowed to learn (some) information from a tag.

The complete set of readers and tags within the system is divided into a hierarchical group structure consisting of groups and subgroups. The top level in the tree is the RFID system itself. The leaves of the tree are individual tags and readers. Fig. 1 shows an example with two main groups α and β, in which group α is further subdivided into subgroups U and V.[1] Both readers and tags are assigned to one subgroup at the lowest level (group U or V) in our example. Entities which are part of a subgroup, automatically obtain membership of the parent group. This inheritance of group membership continues until the root of the group tree has been reached. For example, Reader 3 has been assigned to the lowest level subgroup V and therefore automatically obtained membership of the parent group α. Because he is now part of group α he also becomes part of the top level group, *i.e.*, the RFID system itself.

Once these groups have been set up, tags and reader can start using the protocol described in Sect. 4 to allow readers to verify group membership of tags. The level of detail of group membership a reader can verify depends on the group membership of both the tag and the reader:

---

[1] For clarity we have limited this example to 2 layers of groups, but our scheme allows an arbitrary level of subgroups.

1. The reader and the tag belong to the same lowest level group in the tree. In this scenario, the reader will be able to verify all group memberships of the tag, including the identity of the tag itself. For example, Reader 3 in Fig. 1 can verify that Tag D is part of the RFID system, part of group α, part of subgroup V and has identity D.

2. The reader and the tag do not belong to the same lowest level group, but do share a higher level group. In this scenario, the reader will be able to check group membership of the tag *up to the level of group they share – plus one, starting from the top*. For example, Reader 3 in Fig. 1 can verify that Tag A is part of the RFID system, part of group α, and part of subgroup U. But because they are not part of the same subgroup at the lowest level, Reader 3 is not able to obtain/verify the identity of Tag A.

3. The reader and the tag are not part of the same RFID system (i.e., reader and tag do not share any group). In this scenario, the reader is not authorized and is not able to obtain any information on the tag.

Key setup. We will now introduce the key setup that is used in our protocol (described in Sect. 4). To illustrate the notation discussed above, let us revisit the example. Figure 2 shows the group structure and the private keys associated to the groups and subgroups. First, consider the readers in the system. Every reader obtains the private key $y_{i,G}$ of the group G of which it is a member at level i. This key is required to check the group membership of tags of subgroups at level i. For example, Reader 3 obtains key $y_{1,V}$ and can use this to obtain the identities of tags D and E. He also obtains key $y_{2,\alpha}$ that can be used to verify membership of either group U or V. Finally, he obtains private key y_3 that can be used to verify membership of either group α or β.

In order to prove membership, tags require a set of private keys. Again, a tag obtains a single private key $x_{j,G}$ at each level j for the group G of which this tag is a member. For example, tag A has knowledge of the private keys $x_{1,A}$ (to prove its identity), $x_{2,U}$ (to prove membership of group U), and $x_{3,\alpha}$ (to prove membership of group α). Table 1 give a complete overview of the private keys stored by the different entities in the example RFID system.

Protocol use. Before explaining the details of the protocol, we will demonstrate how the protocol is used to obtain the group membership of a particular tag. Take for example the case in which Reader 3 interrogates tag E in Fig. 2. First, the tag will generate a proof that it is part of group α using the private key $x_{3,\alpha}$. Because the reader has key y_3, it is able to verify this claim. Next, the tag constructs a proof of membership of group V using the private key $x_{2,V}$. The reader can verify this using the private key $y_{2,\alpha}$. Finally, the tag will prove its identity using the private key $x_{1,E}$. The reader opens this proof using the private key $y_{1,V}$. This tree traversal is indicated with the dotted arrow in Fig. 2.

To simplify the notation, we will denote the identity of the tag, or the group where it belongs to, by its private key. In the example above, the identity of tag A will be denoted by $x_{1,A}$, and the identity of group U by $x_{2,U}$. Note that, although the name suggests that it can be publicly known, the identity of a group or a tag should be kept secret (as these are equal to the corresponding private keys). To

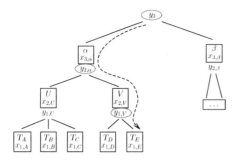

Fig. 2. Example RFID group structure showing groups (α, β, U, V), private keys required to check group membership $(y_{i,G})$ and private keys to prove group membership $(x_{j,G})$.

Table 1. Private keys stored in tags and readers

Entity	Group	Private keys		
Tag A	U	$x_{1,A}$	$x_{2,U}$	$x_{3,\alpha}$
Tag B	U	$x_{1,B}$	$x_{2,U}$	$x_{3,\alpha}$
Tag C	U	$x_{1,C}$	$x_{2,U}$	$x_{3,\alpha}$
Tag D	V	$x_{1,D}$	$x_{2,V}$	$x_{3,\alpha}$
Tag E	V	$x_{1,E}$	$x_{2,V}$	$x_{3,\alpha}$
Reader 1	U	$y_{1,U}$	$y_{2,\alpha}$	y_3
Reader 2	U	$y_{1,U}$	$y_{2,\alpha}$	y_3
Reader 3	V	$y_{1,V}$	$y_{2,\alpha}$	y_3

check the identity of a group or a tag, the corresponding public key is computed by the reader. For further simplification of the notation, we will assume that both the reader and the tag are part of the same lowest level subgroup and thus that the tree traversal will go from the top until the bottom of the tree. This means that for every private key $x_{j,G}$ of the tag, the reader will have the corresponding verification key $y_{i,G}$. This means that we can omit the second subscript G in the notation of these keys.

4   Hierarchical Authentication Protocol

4.1   Security and Privacy Requirements

The goal of this paper is to propose a hierarchical RFID authentication protocol, in which a tag can prove to a reader to which group it belongs and/or its identity. The protocol should offer *impersonation resistance*. It should be impossible for a tag to spoof the identity of another tag, or spoof the membership to another group than the one to which it belongs (i.e. membership to a group for which it does not possess the correct private keys). Note that it is impossible to prevent an attacker from (falsely) proving membership to a particular group of which he has obtained the corresponding private key (e.g., stolen from a tag that belongs to that group).

Besides impersonation resistance, our protocol should also offer *untraceability*, in which the (in)equality of two tags must be impossible to determine. Only a trusted reader should be able to check the identity and groups of the tags. To evaluate the privacy of RFID systems, several theoretical models have been proposed in the literature [1,17,24,26]. We particularly focus on two characteristics of attackers from the theoretical framework of Vaudenay [26]: *wide* (or *narrow*) attackers and *strong* (or *weak*) attackers. If an attacker has access to the result of the authentication protocol (accept or reject) in the verifier, he is a *wide* attacker. Otherwise he is a *narrow* attacker. If an attacker is able to extract a tag's secret and reuse it in an authentication protocol instance, he is a *strong* attacker. Otherwise he is a *weak* attacker. Vaudenay demonstrated that one needs to employ public-key cryptography to achieve strong privacy requirements [26]. Because of this observation, our narrow-strong privacy-preserving hierarchical RFID authentication protocol relies on public-key cryptography. For efficiency reasons, we will particularly use ECC.

It is important to stress that the notion of narrow-strong privacy only refers to the identity of a tag. Untraceability regarding the membership of a group can only be achieved partially. Readers can always check the membership of a tag to (sub)groups to which they also belong. If the reader does not belong to a particular (sub)group, then that reader should not be able to check that a tag belongs to this (sub)group. For example, in the scenario depicted in Fig. 1, a reader of group β should not be able to verify that tag A belongs to group U.

4.2   Protocol Description

We describe here our basic privacy-preserving hierarchical authentication protocol, where each tag belongs to one group. There are no subgroups defined, so each tag has an identity x_1 and belongs to a group x_2. Such a hierarchical scheme can be trivially designed as follows:

- In Sect. 2, we discussed several RFID authentication protocol. Out of this list, choose the appropriate protocol, according to the required privacy and security requirements.
- Carry out this protocol twice. The first protocol run uses the group's private key x_2 and the public key Y_2 of the reader, and is used to prove the group where the tag belongs to. The second protocol run uses the tag's private key x_1 and the public key Y_1 of the reader, and is used to prove the tag's identity.

Although the approach discussed above works, it is not efficient. Therefore, we propose a hierarchical authentication protocol in which only one protocol run will be carried out. After receiving a challenge from the reader, the tag will reply with a single response. Depending on the key used to check the correctness of the response, the reader will be able to verify the group where the tag belongs to, the identity of the tag, or even nothing at all. Figure 3 shows the basic protocol.

The protocol starts by the tag generating two random numbers r_0 and r_1. Next, it computes three points on an elliptic curve: T_0, T_1 and T_2, and sends them to the reader. Then, the reader responds with a random challenge c. After receiving this value, the tag computes the response v using the challenge c and the private keys x_1 and x_2. The tag first checks that the challenge is not equal to zero in the group or the order of the point P. Next, the response is sent back to the verifier, to prove the tag's identity and/or being part of a group.

After having received the response v, the reader is going to perform several checks. First, it checks the group where the tag belongs to by performing the

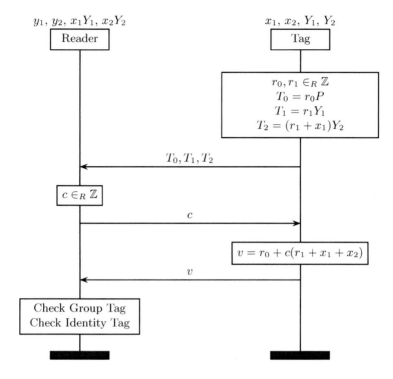

Fig. 3. Basic hierarchical RFID authentication protocol

following computation, using its private key y_2:

$$c^{-1}(vY_2 - y_2T_0 - cT_2) = x_2Y_2$$

If the correct private key y_2 is used (*i.e.*, the reader belongs to the same RFID system as the tag), the result of the computation will be equal to x_2Y_2. This point on the curve is defined as the public key of group x_2. If the incorrect key is used, the output of the computation will be random (*i.e.*, output cannot be used to identify or track the tag or the group of tags).

Next, the reader checks the identity of the tag, using the private keys y_1 and y_2. It performs the following computation:

$$(y_2^{-1}y_1)T_2 - T_1 = x_1Y_1$$

Since the reader already checked the group x_2, it knows that the key y_2 was correct. If the correct private key y_1 is used (*i.e.*, both the reader and the tag belong to the same group x_2), the output of the computation will be equal to x_1Y_1. This point on the curve is defined as the public key of the tag. If the incorrect key is used, the output of the computation will be random (*i.e.*, the output cannot be used to identify or track the tag or the group of tags).

Note that it is very important that the reader first checks the group of the tag, and only then the identity. This order should not be altered. If the reader cannot compute the public key of the group, because the reader has the incorrect private key, it should immediately stop the verification procedure and not compute the identity of the tag. Otherwise, the protocol would become vulnerable to a replay attack.

To avoid timing attacks, the time needed by the reader to carry out the verification steps should be randomized. Otherwise, the outcome of the verification procedure and even the identity of the tag depends on this verification time, which would break the privacy properties of our scheme. For example, if the reader searches linearly in the database of the tags' public keys, then it takes less time to check the correctness of the public keys which are stored in the beginning of this database.

4.3   Extension to n Levels of Subgroups

The basic protocol can be extended to the setting where there are $n - 1$ levels of subgroups. As discussed in Sect. 3.2, x_1 is the identity of the tag, the group x_2 is the subgroup at the lowest level in the hierarchy, and x_n the group at the top level in the hierarchy. The protocol is shown in Fig. 4.

As in the basic protocol, the tag first generates two random numbers, and then computes the points $T_0, T_1, \ldots, T_n$. The reader then generates a random challenge and sends it to the tag. After receiving this value, the tag computes the response v using the challenge c and the private keys $x_1, x_2, \ldots, x_n$. This response is sent back to the verifier, to prove the tag's identity and/or being part of a particular subgroup.

After having received the response v, the reader is going to perform several checks. First, it checks the top-level group where the tag belongs to (x_n) by performing the following computation, using its private key y_n:

$$c^{-1}(vY_n - y_nT_0 - cT_n) = x_nY_n$$

If the correct private key y_n is used (i.e., the reader belongs to the same RFID system as the tag), the result of the computation will be equal to x_nY_n, the public key of the group x_n. If the incorrect key is used, the output of the computation will be random (i.e., the output cannot be used to identify or track the tag or the group of tags).

Next, the reader checks the tag's membership to the subgroup at the second highest layer in the hierarchy (x_{n-1}), using the private keys y_{n-1} and y_n:

$$(y_n^{-1}y_{n-1})T_n - T_{n-1} = x_{n-1}Y_{n-1}$$

Since the reader already checked the group x_n, it knows that the private key y_n was correct. If the correct private key y_{n-1} is used (i.e., both the reader and the tag belong to the same group x_n), the output of the computation will be equal to $x_{n-1}Y_{n-1}$, the public key of the group x_{n-1}.

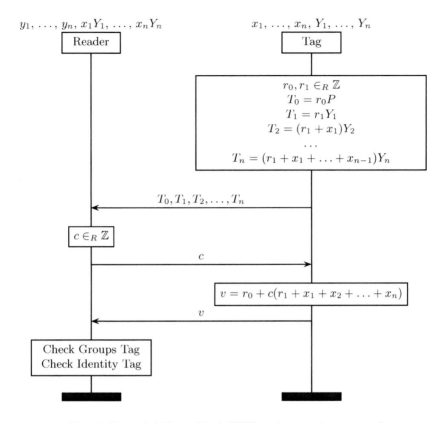

Fig. 4. Extended hierarchical RFID authentication protocol

In the next stage, the reader checks the subgroups $x_{n-2}, \ldots, x_2$ until the verification is not successful. As an example, we show the equation needed to check the membership to subgroup x_{n-2}:

$$(y_{n-1}^{-1} y_{n-2}) T_{n-1} - T_{n-2} = x_{n-2} Y_{n-2}$$

If the reader belongs to the subgroup x_3, all these checks will be correct. If it also belongs to subgroup x_2, the reader can try to check the identity of the tag, using the private keys y_1 and y_2 as follows:

$$(y_2^{-1} y_1) T_2 - T_1 = x_1 Y_1$$

Since the reader already checked the subgroup x_2, it knows that the key y_2 was correct. If the correct private key y_1 is used (*i.e.*, both the reader and the tag belong to the same subgroup x_2), the output of the computation will be equal to $x_1 Y_1$, the public key of the tag.

As in the basic protocol, it is of uttermost importance that the reader first checks the group x_n, then the subgroup x_{n-1}, *etc.* This order should not be altered and the protocol should stop when one of these checks fail (since subgroups at a lower level cannot be checked by that reader). Only when all the checks are correct (because the reader has all the correct private keys), it should check the identity of the tag. As before, the time needed by the reader to carry out the verification steps has to be randomized to avoid timing attacks.

5   Analysis

In this section we give the security and privacy analysis of our basic scheme ($n = 2$). Both proofs are related to the basic protocol of Fig. 3, but can be easily extended to the more general case where the hierarchical group structure has depth n (shown in Fig. 4). First, we remind to some common computational assumptions.

5.1   Computational Assumptions

The security of ECC protocols is founded on the ECDL problem, which is defined as follows:

Definition 1 (ECDL problem). *Let E be an elliptic curve over $\mathbb{F}_q$ and let $P \in E$ be a point of order k i.e. $ord(P) = k$. Let $Q \in \langle P \rangle$ and $Q = \alpha P$ for $\alpha \in [0, k)$. The problem of finding the logarithm α for given P and Q is called the elliptic curve discrete logarithm problem (ECDLP).*

Here $\mathbb{F}_q$ denotes the finite field containing q elements, where q is a prime power. In practice, commonly used finite fields are a prime field $\mathbb{F}_p$ or a binary field $\mathbb{F}_{2^n}$. In addition, $\langle P \rangle$ denotes a group of points on an elliptic curve generated by P.

Definition 2 (Decisional Diffie-Hellman (DDH) problem). *Given 3 random multiples of P on an elliptic curve αP, βP, γP; it is intractable to distinguish the case where $\gamma = \alpha\beta$ or where γ has been selected at random.*

In the proof of privacy of our scheme, we make use of the "extended" DDH assumption, which we can informally define as follows:

Definition 3 (Extended DDH assumption). *Given 5 random multiples of P on an elliptic curve $y_1 P, y_2 P, r_1 P, \gamma_1 P, \gamma_2 P$; it is intractable to distinguish the case where $\gamma_1 = y_1 r_1$ and $\gamma_2 = y_2 r_1$ or where at least one γ has been selected at random.*

Furthermore we assume the following theorem holds:

Theorem 1. *Assuming the hardness of the DDH problem, then the "extended" DDH problem is also hard.*

5.2 Security Analysis

We observe that our scheme is clearly correct as a legitimate tag is accepted with probability 1. We can prove that it is also secure against an active adversary by using the fact that the Schnorr scheme, as shown in Appendix A, is secure against active impersonation attacks under the OMDL assumption. This fact was proved in [2]. Our scheme is a modification of the Schnorr scheme. Therefore, a relevant adversary against our scheme can be transformed into a relevant adversary against the Schnorr scheme.

The proof is inspired on the *security game* defined in [2], and the security proof given in [6]:

Security Game: Assume an adversary is able to interrogate a system of tags via the protocol described in Fig. 3. In a first phase, the adversary pretends to be a verifier (reader) and is allowed to communicate with all tags. In a second phase, the adversary tries to impersonate a tag while communicating with a genuine verifier. The adversary wins if he is accepted as genuine by this verifier.

Definition 4 (Security). *A scheme is secure against active impersonation attacks if any adversary is not able to win the game, except with a negligible probability.*

In order to prove that our scheme is secure against active impersonation attacks, we first define the reduced basic hierarchical RFID authentication protocol (denoted by RHP). This scheme differs from our basic scheme, defined in Fig. 3, in the following way:

- Instead of sending the EC point T_1 to the reader, the tag sends the random number r_1.
- The reader checks the identity of the tag as follows: $(y_2^{-1}y_1)T_2 - r_1Y_1 = x_1Y_1$

Theorem 2. *Assuming RHP is secure against active impersonation attacks, then our basic scheme (Fig. 3) is secure against active impersonation attacks.*

Note that sending r_1 instead of T_1 to the reader only affects privacy, and does not increase the impersonation resistance of RHP compared to our basic scheme.

Theorem 3. *Assuming the Schnorr scheme, as shown in Appendix A, is secure against active impersonation attacks, then RHP is secure against active impersonation attacks.*

Proof: We will prove this last theorem by contradiction. Let us assume that there exists an active adversary $\mathcal{A}$ relevant against RHP, while there exists no adversary $\mathcal{A}^{\mathcal{S}}$ relevant against the Schnorr scheme (shown in Appendix A). In the following, we will show how to convert $\mathcal{A}$ into $\mathcal{A}^{\mathcal{S}}$.

During the first phase of the attack, $\mathcal{A}$ interrogates a genuine tag that executes the Schnorr protocol. Let us assume that the private key of this tag is equal to x_2 and its public key to x_2Y_2. The Schnorr protocol starts by the tag outputting T_0 (denoted by T in Appendix A). We intercept T_0, randomly generate r_1 and

x_1, and compute $T_2 = (r_1 + x_1)Y_2$. Next, we send T_0, r_1, and T_2 to $\mathcal{A}$. After $\mathcal{A}$ has sent c, the tag outputs v. We intercept this value and we send $v + c(r_1 + x_1)$ to $\mathcal{A}$. Because of our interceptions, $\mathcal{A}$ is convinced that it executed RHP.

During the second phase of the protocol, $\mathcal{A}$ tries to impersonate the tag it has interrogated in the first phase towards a genuine reader executing the Schnorr protocol. As before, we will intercept the communication. $\mathcal{A}$ starts by outputting T_0', r_1', and T_2'. We intercept these values, and only forward T_0' to the reader. The latter replies with a challenge c', which we forward to $\mathcal{A}$. Next, $\mathcal{A}$ responds with a value v' for which the following holds: $x_2 Y_2 = c'^{-1}[v'Y_2 - y_2 T_0' - c'T_2']$ and $T_2' - r_1'Y_2 = x_1 Y_2$. We intercept v', compute $v" = v' - c'(r_1' + x_1)$ and send $v"$ to the reader. One can verify that the reader will accept this value $v"$, since $c'^{-1}[v"Y_2 - y_2 T_0'] = x_2 Y_2$. This means that we have successfully transformed $\mathcal{A}$ into $\mathcal{A}^S$. This contradicts our assumption and the statement is proven.   □

5.3   Privacy Analysis

We now explain why our scheme is narrow-strong private. In our privacy analysis, which is inspired by [6], we will use the *privacy game* from [26]. In this game there are tags, an adversary, and a **blinder**. The blinder sits in between tags and the adversary, hiding the former from the latter. The model dictates that the blinder does not know which tag it is simulating and it cannot interact with genuine tags. For the details of the privacy game, we refer to [26]. Briefly, the game consists of two phases:

Privacy game: Assume every tag is known to the attacker by its pseudonym. First, the adversary is allowed to communicate with (or eavesdrop on, if he is passive) genuine tags. After this phase, the attacker receives the map $\mathcal{T}$ of pseudonyms to real IDs of all the tags. After some analysis, the adversary is asked to output either true or false. The adversary wins the game if he outputs true[2]. In the second phase, the adversary is only allowed to communicate with the blinder, who is simulating the tags' outputs. Again, the adversary is given the map $\mathcal{T}$ and asked to output either true or false.

Definition 5 (Privacy). *A scheme is private if there exists a blinder such that no adversary has an advantage (except with negligible probability) between the two phases of the privacy game.*[3]

"Informally, an adversary is trivial if it makes no effective use of protocol messages. Namely, these messages can be simulated without significantly affecting the success probability of the adversary [26]." In other words, a scheme is private if it is possible to build a simulator that is indistinguishable from genuine tags. Although a narrow-strong adversary has knowledge of the secrets of all tags, we can show that he cannot distinguish a genuine protocol run from a simulated run in the privacy game. This shows that the adversary is not able to link the tags' outputs and their secrets under the "extended" DDH assumption (defined above):

---

[2] Note that there are a number of trivial adversaries, such as the one that always outputs true.

[3] This definition is sufficient to prove the privacy of a scheme in Vaudenay's model.

Theorem 4. *Assuming the hardness of the "extended" DDH problem, the scheme described in Fig. 3 is narrow-strong private.*

Proof: In order to prove the scheme, we have to show that we can build a simulator (blinder) that can simulate the tag's outputs and that these simulated outputs cannot be distinguished from genuine outputs by a narrow-strong attacker.

A genuine protocol run between a tag and a reader are of the form $T_0 = r_0 P$, $T_1 = r_1 Y_1$, $T_2 = (r_1 + x_1)Y_2$, c, and $v = r_0 + c(r_1 + x_1 + x_2)$. A simulator outputs random instances A_0, A_1, A_2, c, α. In order to win the game, an adversary has to distinguish these random instances from genuine instances $r_0 P, r_1 Y_1, (r_1 + x_1)Y_2, c, r_0 + c(r_1 + x_1 + x_2)$. This is equivalent to distinguishing between $A_0, A_1, A_2' = A_2 - x_1 Y_2, c, \beta = \alpha - c(x_1 + x_2)$ and $r_0 P, r_1 Y_1, r_1 Y_2, c, r_0 + cr_1$. Note that both A_2' and β are as random as A_2 and α respectively. Note also that the adversary has knowledge of x_1, x_2 and the public parameter Y_2. We will now show that distinguishing legitimate quintets from simulated quintets is harder than solving the "extended" DDH problem.

Given an instance $y_1 P, y_2 P, r_1 P, \gamma_1 P, \gamma_2 P$ of the "extended" DDH problem, we randomly choose the values β and c, and compute $A_0 = \beta P - cr_1 P$. One can now see that the quintet $A_0, \gamma_1 P, \gamma_2 P, c, \beta$ are equivalent to a simulation of a protocol transcript. If $\gamma_1 = r_1 y_1$ and $\gamma_2 = r_1 y_2$, we have $\beta y_1 P = y_1 A_0 + c\gamma_1 P$ and $\beta y_2 P = y_2 A_0 + c\gamma_2 P$ and thus the quintet comes from a valid transcript. Otherwise it is a random quintet because either γ_1 or γ_2 is random. For this reason, if there exists an adversary able to distinguish between simulated protocol runs and genuine ones, he can solve the "extended" DDH problem. □

Similarly, one can prove that an adversary with knowledge of the private key y_2 (the verifier's private key of the group x_2) is not able to learn anything about the personal private key x_1 of any tag.

6   Performance Results

Cost reduction is an important requirement when designing RFID authentication protocols. In the hierarchical authentication protocol proposed in this paper, a RFID tag has to carry out point multiplications, field multiplications and additions. Of these operations, the former is by far the most complex and energy consuming. Therefore, the number of EC multiplications has to be reduced to a minimum. The Randomized Schnorr protocol proposed by Bringer *et al.* [6], which does not include the concept of groups, requires two EC point multiplications on the tag side. Our basic hierarchical authentication protocol, described in Fig. 3, requires three EC point multiplications. For each extra level introduced in the group hierarchy, the number of EC point multiplications is increased by one. So in the extended protocol shown in Fig. 4, the tag has to compute $(n+1)$ EC point multiplications. This makes our solutions scalable for the setting where many hierarchical group levels need to be defined.

Although the reader has more computational resources than the RFID tag, its resources are not inexhaustible. In the Randomized Schnorr protocol proposed by Bringer *et al.*, the reader has to compute three EC point multiplications. In our basic hierarchical authentication protocol, shown in Fig. 3, the reader also has to perform three EC point multiplications. For each extra level introduced in the group hierarchy, the number of EC point multiplications is increased by one. So in the extended protocol shown in Fig. 4, the reader has to compute $(n + 1)$ EC point multiplications.

This amount of computation is assumed feasible for RFID tags. The advantage of both approaches mentioned above is that the schemes require no additional primitives as they use ECC-only operations. Let us for example consider the ECC hardware processor of Lee *et al.* [22], since its architecture allows for the execution of our protocols. Assuming ECC over a binary field $\mathbb{F}_{2^{163}}$, the special curve as in [22], projective coordinates and the use of a Montgomery ladder for point multiplication, we get the following estimates for the protocol. We adjust the clock frequency in order to produce an acceptable performance, which we estimate to 200 *ms* for 1 point multiplication. To have this latency, a frequency of 293 *kHz* is required, as the arithmetic unit has a digit size of 4, resulting in a total number of 58,678 cycles for one point multiplication. In this way, the basic version of the protocol (with $n = 2$) would require 400 *ms* for completion. These numbers show the feasibility of our protocols even for a passive tag and prove the suitability of ECC-based solutions for RFID applications. The implementation details are left out due to the space limitation, but we refer to [20] for a description of an ECC processor (described in detail in [22]) that can perform all operations required. Furthermore, the increase in storage is linear when the depth of the hierarchical group structure (*i.e.* the parameter n) is increased. In particular, for each extra level in the group hierarchy, we have to add additional 163×4 bits for key storage (a scalar for a private key and a point $P(X, Y, Z)$ for a public key).

Table 2 gives a comparison in the number of point multiplications. These results demonstrate that our scheme requires significantly less point multiplications (on both sides) than the trivial solution where the Randomized Schnorr protocol is executed n times.

Table 2. Feasibility and Privacy Summary

Protocols	Privacy	EC point mult.	
		Server	Tag
n instances of Randomized Schnorr	Narrow-strong	$3n$	$2n$
Our hierarch. protocol (hierarchy level n)	Narrow-strong	$(n + 1)$	$(n + 1)$

7   Conclusions and Future Work

In this work the concept of RFID groups and a hierarchical authentication protocol is introduced. During its lifetime a RFID tag encounters various readers, each of which is not necessarily supposed to learn all the details of the tag.

As a solution to this problem we propose a hierarchical authentication protocol that allows a RFID tag to tune its identification process to the type of reader it is communicating with. Hence, only a (designated) subset of readers can learn the identity of a particular tag, while others can only acquire information on the group to which the tag belongs. We also demonstrate that the concept is extendable to multiple number of levels in the group hierarchy.

Furthermore, we prove the security against active adversaries and the privacy properties of our protocols. More precisely, our protocols offer impersonation resistance under the OMDL assumption and are narrow-strong privacy-preserving. Using the performance results for a suitable ECC-based hardware architecture we also demonstrate the feasibility of our proposed protocols for RFID tags.

For n levels in the group hierarchy, our protocol reduces the number of EC point multiplications at the tag and server by respectively a factor 2 and 3, compared to the trivial solution where n instances of an RFID authentication protocol are carried out. The tag has to store n private keys, corresponding to its unique identity and the subgroups where it belongs to. It remains an open problem how to construct a hierarchical RFID authentication protocol where each tag only has one private key. Tags belonging to the same subgroup could have keys which are mathematically related. This relation could then be used by an authorized reader to check the subgroup where the tag belongs to, while any other party should not be able to verify this mathematical property or compute the identity of the tag.

Acknowledgments. This work was supported in part by the IAP Programme P6/26 BCRYPT of the Belgian State, by FWO project G.0300.07, by the European Commission under contract number ICT-2007-216676 ECRYPT NoE phase II, by the K.U.Leuven-BOF (OT/06/40), and by the Research Council K.U.Leuven: GOA TENSE.

References

1. Avoine, G.: Adversarial Model for Radio Frequency Identification. In: Cryptology ePrint Archive, Report 2005/049 (2005), http://eprint.iacr.org/
2. Bellare, M., Palacio, A.: GQ and Schnorr Identification Schemes: Proofs of Security against Impersonation under Active and Concurrent Attacks. In: Yung, M. (ed.) CRYPTO 2002. LNCS, vol. 2442, pp. 162–177. Springer, Heidelberg (2002)
3. Brickell, E., Camenisch, J., Chen, L.: Direct Anonymous Attestation. In: Proceedings of the 11th ACM Conference on Computer and Communications Security (CCS 2004), pp. 132–145. ACM (2004)
4. Bringer, J., Chabanne, H.: Trusted-HB: A Low-Cost Version of HB^+ Secure Against Man-in-the-Middle Attacks. IEEE Transactions on Information Theory 54(9), 4339–4342 (2008)
5. Bringer, J., Chabanne, H., Dottax, E.: HB^{++}: a Lightweight Authentication Protocol Secure against Some Attacks. In: Security, Privacy and Trust in Pervasive and Ubiquitous Computing (SecPerU 2006), pp. 28–33. IEEE Computer Society (2006)
6. Bringer, J., Chabanne, H., Icart, T.: Cryptanalysis of EC-RAC, a RFID Identification Protocol. In: Franklin, M., Hui, L., Wong, D. (eds.) CANS 2008. LNCS, vol. 5339, pp. 149–161. Springer, Heidelberg (2008)

7. Camenisch, J., Lysyanskaya, A.: Signature Schemes and Anonymous Credentials from Bilinear Maps. In: Franklin, M. (ed.) CRYPTO 2004. LNCS, vol. 3152, pp. 56–72. Springer, Heidelberg (2004)
8. Chaum, D.: Security Without Identification: Transaction Systems to Make Big Brother Obsolete. Communications of the ACM 28(10), 1030–1044 (1985)
9. Deursen, T., Radomirović, S.: Attacks on RFID Protocols. In: Cryptology ePrint Archive: Listing for 2008 (2008/310) (2008)
10. van Deursen, T., Radomirović, S.: EC-RAC: Enriching a Capacious RFID Attack Collection. In: Ors Yalcin, S.B. (ed.) RFIDSec 2010. LNCS, vol. 6370, pp. 75–90. Springer, Heidelberg (2010)
11. Fan, J., Hermans, J., Vercauteren, F.: On the Claimed Privacy of EC-RAC III. In: Ors Yalcin, S.B. (ed.) RFIDSec 2010. LNCS, vol. 6370, pp. 66–74. Springer, Heidelberg (2010)
12. Feldhofer, M., Dominikus, S., Wolkerstorfer, J.: Strong Authentication for RFID Systems Using the AES Algorithm. In: Joye, M., Quisquater, J.J. (eds.) CHES 2004. LNCS, vol. 3156, pp. 357–370. Springer, Heidelberg (2004)
13. Frumkin, D., Shamir, A.: Un-Trusted-HB: Security Vulnerabilities of Trusted-HB. In: International Workshop on RFID Security (RFIDSEC 2009), pp. 62–71 (2009)
14. Garfinkel, S.L., Juels, A., Pappu, R.: RFID privacy: An overview of problems and proposed solutions. IEEE Security & Privacy 3(3), 34–43 (2005)
15. Gilbert, H., Robshaw, M., Sibert, H.: An Active Attack Against HB^+ - a Provably Secure Lightweight Authentication Protocol. IET Electronic Letters 41(21), 1169–1170 (2005)
16. Hein, D., Wolkerstorfer, J., Felber, N.: ECC Is Ready for RFID – A Proof in Silicon. In: Avanzi, R., Keliher, L., Sica, F. (eds.) SAC 2008. LNCS, vol. 5381, pp. 401–413. Springer, Heidelberg (2009)
17. Juels, A., Weis, S.: Defining Strong Privacy for RFID. In: Cryptology ePrint Archive, Report 2006/137 (2006), http://eprint.iacr.org/
18. Juels, A., Weis, S.: Authenticating Pervasive Devices with Human Protocols. In: Shoup, V. (ed.) CRYPTO 2005. LNCS, vol. 3621, pp. 293–308. Springer, Heidelberg (2005)
19. Koblitz, N.: Elliptic Curve Cryptosystem. Math. Comp. 48, 203–209 (1987)
20. Lee, Y.K., Batina, L., Singelée, D., Verbauwhede, I.: Low-Cost Untraceable Authentication Protocols for RFID (extended version). In: Wetzel, S., Rotaru, C.N., Stajano, F. (eds.) Proceedings of the 3rd ACM Conference on Wireless Network Security (WiSec 2010), pp. 55–64. ACM (2010)
21. Lee, Y.K., Batina, L., Verbauwhede, I.: Untraceable RFID Authentication Protocols: Revision of EC-RAC. In: IEEE International Conference on RFID, pp. 178–185. IEEE (2009)
22. Lee, Y.K., Sakiyama, K., Batina, L., Verbauwhede, I.: Elliptic Curve Based Security Processor for RFID. IEEE Transactions on Computer 57(11), 1514–1527 (2008)
23. Miller, V.: Use of Elliptic Curves in Cryptography. In: Williams, H. (ed.) CRYPTO 1985. LNCS, vol. 218, pp. 417–426. Springer, Heidelberg (1986)
24. Ng, C.Y., Susilo, W., Mu, Y., Safavi-Naini, R.: RFID Privacy Models Revisited. In: Jajodia, S., Lopez, J. (eds.) ESORICS 2008. LNCS, vol. 5283, pp. 251–266. Springer, Heidelberg (2008)
25. Schnorr, C.-P.: Efficient Identification and Signatures for Smart Cards. In: Brassard, G. (ed.) CRYPTO 1989. LNCS, vol. 435, pp. 239–252. Springer, Heidelberg (1990)
26. Vaudenay, S.: On Privacy Models for RFID. In: Kurosawa, K. (ed.) ASIACRYPT 2007. LNCS, vol. 4833, pp. 68–87. Springer, Heidelberg (2007)

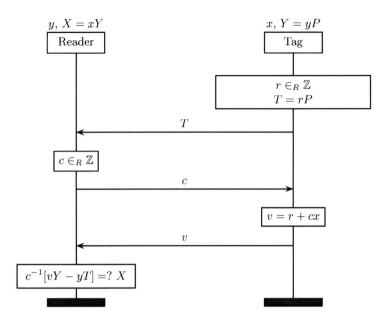

Fig. 5. ECC-based version of the Schnorr identification scheme [25]

A ECC-Based Schnorr Authentication Protocol

Many attempts to design an RFID authentication protocol which relies exclusively on the use of ECC, are based on the Schnorr protocol [25], a conventional
identification scheme that offers resistance to impersonation attacks, as has been
proven by Bellare and Palacio [2]. The protocol of Schnorr is shown above. Note
that the public key X of the tag is defined slightly different than in the original version of the protocol (xY instead of xP), but this modification does not
change the security properties of the protocol. The scheme offers interesting security properties and can be implemented quite efficiently. However, it was not
designed to resist tracking attacks, and does not offer any privacy protection.

Author Index